Still Artful Work

THE CONTINUING POLITICS
OF SOCIAL SECURITY REFORM

SECOND EDITION

Still Artful Work

THE CONTINUING POLITICS
OF SOCIAL SECURITY REFORM

Paul Light

McGRAW-HILL, INC.

New York St. Louis San Francisco Auckland Bogotá Caracas
Lisbon London Madrid Mexico City Milan Montreal New Delhi
San Juan Singapore Sydney Tokyo Toronto

To the Lights in my life

This book was set in Palatino by ComCom, Inc.
The editors were Peter Labella and Fred H. Burns;
the production supervisor was Elizabeth J. Strange.
The cover was designed by Nicholas Krenitsky.
R. R. Donnelley & Sons Company was printer and binder.

STILL ARTFUL WORK
The Continuing Politics of Social Security Reform

This book is printed on recycled, acid-free paper containing 10%
postconsumer waste.

1 2 3 4 5 6 7 8 9 0 DOC DOC 9 0 9 8 7 6 5 4

ISBN 0-07-037949-1

Library of Congress Cataloging-in-Publication Data
Light, Paul Charles.
   Still artful work: the continuing politics of social security
reform / Paul Light. — 2nd ed.
    p.   cm.
   Rev. ed. of: Artful work. New York: Random House, c1985.
   Includes bibliographical references and index.
   ISBN 0-07-037949-1
   1. Social security—United States.   2. Social security—United
States—Finance.   3. Social security—Law and legislation—United
States.   I. Light, Paul Charles. Artful work.   II. Title.
HD7125.L535   1995
368.4'3'0973—dc20   94-17594

About the Author

PAUL LIGHT earned his B.A. in 1975 from Macalester College in St. Paul, Minnesota, and his M.A. and Ph.D. from the University of Michigan in political science by 1980. He has taught at the University of Virginia, Georgetown University, and is now a professor of planning and public affairs at the Hubert H. Humphrey Institute of Public Affairs at the University of Minnesota. He is currently the director of the Surviving Innovation project at the Humphrey Institute.

From 1982–1983 he was an American Political Science Association congressional fellow, serving with Rep. Barber B. Conable, Jr., and Sen. John Glenn. After a year with the Brookings Institution as a guest scholar, he joined the National Academy of Public Administration as director of studies. In 1987, he became special adviser on public management to the U.S. Senate Governmental Affairs Committee where he worked on issues of executive organization, presidential appointments, presidential transitions, and the elevation of the Veterans Administration and Environmental Protection Agency to cabinet status.

Immediately before joining the Humphrey Institute as associate dean, he served as senior adviser and drafted the final report of the National Commission on the Public Service, chaired by former Federal Reserve Board Chairman Paul Volcker. The Volcker report was presented to President Bush in March 1989. He served in a similar role at the National Commission on the State and Local Public Service, chaired by former Governor of Mississippi William Winter. The Winter Commission presented its final report to President Clinton in June 1993.

Light has written seven books, including *The President's Agenda, Vice Presidential Power,* the first edition of *Artful Work: The Politics of Social Security*

Reform, Monitoring Government: Inspectors General and the Search for Accountability, and, most recently, *Thickening Government: Why It Matters, How It Happened, and What to Do About It.* He is a member of Phi Beta Kappa and was honored as a distinguished citizen of Macalester College in 1989. He is a senior fellow of the Washington-based Governance Institute and visiting fellow at the Brookings Institution. Light is frequently quoted in the national media and is a regular commentator on public and nonprofit reform.

It is not a work of art, but it is artful work.
—Representative Barber B. Conable, Jr.
March 1983

Contents

PART SIX
Epilogue   225

Appendixes

Preface to the Second Edition

Looking back from today, the 1983 social security rescue remains a legislative miracle, perhaps all the more so by the inability to solve a host of other pressing national problems. Time has not dulled the achievement: hard truths were faced, tough choices were made. Facing a huge short-term deficit and an even larger long-term crisis, the two branches forged a tough package of pain, leaving no individual or group happy but satisfying all nonetheless. Linking arms for a moment of unique national sacrifice, Congress and the President repaired America's flagship social program and moved on to more pressing business.

Alas, most of that business remains unaddressed eleven years later—the deficit is still huge, America has no energy policy, AIDS still plagues us. The legislative process seems stuck in low gear facing problems that involve too much political pain to move faster—benefit cuts, tax increases, base closures, higher user fees on everything from national parks to driver's licenses. The *de*distributive choices keep coming.

Unfortunately, Congress and the President are much better at giving than taking away. And, truth be told, the American public is much better at receiving than giving back. "Clinton is the innocent who went to some country hollow and got caught between the Hatfields and the McCoys," former Reagan budget director David Stockman explained in 1993. "The job of every President since Reagan—a sunshine boy who didn't want to acknowledge the deficit was his problem—is to distribute and administer pain. Clinton is mired neck deep."[1] Such is the problem of dedistribution.

Thus, the 1983 social security rescue still holds lessons for today, particularly as the President and Congress confront the staggering federal deficit.

---

[1] Sidney Blumenthal, "The Sorcerer's Apprentices," *The New Yorker*, July 19, 1993, p. 29.

There is simply no way to gnaw the deficit down from its $200 billion heights without inflicting pain, and lots of it. As in the case of the social security crisis of the early 1980s, incremental adjustment simply will not suffice, not even of the magnitude envisioned in President Bill Clinton's economic plan.

Unlike the social security crisis, however, the deficit doesn't scare anyone. Granted, there is some consensus that the deficit is a problem worth fixing, and, granted, people seem to like politicians who promise to get under the hood and clean out the barn. Yet, the public appears less committed somehow to solving the problem, at least in the near term, and certainly not if it means closing their obsolete military base or goring their pet program.

The deficit does not have a target for action on which people agree. The signal accomplishment of the National Commission on Social Security Reform was in setting the parameters of the problem. Not that the target was precise— it hovered between $150 and $200 billion. Rather, having a number, even soft $50 billion one way or the other, allowed Congress and the President to move on to the real business of finding a solution. To date in the deficit crisis, no one seems to have decided just how big a deficit is too big.

Finally, the deficit carries no deadline for action. The beauty of the 1983 social security rescue was not just that the commission provided a handy target but that the previous Congress supplied a deadline. The fear that the social security checks would not go out if Congress did not act in time was no small part of the 1983 legislative miracle. There is no such device on the deficit, no mechanism that might lead members of Congress to close ranks, close eyes, and pass a sweeping remedy for the lingering deficits.

This revision of *Artful Work* is not about failure to learn from the social security success, however. It is about the success itself and what it has meant for the politics of social security reform. The 1983 miracle is *Still Artful Work,* a work of legislative art that remains unblemished after a decade of implementation.

The proof of the miracle does not rest only in its legislative history, which is still chronicled in the pages that follow, but in its effectiveness. *It worked!* In a time when government seems incapable of making anything it does work— from B-1 bombers to savings and loan bailouts—the 1983 social security rescue actually fixed the problem. To be fair, of course, the 1983 rescue would not have been needed if a 1977 rescue had not failed. Then again, the 1983 rescue had a much bigger problem to tackle as a result.

Clearly, the 1983 bill rightly belongs on any list of contemporary policy successes—it more than met its fiscal target and did so just in time. The checks continued to go out like clockwork, and the reserve account began building up. By the end of 1992, social security had more than a quarter of a *trillion* dollars in reserve. With 132 million people paying in at higher tax rates, more money—much more, that is—was coming in than going out.

Money is not the only measure of success, however. Many involved in the 1983 miracle had hoped that legislative success would somehow make social security both less political and less of a target for future budget cutters and, in doing so, restore public faith in the program. As the title of this revised edition suggests, those hopes remain just out of reach, in large measure because social security is too big, too important to ever escape politics. It remains America's flagship income security program and is likely to remain so regardless of what happens on health care reform.

Alas, financial health alone could never insulate social security from politics. As the trust fund balance swelled during the 1980s and into the 1990s, its surpluses shielded the federal deficit from even greater scrutiny. The positive balances on social security meant the federal government had less need to borrow money from the private sector and foreign investors, while at the same time masking the true size of the deficit. Technically, Congress and the President could not use the social security trust fund for general purposes— that fire wall between the trust fund and the rest of the budget remains inviolable. However, as Chapter 19 argues, nothing prevented using the social security dollars to make the deficit look smaller, an annual budget ritual that eventually led Sen. Daniel Patrick Moynihan to introduce his 1990 proposal for a social security tax cut.

Ultimately, as Chapter 20 argues, the greatest test of the 1983 social security rescue is still decades away. That is when the first members of the baby boom generation will retire, and social security will begin using up its substantial reserves. The politics of social security reform could make the presidential election of 2016 one of the most volatile in history, pitting 75 million baby boomers against their children and grandchildren.

The outcome depends largely on what happens in the next few years. Will Congress and the President knock down the deficit? Will America regain its economic momentum? Will the baby boom's children get the kind of high-quality education needed in the global marketplace of tomorrow? The answers will dictate the contours of the 2016 election. With baby boomers now in the White House as President and Vice President, America finally has a new generation of leaders. If the baby boomers fail to act on the pressing problems of today, their children will be right to ask whether they should pay the kinds of tax increases likely needed to sustain a reasonable level of social security benefits through the 2020s and beyond.

Thus does the story of the social security rescue come full circle. Learning the right lessons about *how* the bill passed—and applying those lessons to the backlog of unsolved problems—can help America avoid the need for another social security rescue twenty-five years hence. The 1983 social security rescue stands as a model for achieving the kinds of dramatic political breakthroughs that Washington so desperately needs.

Paul Light

Acknowledgments
for the Second Edition

This edition of the book benefits directly from the input of various reviewers and colleagues over the past ten years. First on a long list are Andrew Achebaum, Fay Lomax Cook, and Eric Kingson. The book could not have been revised, however, without the input of Robert Myers, former Chief Actuary of Social Security. His comments and corrections substantially improved several key sections and helped propel me toward doing the revision in the first place. Thanks also go to Robert Ball, former Commissioner of Social Security, who offered valuable corrections even as the first edition was in press. Despite their input, they may still disagree with some of my conclusions and I must take responsibility for all that follows. Margaret Trostel, my research assistant here at the Humphrey Institute, provided enormous help as we assembled the core materials for the revision, and my family, as always, provided patient encouragement as I did the work.

Paul Light

Preface to the First Edition

Social security will always be a hot political issue. It is simply too large to ignore, too important to neglect. It will always be part of the struggle over who gets what, when, where, and how. Because it shifts almost $200 billion mostly from the young to the old each year, and because it affects nearly 150 million taxpayers and beneficiaries, it will always be on the national agenda. Elderly Americans will continue to rely on social security for the bulk of their retirement income; younger Americans will continue to pay more taxes throughout their working lives.

Anyone who wants to understand American politics must first understand social security. Those who care about budget deficits must know something about the single largest program on the domestic ledger; those who care about electoral politics must know something about the central concern of older voters; those who care about trust in government must know something about the lack of confidence in social security among young and old Americans alike; those who care about poverty must know something about the most important program for helping elderly women and minorities; and those who wonder how Congress and the President will solve the coming budget and Medicare crises must know something about how the nation squeaked through the last social security rescue.

Moreover, social security will always be in trouble—either in another crisis or as the target for deeper cuts, either in repair or as the topic of a presidential campaign. The program will always be in flux, if only because it was designed for a society that no longer exists. And when it gets into trouble, it will demand attention, if only because it is so remarkably large.

Yet, social security can only be understood within its political context. It is not a simple insurance program or a mere retirement plan. It is the product of decades of political conflict and compromise and reflects the ebb and flow of presidential and congressional power. It is the result of both legislative tinkering and major expansion and involves the clash of House versus Senate, Democrat versus Republican, Boll Weevil versus Gypsy Moth.

Thus, this book is written for those who want to learn about social security as a political program. The book starts with an introduction to how Congress and the presidency work and asks how they might provide leadership on painful policy issues. It then turns to the nature of social security itself, offering a basic primer on the program. It examines the technical assumptions that drive the program from year to year and reviews the public and interest group opinions on social security. The book looks at why the program gets into trouble and how it got out of its most recent crisis. The book serves as a broad introduction to the American political system and its largest domestic commitment.

More specifically, the book examines the 1983 social security rescue and its lessons for the coming budget and Medicare crises. It looks at how President Reagan tried and failed to set the social security agenda and how a small band of social security leaders set the deadline for him. It offers the first details on the secret meetings that produced a final social security package and asks why the National Commission on Social Security Reform collapsed and what happened in the final House-Senate conference committee just before the rescue passed.

The book is meant for students and lay readers alike and tells a story that will influence American politics for decades to come. Indeed, as a result of the 1983 social security rescue, every college student who reads this book will be encouraged to retire at age 67 instead of 65. Those who want to know how this happened—why an entire generation will work two more years—must first understand the basic structure of social security, the nature of American politics in a new era of cutbacks, and the artful work of congressional compromise. Those who want to know how taxes were raised on over 115 million workers, how benefits were cut on another 36 million, and how federal employees were finally brought under the umbrella of social security coverage must also understand how Congress and the President can hide the pain needed to solve a new breed of policy breakdowns.

This book is intended as a lesson on how leaders can make the tough choices needed in coming years. Facing a series of policy breakdowns in other programs, Congress and the President will surely need help. They appear incapable of acting in the sunshine of the new legislative system. Whether they can find the courage to make the difficult choices for the budget and Medicare remains open to question. The 1983 social security rescue provides some clear advice. Whether the leaders will notice remains unanswered.

Paul Light

Acknowledgments
for the First Edition

Acknowledgments are always a pleasant part of writing a book. They are written only at the very end and offer a rare chance to thank all the people and places who have helped. Though acknowledgments rarely do justice to the depth of support, they are one way to say thanks.

My first thanks must go to Rep. Barber B. Conable, Jr., who gave me his time and patience as the social security rescue worked its way through the National Commission and Congress. He will always have my deepest appreciation and respect. So will his personal staff: Harry Nicholas, Linda McLaughlin, Nancy Marks, Joan Janshego, Marjorie Vanderbilt, Sigi Woolbert, Marian Wallace, Jo Ann Burton, and Sharon Wells.

Thanks also go to the American Political Science Association's Congressional Fellowship program, which gave me a year on Capitol Hill to watch the legislative process, and to its director, Cathy Rudder. Without the fellowship, I could not have written this book. Thanks go to the Brookings Institution for guest privileges and space and to the Earhart Foundation for the needed financial support during the writing year. Thanks also go to my friends and colleagues at Brookings, Georgetown University, George Washington University, and other places far and near. Steven Smith, James Lengle, David O'Brien, Bruce Jacobs, David Sears, Susan Lawrence, and Paul Petersen all lent their encouragement. Special thanks go to Stephen J. Wayne, who gave me the idea for the book in the first place and read every word of it. His editorial comments and friendship made this book much easier to write. Thanks to the small group of anonymous reviewers who offered their insights on how to improve the book. Thanks also go to the Ability Group for their quick editing and word processing. Finally, thanks go to my small band of close friends who have surrounded me with their kindness and encouragement during past years.

All of these people and organizations helped with the artful work that goes into writing any book. Whether this particular book turns out to be a work of art, of course, is ultimately my responsibility.

Paul Light

1

Introduction

This is a story about a legislative miracle. Under extreme time pressure in 1983 (and largely because of it), Congress and the President finally passed a social security rescue bill. Two years in the making, the legislation arrived just moments before the social security trust fund was to run dry. Without the $170-billion package of tax increases and benefit cuts, millions of checks would have been delayed.

Yet more than social security was involved. According to one senator, "our basic capacity to govern" was at stake. Without a bill, public confidence in social security would have plunged to new lows. Support for the system would have been stretched to the limit.

Despite the pressures, the solution was always in doubt. Key players tried to draft an agreement and failed repeatedly: first in the House; next in the agencies; then in the White House, the Senate, a House-Senate conference committee, and the budget committees; and finally in a national commission. None seemed capable of reaching an accord—either on the size of the coming collapse or on the range of possible solutions—and the courts had no authority to respond.

It was only at the very last moment that Congress and the President decided to act, and then only under extreme political and time pressure. Caught between the obstacles to change—which are so much a part of the American system of separate powers and checks and balances—and the need to move—which is so much a part of the current budget and economic climate—the legislative and executive branches finally began the secret negotiations that would produce a package. An American system of government that had been originally designed more for stalemate than action was finally able to produce an agreement. That was the miracle.

This is the story of how the compromise was crafted; how it was built from repeated failures, legislative illusions, political "gridlock," and the battle over assumptions. This is the story of how two aging political opponents, President Ronald Reagan and the late House Speaker Thomas P. ("Tip") O'Neill (both eligible for social security in their own right), finally reached an agreement more out of mutual fear than the public interest and how a small band of congressional leaders created a social security crisis that would either save the program or destroy it. This is the story of the National Commission on Social Security Reform. Created as a way to cool off the issue in 1981, it was deadlocked by partisan infighting in late 1982. This is the story of the secret Gang of Nine that followed, an ad hoc group that built the final social security compromise in the first weeks of 1983. Operating behind the cover of the formal commission, the gang provided an important opportunity to talk behind closed doors. The miracle was that the American system worked, if only at the last instant.

Yet by 1984, it was far too early to tell if the story had a happy ending. This is a book about artful political work, but only time will tell if the social security compromise was a work of legislative art. The program would still falter as early as 1986 if the economy did not improve quickly. Social security would still face a severe test when the baby boom generation started to retire in the first quarter of the twenty-first century. Whether this is the story of a policy miracle that will save social security well into the coming years or merely the story of a political compromise remains very much in doubt.

TOUGH CHOICES

Ultimately, this is a story about how Congress and the President handle tough issues. Government has always been good at saying yes, particularly when it distributes or redistributes new and larger programs to society. It has not been as good at saying no. Unfortunately, social security was only the first in a string of programs that test government's courage to "dedistribute," to cut back by raising taxes and reducing benefits at the same time. Though many of these programs involve cherished goals—medical care for the poor and elderly, quality education for all, environmental protection, the elimination of poverty, new jobs, a strong defense, and so on—economic and demographic changes will force government to choose. Some programs will be saved; others will be dedistributed.

The problem, of course, is that tax increases and benefit cuts generate intense public opposition. The public might agree on the need for balanced budgets or help for the poor but not on the specific cuts or tax increases to reach these goals. On social security, for example, the public clearly wanted to save the program but was opposed to tax increases and benefit cuts, the only major rescue options. With no one in favor of change, Congress and the President had to either cancel out the opposition or hide the painful solutions.

Unfortunately, the American system is not well designed to set priorities among competing goals. Congress and the presidency are quite sensitive to interest group pressure; both provide ample opportunities for legislative meddling. The presidency, once all but immune to lobbies, now actively cultivates interest group support. As the White House reaches further out, however, interest groups reach further in. Congress, once partly shielded from interest groups by strong committees and closed doors, now operates with a highly decentralized subcommittee system. Power has been dispersed to all 535 members. With greater staff support, each one has become a legislative broker.

Moreover, with every word on the record, it is more difficult to sit down and negotiate on most issues. As one reaction to Watergate and the Vietnam War, Congress opened many of its once secret hiding places. By bringing "sunshine" into the legislative process, many reformers hoped to make Congress more accountable. There would be no more smoke-filled rooms. The only problem was that Congress and the President still needed an occasional hiding place, particularly on dedistributive issues. Sunshine was a noble goal, generating greater public access, but it also put Congress on the spot. It was difficult to vote for spending cuts or tax increases with every interest group watching.

If the past decade of poor economic performance is any harbinger of the next, the choices must be made. It is no longer possible to do everything, however well or poorly. The nation may not be able to afford both clean air and B-1 bombers, the MX missile and hazardous waste control, balanced budgets and student loans. At least in this era of tight budgets, government must decide. In the words of Rep. Barber B. Conable, Jr.:

> Some things just aren't pretty to watch or easy to do. I've never seen a glamorous opossum or a graceful giraffe. Divorces are never comfortable. The seriously overweight should stay away from short shorts. Deep mud doesn't make for light movements. A politician has a hard time looking relaxed when found with his hand in the cookie jar.
>
> In the same way, government, which has a great time making people happy by allocating surpluses, always looks awkward—and sometimes downright foolish—when it tries to deal with shortages. If that government is a democracy, it will go through the most remarkable contortions to avoid unpleasant duties, even when everyone understands the necessity and yearns for grace under pressure.

There should be little doubt that policymakers will face an increasing number of such awkward choices in the coming decades. Indeed, with the social security crisis finally at rest in 1983, Congress turned to the Medicare program and its staggering ten-year $300-billion deficit, a new crisis in American education, acid rain and hazardous wastes, El Salvador, $200-billion deficits, and a rapidly growing defense budget. Once again, the choices would be painful.

The question, then, is what the social security story might tell Congress and the President about other tough issues. How did government cut benefits for 36 million current retirees, raise taxes on 115 million workers and all businesses, cover most federal employees under social security for the first time in history, boost the retirement age from 65 to 67, and put a tax on social security benefits? The answers may help Congress and the President package other tough choices into legislative miracles.

THE AMERICAN SYSTEM

Before telling the story of the social security compromise, it is important to understand one feature of the American system of government: it was not designed to be efficient. As a defense against tyranny, the founders created a system that often encourages stalemate. No majority, however large, could gain control of government by simply winning in one branch.

By creating a system of "separate institutions sharing power," the founders also made sure that any major changes in the status quo would come only with some level of consensus among the competing branches. By endowing these branches with checks and balances, the founders also made sure that each one could protect itself against the others. Even the checks had counterchecks. The President had the veto, but Congress had the override. Further, by adopting separate terms of office and different rules of election, the founders made sure that the fortunes of one institution would never rest completely with the others. And by creating a bicameral Congress, the founders made sure that legislation would move slowly, if at all.

The government was clearly designed to be inefficient and was well equipped for frustration. Ambition would counteract ambition, the founders said. Nothing would happen unless all of the branches reached agreement. Proponents would have to win repeatedly en route to any major changes; opponents would have to win only once. Stalemate was a small price to pay for freedom.

The system worked quite well during the first 180 years or so. Very little happened without a consensus. The system protected the public against change. Despite periods of intense legislative activity—the New Deal and the Great Society—standoff was the rule, not the exception. The system did its job by not moving too fast. Stalemate winnowed the long list of potential laws and constitutional amendments to a select few. It was survival of the fittest.

Yet the system carried certain risks, particularly when government needed to move quickly. Stalemate could become a threat, delaying action on policy emergencies. Though the system protected the public against ceaseless change, it also stymied efforts to repair damaged programs, particularly as they started to break down in the late 1970s and early 1980s. Some of the emergencies were caused by the simple passage of time. Programs designed for a society of the 1930s did not do so well in a society of working women, smaller families, new technologies, and so on. Other emergencies were caused by errors in the original legislation. Programs that worked well with few beneficiaries did not do so well when the population changed.

These were just the kinds of problems that only got worse with waiting. If the social security crisis was not solved one year, it only got more painful the next, boosting the benefit cuts and tax increases needed to plug the holes. If the budget deficit was not answered one year, it only got bigger the next, multiplying the annual interest on the national debt.

The leadership dilemma was clear: the public still needed protection against tyranny, while the government needed the freedom to answer pressing problems as quickly as possible. Contrary to those who called for sweeping constitutional reform to make government more efficient, the system still worked as intended. Unfortunately, the system sometimes got in the way of needed repairs. Programs took on a life of their own, technical advice went wrong, the public did not understand the issues, and interest groups exploited the potential for stalemate.

THE STORY

This is a story of how Congress and the President finally handled one of the most serious policy emergencies of the 1980s: social security. The story itself breaks into four parts. The first deals with a short discussion of Congress and the presidency. How were they equipped to deal with the social security issue? What were the opportunities for leadership? Both institutions faced serious problems mustering the courage to tackle problems in the face of overwhelming public and interest group opposition.

The second part of the story deals with the obstacles to change. How did the social security program work, and how did its size limit the chances for rescue? How did the failure of key economic and demographic assumptions heighten the political conflict and uncertainty? What did the public know about the issues, and how did their panic shape the compromise? How did the interest groups represent the public, and how did their unwillingness to compromise affect the final bill? Given the obstacles, it was almost impossible to move within the normal legislative process.

The third part of the story deals with the social security crisis itself. What were the problems facing the system, and what were the solutions? Social security was facing a serious "bust" in the early 1980s. The problems were deep and getting worse, while the solutions were becoming more painful with each delay.

The fourth and final part of the story deals with the events leading to the social security compromise. This part starts with the inauguration of Ronald Reagan in January 1981 and ends with a bill-signing ceremony in April 1983. The two-year chronology covers eight separate events:

1. Reagan's proposal to solve the social security crisis through deep benefit cuts in May 1981
2. Passage of a scarcely noticed bill in December 1981 that would trigger a social security emergency in mid-1983
3. An attempt to tackle social security through the budget in April 1982
4. A break for the midterm congressional elections
5. The birth and death of the National Commission on Social Security Reform in 1982

6. The rise of a secret negotiating "gang" as a shield for talks between Reagan and O'Neill in January 1983
7. Navigation of the social security agreement through the interest group-infested waters on Capitol Hill in early March 1983
8. The final House-Senate conference just before the Easter recess in 1983

A more detailed chronology is presented in Appendix A, while a list of key players is presented in Appendix B.

That the bill was actually signed into law in time to save the program was, indeed, artful work. The question is how it happened. The short answer is that Congress and the President moved the debate outside the normal legislative process. Responding to the obstacles inside the constitutional framework, they created a new form of government.

THE TELLING

Much of the story is based on my work as an American Political Science Association Congressional Fellow in 1982–1983. The fellowship gave me a year on Capitol Hill to spend as I wished. After looking over the list of members and range of issues, I picked Barber Conable and social security. I bet a year of my time that Conable would be in the eye of the legislative storm and would tell me what was happening.

Clearly, this book hinges on whether Conable was actually involved in the social security debate and whether he was honest with me. I know he was in the center of the debate, and I have no reason to doubt his candor. Conable was involved in virtually every major decision on the social security rescue and had been a key player on the issue for almost twenty years. He was a member of every social security negotiating group, as well as the Ways and Means Committee and the National Commission on Social Security Reform. He was a participant in the 1982 budget talks and was a regular at White House leadership/strategy meetings. He kept a detailed journal of his activity and was willing to open his files for my work. More important, he was willing to field my questions. I followed him to all of the social security negotiations, talked with him as often as possible, hounded him at times, and sat in on many meetings as his staff assistant. Though I rarely offered more than trivial advice, he gave me invaluable access and information. More than anyone else, Conable was my social security teacher.

However, in order to enrich Conable's perspective, I also interviewed other social security players. After all, Conable was a Republican House member and was neither privy to Democratic secrets nor interested in Senate strategies. To compensate, I talked regularly with a small group of 20 or so Democrats and Republicans during my year and expanded my list of respondents after the final rescue bill was signed. In all, I talked with over 100 people, most of whom were either central participants themselves or senior staffers. With Conable's help, I was able to interview nine of the fifteen commission members; seven of the nine secret negotiators who built the final agreement; eight key members of the Ways and Means Committee; a small number of senators; all of the top House, Senate, and White House social security advisers; and most of the key interest group leaders. All of the interviews were off the record. Because I promised my respondents complete confidentiality as a condition of the interviews, most of the quotes are not identified by name. Where quotes are identified in the book, they were either on the record at the time or are used with the respondent's permission.

Thus, this book rests on two separate research strategies: the first involving my own participant observations, and the second involving personal interviews. Because most of the story has not been told elsewhere, and because the telling reflects my own records and confidential interviews, there are few footnotes in the book. Readers will have to trust either that I was in a position to see what happened or that I talked with someone who was.

CONCLUSION

By now it should be clear what this story is and is not about. Those who search for a full explanation of what the social security program does and does not do will not find it here. Perhaps such an explanation can never emerge from the complicated history of the system. Those who search for a detailed analysis of the technical aspects of the program—whom it helps, whom it hurts—will not find it here either. Though technical issues were important, particularly when they were manipulated by skillful players, this is a book about the political work, not about actuarial tables and benefit formulas. Those who search for an endorsement of alternatives to social security will also search in vain. This is a story about politics and should be taken as such. This is a story about how the American system works, whether producing stalemate in the old constitutional framework or dedistributive choices in new forms of government.

Separate
Powers

2

A Leaderless Branch?

"Congress lives by four horrid aphorisms," a member of Congress once remarked. "Never adopt a political philosophy that won't fit on a bumper sticker. If you have to explain something, you're already in trouble. When you're drowning in a sea of economic illiteracy, don't drink the water. . . . Swim prettily. Any rooster who sticks his head above the tall grass will get hit by a rock." In short, Congress is better equipped for stalemate than leadership. "It's good to be in the middle of things, and Congress clearly is a place of action," Conable said. "It's a frustrating place for people who want to push a button and make things happen, though, and any realist better not talk too much of power or influence among Congressmen."

Though most members want to pass good laws, they also want to win reelection. In recent years, the electoral pressure has grown so intense that good policy is sometimes neglected, particularly in even-numbered years. Sometimes, it is easier to pretend that problems do not exist rather than make redistributive choices. Other times, it is impossible to tell just what good policy is. No one wants to pass programs that will fail, but government increasingly finds it hard to build programs that will succeed.

A REACTIVE CONGRESS

Clearly, separated powers and checks and balances make it more difficult to win passage of important legislation. As President John Kennedy once said, "It is very easy to defeat a bill in Congress. It is much more difficult to pass one." The President must usually win at least ten times to hope for final passage: (1) in one House subcommittee, (2) in the full House committee, (3) in the House Rules Committee to move to the floor, (4) on the House floor, (5) in one Senate subcommittee, (6) in the full Senate committee, (7) on the Senate floor, (8) in the House-Senate conference committee to work out the differences between the two bills, (9) back on the House floor for final passage, and (10) back on the Senate floor for final passage. If the issue involves more than one House or Senate committee, of course, the number of steps can easily double or triple.

A New Congress

This potential for stalemate was not an accident. The constitutional founders wanted government to move slowly, if at all. Yet recent changes in Congress have made action more difficult, particularly when government must cut back. Congress has never spoken with one voice, but there was a time when party leaders could direct the chorus. Now there are 535 power centers, most of them equipped with the staff and subcommittee assignments to fight party leaders and the President on even the most trivial issues. Members of Congress still believe in doing what is right on most issues. It is just that there are more opinions that count.

Moreover, following a decade of reform, Congress must now work in the sunshine. As Congress opened its workings to the public and interest groups, the smoke-filled rooms began to disappear. Unfortunately, so did many of the closed rooms that are so important to legislative action. Under the hot lights of television, with every word in a transcript and every vote on the record, members of Congress became less willing to take a stand on painful issues. And with so many open meetings, leaders had fewer chances to sit down and talk. No one wanted to make the first move, especially if it might become an issue in the next campaign.

The dispersion of power to the subcommittees and individual members was complicated by the rise of a new congressional budget process, passed in 1974. The budget has taken over in Congress, absorbing vast amounts of time and energy at the expense of other issues. As Alice Rivlin, former director of the Congressional Budget Office and a senior member of the Clinton administration ten years later, argued in 1983, the current process is "too long and complicated. It demands too many decisions—more than can be made in the time allotted."[1] Unfortunately, more time on the budget means less time on other issues. Some problems cannot be handled in the budget process without raising fears that popular domestic programs are being sacrificed for increased defense spending and so forth.

As a product of these changes, Congress has become a reactive legislature, moving only when forced and then only at the last moment. Because the two houses of Congress are different, however, it is important to look at each separately. The House, composed of 435 members, relies on rules to a much greater extent than the Senate. Such rules are one way to control the larger number of people. The Senate, composed of 100 members, allows much greater

---

[1]Quoted in *The Brookings Review*, Fall 1983, p. 27.

individual freedom. Despite the differences, both chambers have become "crisis-activated" bodies, responding only when some policy or political crisis is imminent and unavoidable. "Congress will do what it has to do," a member of the House Ways and Means Committee said, "but only at the last moment."

The problem is that Congress sometimes has great difficulty knowing when that moment has arrived. What might be a serious crisis to Democrats may be little more than a passing storm to Republicans, and vice versa. What might be a pressing problem in the headlines may be little more than a slight disturbance on Capitol Hill. Thus the first step in solving a policy emergency is simply admitting that the emergency actually exists.

The Government Giveth . . .

Though sunshine and decentralization had important impacts, they came at a time when Congress began to confront a new set of policy issues. Congress always worked well when it had a chance to distribute new programs to the nation and even functioned when it had to redistribute benefits from one group to another. There were occasional delays en route to passage, but Congress was able to lead.

Toward the end of the 1970s, however, Congress had to start cutting back. Long before Reagan's tax cuts, government was facing a serious budget crisis. It was no longer possible to do everything. Congress began to face more and more *dedistributive* policy issues. And as Conable noted, "We in Congress are very good at giving people relative advantages but incredibly inept at assigning relative disadvantages. In social security, we've run out of goodies to pass out, and we have no choice but to ask some part of all the people involved to lower their expectations."

Dedistributive issues present special problems for Congress. Because these issues are politically hot, staff involvement must be kept to a minimum. The dangers of a mistake are so great that most members of Congress try to keep their opinions to themselves. It is particularly hard to discern a developing consensus in favor of any options, giving leaders little guidance on how to package a bill. On social security, for example, one Republican House member accused his colleagues of a "conspiracy of silence" on the issue. Little wonder, given the electoral risks.

Because dedistributive issues also involve considerable pain for constituents, there are great temptations to avoid action until after the next election. Since political opponents can easily exploit public opinion without offering their own alternatives, members of Congress often remain on the defensive throughout the term. Whereas most other legislative action occurs at the very end of a legislative session, dedistributive issues must be tackled at the very beginning or not at all. Action must take place at the point furthest from the next campaign. Yet most members of Congress would rather delay action until the last possible moment or hide the decisions from the public entirely. Given the blinding sunshine on Capitol Hill, it is no surprise that the most frequent answer has been delay, not action.

THE HOUSE

Each chamber of Congress had its own problems in dealing with dedistributive issues in the early 1980s. In the House, neither the Democrats nor the Republicans could count on the support of their party members. Indeed, as one House member said, the House was having an "insect crisis." By the end of 1982, there were at least three major splinter groups in the House: the Boll Weevils (conservative Southern Democrats), the Gypsy Moths (liberal Northern Republicans), and the Yellow Jackets (conservative Reagan Republicans). Though the three groups were not large (26 Gypsy Moths, 46 Boll Weevils, and 64 Yellow Jackets), they had enough votes to swing the balance on key bills. As one member suggested, "We ought to have a Praying Mantis caucus so we can eat all the other insects. We've had too much entomological trouble up here."

The rise of these House factions meant that neither the Democratic nor the Republican party leadership could count on the full support of their membership. "By golly," Democratic Majority Leader James Wright remarked in April 1982, "sometimes, when I'm trying to corral this gang of Democrats, I know just how those little old banty hens felt." Earlier in the year, he had complained, "You might as well have Donald Duck leading this pack."[2]

Clearly, the problem was more important for the Democrats, if only because they were the majority party. If they could not lead in 1981 with 243 members, who could? With a Republican in the White House, the Democrats could not rely on outside leadership to build a party majority. However, as Wright finally concluded, "You've got a hunting license to persuade, that's all you've got. We don't have punishments and rewards that we can hold in some cookie jar somewhere. That's not the way the system works. Perhaps it did at one time, but it doesn't anymore."

The question was whether the House could ever become a reliable source of social security leadership, or whether it would become a source of frustration and disagreement. At least in the early 1980s, the answer was frustration, not leadership.

A House Divided

The House leadership crisis involved more than the rise of the insects. It was the natural result of the nation's diversity. Representing so many different districts, House members were pulled in a variety of directions. Southern Democrats could easily point to opinions back home and claim support for budget cuts; Northern Republicans could point to unemployment back home and claim support for a huge jobs program.

It was also the simple product of the size of the House. Getting 435 individual politicians to agree even on occasion is a legislative feat. As Conable argued, "Power exists here, but it is so diffused that it can be exercised only by

---

[2]Quoted in *The New York Times*, April 27, 1982, p. A16.

consent; and nobody, not even a Speaker or majority leader has consent for more than a moment under sharply delimited procedural standards. The elected leaders of a modern Congress have very little to give and therefore very little to withhold in the exercise of discipline within the group that elects them." In short, leadership is more an art of "followership" than anything else; if your followers do not know where they are going, it is difficult to get there first.

Other factors complicated leadership problems in the early 1980s. One involved the rise of subcommittee government. The total number of subcommittees doubled in the course of two short decades, so that by 1980 the number of power centers had increased, too. With more and more legislative work taking place at the subcommittee level, it became harder for party leaders and committee chairs to influence the movement of important bills. By 1980, over half of the Democrats in the House held a chair of a committee or subcommittee, creating almost 150 overlapping fiefdoms. The growth of subcommittees created greater confusion over jurisdictions, less discipline on the floor, and less accountability for mistakes and delays. It certainly made full House leadership more difficult. As bills entered the maze of subcommittees, it became harder to pull them back together for final passage.

The leadership crisis also involved reelection pressure. Though most incumbents win reelection if they run, there are always just enough defeats to frighten the rest of the House. Congressional elections are not games; they involve the potential loss of a valued career. Including voluntary retirements (often in anticipation of defeat), 1 out of 7 House members leaves after each election. In 1982, for example, 81 members were replaced. It does not take too many elections to replace a sizable chunk of the House. Moreover, because House members run every two years, the odds of losing may compound over time. Like aging prizefighters, members of Congress may face greater risks with each passing victory.

Regardless, as one political scientist argues, House seats are "unsafe at any margin." No matter how impressive the most recent victory, members must be on guard. And those fears rise whenever a prominent member loses. Since many defeated members return to the Hill as lobbyists, their lingering pain is always present. "It makes you think about your own chances," one Ways and Means Committee member remarked after spying a former chairman in the hearing room. "You see the old guys in the halls talking to other lobbyists and it reminds you of your own mortality."

A third part of the leadership crisis involved the unusual shape of the Ninety-seventh Congress, elected in 1980. House Republicans had just enough seats to form a conservative majority with the Boll Weevils on the floor, but not enough to alter the balance of power in the committees and subcommittees. Because the Democratic party controlled committee ratios and its own assignments, most of the major committees were stacked against the conservative coalition. As a result, the committees continued to produce liberal legislation, only to see it defeated and/or replaced on the floor. The stalemates began early in the Ninety-seventh Congress and continued through 1982. "This was the most frustrating session of Congress I've ever served in," a Republican complained at the end of 1982. "We were so much closer in the House and had a majority in the Senate, but we didn't control any of the committees. We were close, but not close enough." According to one Republican Senate aide a larger Democratic majority in the House might have been better for social security: "It could be that having a more liberal House would improve the chances for some social security legislation. The Congress is pretty good at settling arguments between strong opponents. But the House has been so weak inside that we've had trouble negotiating with anyone. The liberals might be able to pass something in 1983 if they win more seats in 1982. That way, we could use our strength in the Senate to get some real reform."

Who Moves First?

If the House was to lead on social security, the initiative would have to come from the Ways and Means Committee. Ways and Means had jurisdiction over social security and had no competition from other committees. "Who else would do it?" one Ways and Means staffer asked. "The Aging Committee? It's not empowered to create legislation, just to hold hearings and raise issues. The Rules Committee? It's not empowered to create bills either. . . . It has to be Ways and Means because there isn't anyone else." If Ways and Means failed to move, leadership would have to come from outside the House. Yet, under the Constitution, the House of Representatives has to be the source of any revenue-raising bills. If the social security rescue involved any kind of tax increase, Ways and Means would have to move before the Senate.

In taking control of the issue, Ways and Means had one advantage: the lack of knowledge among the rest of the House membership. As a result of the rise of subcommittee government, members had grown more specialized over time, becoming experts in very narrow policy areas. This specialization had led to an increase in what some political scientists have called cue taking, where large numbers of House members follow the lead of recognized experts at the committee and subcommittee level. Thus the more technical the legislation became, the less most members would understand. If Ways and Means passed a complicated bill and received a ticket to the floor from the Rules Committee, the chances of success would improve dramatically.

But unfortunately for social security, Ways and Means had lost considerable power in the early 1970s. Liberal Democrats had stripped the committee of its leadership tools, weakening its influence over such key issues as social security and tax increases. Ways and Means had once controlled all committee assignments in the House. In exchange for good assignments, House members would often support the committee on the floor, even on painful votes. Moreover, the 25-member committee was allowed to operate without subcommittees, eliminating extra delays. Under the reforms, Ways and Means not only lost the committee assignment power but was forced to expand to six subcommittees and 35 members. The committee grew unwieldy and began to do more of its legislative business in the subcommittees. More important, because Ways and Means had little to trade in return for support on painful legislation, it now found full committee action more difficult. Thus if Ways and Means was to be the leader on social security, it would have few weapons at its disposal to enforce its will on the House floor.

THE SENATE

The Senate also had a leadership crisis in the 1980s. As Sen. Robert Dole joked at the start of the Senate Finance Committee hearings on the social security rescue bill in 1983, "We have a lot of self-starters up here. The last time I counted, there were 100." Indeed, the Senate actually seemed perfectly designed for individual action. If a senator wanted to introduce a dozen amendments on a social security rescue bill without even the slightest understanding of the issue, there was no rule against it. As Dole explained, "We are very disciplined. We always try to limit ourselves to two or three amendments . . . apiece. That's a total of 300." Because the Senate did not have strict rules for floor debate, it was often easier to delay action than to promote it. As Majority Leader Howard Baker once said, the Senate was often as unruly as "hogs on ice."

A Deliberative Body

The Senate leadership crisis involved more than just a lack of rules for floor debate. Some senators blamed the leadership crisis on sunshine. One Democrat argued that "ten years ago, I could sit in a closed committee meeting and say that I couldn't go along with something, but if they let me demagogue it for a while, I wouldn't stand in the way. Now I would have to carry it out much further."[3] Others blamed the erosion of Senate courtesy. As one remarked, "There's much less civility than when I got here ten years ago. There aren't as many nice people as there were before. It makes working in the Senate difficult. Ten years ago you didn't have people calling each other sons of bitches and vowing to get each other."[4]

Still other factors complicated leadership problems in the Senate. One involved the rise of the Senate as an incubator of presidential candidates. In 1984, for example, six of the eight contenders for the Democratic presidential nomination were current or former senators, and the bulk of potential contestants for the 1988 Republican nomination were also from the Senate. Those presidential ambitions had a predictable impact on the Senate. Senators were not willing to remain passive participants in the legislative process. They had to establish their reputations quickly and build national exposure. If that meant an occasional filibuster or endless delays on crucial bills, so be it. The intense media attention inside the Senate incubator also made it more difficult to build legislative coalitions on the floor.

[3]Congressional Quarterly *Weekly Report,* September 4, 1982, p. 2176.
[4]Ibid., p. 2182.

The leadership crisis also involved the collapse of committee government. As in the House, the decline of strong committees reflected individual demands for more power. But unlike in the House, the loss of committee government did not mean a rise of subcommittee power. The Senate simply shifted to 100 separate committees—each one an individual senator with a staff to rival the larger House committees; each one without boundaries, free to roam from issue to issue. Indeed, between 1947 and 1980, the average Senate staff jumped from five to forty-three. The increase made it easier to ignore the committees and the leadership, creating individual fiefdoms in each Senate office. "It's every man for himself," said a former Kansas Republican. "Every senator is a baron. He has his own principality. Once you adopt that as a means of doing business, it's hard to establish any cohesion."[5] The decline of Senate committees meant that legislation often came from individual staffs. On the easy issues, there were competing bills to choose from. On the hard issues, there were often none. If there was no payoff in an issue, there were few takers. It was up to the committees, however weak, to generate legislation on the difficult questions, whether taxes or social security.

A third part of the leadership crisis involved the low reelection rates in the Senate. Unlike in the House, where incumbents were reelected nine times out of ten, the chances in the Senate were barely fifty-fifty. In 1976, 9 incumbents were defeated, another 10 in 1978, another 13 in 1980. The picture improved in 1982, but even the most secure senator had reason to fear in 1984 or 1986. Senate contests attract better challengers, more media exposure, and more money, leading to higher odds against reelection. One senator summed up the atmosphere in the Senate in 1982 as follows: "The founding fathers gave senators six-year terms so they could be statesmen for at least four years and not respond to every whim and caprice. Now a senator in his first year knows that any vote could beat him five years later. So senators may behave like House members. They are running constantly."[6]

Who Moves Second?

If the Senate was to lead on social security, the initiative would have to come from the Finance Committee. Like Ways and Means in the House, Finance had jurisdiction over social security and had no competition from other committees.

The best example of the Finance Committee's potential for leadership came in the summer of 1982, when Chairman Dole steered a $99-billion tax increase through a reluctant committee, past a divided Senate floor, through a House-Senate negotiating committee, and onto the President's desk. It was a legislative miracle of sorts, but it offered little hope for social security. First, the tax bill was a product of closed-door meetings, with little input from the Democrats. That style would not work on social security; Republicans did not want sole responsibility for a package of tax increases and benefit cuts. Second, the bill

[5]Ibid.
[6]Ibid.

barely passed the Senate on a straight party-line vote of 50–47. Again, that style would not work on social security; it had to be a bipartisan effort. Third, when the issue arose in the House, the Democrats could not pass their own tax bill and entered the final negotiations empty-handed. That would not happen on social security; the House would have a bill.

Thus the 1982 tax increase offered few lessons to the Finance Committee on how to draft a major social security rescue bill. Indeed, the inability of the House Democrats to draft their own tax bill and the straight party votes in the Senate seemed to suggest that a social security bill could not be drafted without intense conflict. Further, if the Finance Committee did not lead in the Senate, that left a power vacuum for individual senators.

CONCLUSION

"Don't expect leadership from us," a Ways and Means member said in 1982. "Congress isn't equipped to lead. It's a representative institution, with all that means for a stalemate." Though both the House and Senate had committees for drafting legislation, it was not clear that either body could use them. Though both the House and Senate had formal leaders at the top of the parties, it was not clear whether either side knew enough about where it was going to get there first. The budget was taking more and more time away from other issues, and the sunshine was too intense for even the most responsible members.

If not in the House or Senate, then where? According to one observer, "Congress is not well adapted for dealing with complex issues that also have high political risks *unless* the President becomes involved. The Democrats and Republicans can negotiate all they want, but at some point they have to ask 'Can you deliver the President?'" At the start of the term, Congress is willing to give the President at least one chance to set the legislative agenda. If the President becomes involved, the House and Senate have a better chance to forge internal coalitions. If not, individual members take over, using their institutions more to win elections than to make needed choices.

3

The One-Shot Presidency

"Ron Reagan is a great guy, a real charmer," a House member said. "He's got a great sense of humor, always has an anecdote for the occasion. But I'd never vote for his program on that basis. I'd no more vote for his legislation because he's a nice guy than I'd walk over hot coals for a handful of jellybeans." The President was always welcome to give advice to Congress, but nothing compelled Congress to move on his behalf. Stalemate was always an option. Clearly, there are few senators or representatives who would refuse a phone call from the President; there are fewer still who would turn down a trip to the presidential retreat at Camp David or box seats at the Kennedy Center for the Performing Arts.

Yet even though members of Congress will listen politely, they do not have to respond. As President Lyndon Johnson learned early in his career, "You can tell a man to go to hell, but you can't make him go." Johnson remembered that line many times in building his Great Society: "It seemed particularly apt when I found myself in a struggle with the House or Senate," he wrote. "I would start to speak out . . . and remember that no matter how many times I told the Congress to do something, I could never force it to act."[1]

There are a number of reasons why Congress might refuse to listen. First, the branches are on different timetables. House and Senate members can continue to serve until they are defeated; the Twenty-second Amendment restricts the President to two consecutive terms in office, a total of eight short years. Second, the branches represent different constituencies. House members are elected from narrow districts, covering an average of 520,000 people each; senators are elected from the states, ranging in size from hundreds of thousands to millions; Presidents are elected by the nation, or at least the coalition of

---

[1]Lyndon Baines Johnson, *The Vantage Point* (New York: Holt, Rinehart and Winston, 1971), p. 461.

districts and states that provide an electoral college majority. Finally, the branches have different policy concerns. Presidents face a wide range of issues dictated by law and custom, and they need congressional support on virtually every item; members of Congress are free to pick and choose their agendas on the basis of reelection or what they see as good policy.

Yet there are also reasons why Congress might choose to listen. It is not enough merely to stalemate the President for four years. The President's public approval ratings affect public support for members of Congress, too. According to opinion polls, the politicians rise and fall together, regardless of the party. When the President is sinking in the polls, members of Congress sink, too. Certainly, if members of Congress run for reelection, the President can be a valuable ally or potent enemy, particularly when it comes time to fund a local project or close a military base back home.

PRESIDENTIAL POWERS

By the 1980s, Presidents had a number of tools for leading Congress on the tough and not-so-tough issues. Some were formal, others informal. Still, even the strongest weapon was little more than a temporary advantage in the ebb and flow of presidential power. As Richard Neustadt argues, "With the array of vantage points at his disposal, a President may be far more persuasive than his logic or charm could make him. But outcomes are not guaranteed by his advantages. . . . It is well that the White House holds the vantage points it does. In such a business any President may need them all—and more."[2]

The Strengths

Reagan had three formal advantages as he opened his administration. First, under the Constitution, the President is required "from time to time" to "give to Congress information on the state of the union, and recommend to their consideration such measures as he shall judge necessary and expedient." In short, the President has at least one chance to set the national agenda. By the twentieth century this advantage had evolved into an annual event, composed of dozens of messages and reports to Congress on possible legislation. Foremost among the messages was the State of the Union address, listing the President's legislative program. Sometimes, the address focused on a small set of priorities; other times, it was little more than a "laundry list" of requests. Because the message was delivered at the start of each year, it gave the President a prime opportunity to focus congressional attention.

Second, Reagan had the veto power, allowing him to stalemate Congress. Though Congress could override a presidential veto with a two-thirds vote in each house, it was difficult to do so. Of 1,400 vetoes from Washington to

---

[2]Richard Neustadt, *Presidential Power* (New York: Wiley, 1980), pp. 28–29.

Reagan, Congress overrode fewer than 100. Moreover, as Reagan knew, the veto is particularly valuable when Presidents are in trouble. During Gerald Ford's brief term in office, for example, he vetoed 66 bills but was overridden on only 12. Ford did not have the votes to pass his own legislation, but he had more than enough to stop large Democratic majorities in both chambers. After all, Ford needed only one-third plus one of either house to block action. Presidents sometimes find it easy to defeat a bill, too.

Third, as administrative chief, Reagan had some control over the legislative agenda. Whether through executive orders, reorganizations, or political appointments, he could shape government action without congressional consent. His appointment of James Watt as Secretary of the Interior, for example, had a major impact on environmental policy. Even if Reagan's environmental program could not pass in Congress, Watt could move forward in the executive branch. Moreover, Reagan's administrative control appeared to be strengthened by a 1983 Supreme Court decision declaring the legislative veto unconstitutional. In striking down the legislative veto, the Court declared 126 laws unconstitutional, voiding more laws in that one decision than in its entire history.

Beyond these formal advantages, Reagan also had at least three informal tools for focusing congressional attention on his priorities. First, he started his term with high public approval. His standing in the public opinion polls affected congressional support for key programs. As long as he was popular, Congress would have to listen. Threats to campaign for or against members of Congress took on more meaning while Reagan was riding the crest of public support, giving him the power to reward friends and punish enemies. When a popular President talks, Congress listens. Though public approval is always measured by a very simple question—in this case, "Do you approve or disapprove of the way Reagan is handling his job as President?"—it has a major bearing on how Congress reacts to specific legislation.

Second, Reagan had a Republican party majority in the Senate and an ideological majority in the House. Obviously, a majority party was more valuable to the President than a minority. Because the majority party controls the committees and subcommittees, it can control the movement of legislation to the floor. Thus Reagan's Republican Senate was more often the source of conservative bills than was the Democratic House. Yet even there, Reagan had a conservative floor majority, composed of Republicans and conservative Democrats. Though that ideological majority did not control the committees, it did provide the margin of victory on Reagan's budget and tax cuts.

Third, though public approval and party seats were critical, Reagan had his own lobbying skills. His persuasive abilities could stretch public approval and party support. Reagan's speaking ability, personal charm, vote trading on key bills, arm twisting, and campaign support were all tools for focusing congressional attention on his priorities. Nevertheless, whatever his public approval and party seats, Reagan was but one suitor among many on Capitol Hill. He had to bargain, cajole, threaten, horse-trade, manipulate, and stroke Congress on his top legislation. As Johnson once argued, there is "but one way for a

President to deal with the Congress, and that is, continuously, incessantly, and without interruption. If it's really going to work, the relationship between the President and Congress has got to be almost incestuous."[3] Indeed, for Johnson, "merely placing a bill before Congress is not enough. Without constant attention from the administration most legislation moves through the congressional process at the speed of a glacier."[4]

The Weaknesses

The problem with all of the President's strengths was simply that they did not go as far in the 1980s as before. Congress had changed. As former President Ford concluded in 1980, "Party members now go off in ten different directions. They seem to follow the public surveys rather than the party philosophy. And the net result is no leader in the Congress, Democrat or Republican, can say 'My party is going to follow this party position.'" Gone were the days when the President could sit down with the party leaders and hammer out a bill that would pass through Congress. There were too many interests, too many committee and subcommittee chairs, too little floor discipline. And even if the leaders wanted to negotiate, the public spotlight might blind them. Further, as the campaign season grew longer and the national parties grew weaker, Presidents had even less time to think before having to announce their own intentions. It was not an environment designed for careful decisions.

Thus, despite their similar mastery of Congress, Johnson and Reagan operated in different presidential times. Though both Presidents set clear priorities in Congress, used their public approval and party seats as building blocks for passage, and created a climate of support in Washington, Reagan's victories did not spell a return of power to the presidency. His victories owed more to legislative maneuvers and first-year public support than to formal advantages. The House and Senate remained as fragmented and leaderless after 1981 as before. That Reagan was able to win on the budget was a testament to his legislative skills; that he was able to win on the tax cut was a testament to his outbidding the Democrats; and that he was stalemated on both issues within a year was a tribute to the dispersion of power in the congressional system.

There were at least two basic differences between Johnson and Reagan that reflected changes in both Congress and the issues over the 1970s. First, unlike Johnson, Reagan went to the public early and often, using his communications skills to marshal public support. From the very opening of Reagan's term, he pressed the public to show Congress grassroots support. The problem was that the public rose to Reagan's support only for a time, growing impatient and uninterested as the term wore on. Second, at least on his budget, Reagan relied on a packaging maneuver to end-run the legislative committees and subcom-

---

[3]Doris Kearns, *Lyndon Johnson and the American Dream* (New York: Harper & Row, 1976), pp. 236–237.
[4]Johnson, *The Vantage Point*, p. 461.

mittees. His budget was put together as an omnibus resolution containing over eighty different cuts and never moved through the normal process. It was passed in a single up-or-down vote. Unlike Johnson, who built his victories from the committees up, Reagan finessed Congress on the budget. On most other issues, including social security, Reagan would have to build from the ground up, winning many times en route to final passage. Packaging devices might work on the budget, but not on substantive bills.

A FIRST-YEAR PRESIDENCY

If there was one lesson in recent history for Reagan on social security, it was to move quickly. Even though Johnson had enjoyed the largest Democratic majorities since Franklin Roosevelt, he still moved fast. As Johnson said at the time, "I keep hitting hard because I know this honeymoon won't last. Every day I lose a little more political capital. That's why we have to keep at it, never letting up. One day soon, I don't know when, the critics and the snipers will move in and we will be at stalemate. We have to get all we can now, before the roof comes down."[5]

Office of Management and Budget (OMB) director-to-be David Stockman echoed those words fifteen years later in a transition memo to President-elect Reagan warning of a "GOP economic Dunkirk": "If bold policies are not swiftly, deftly and courageously implemented in the first six months, Washington will quickly become engulfed in political disorder commensurate with the surrounding economic disarray. A golden opportunity for permanent conservative policy revision and political realignment could be thoroughly dissipated before the Reagan administration is even up to speed."[6] In short, Reagan's strength would decline over time. His formal advantages would be rendered meaningless, and his formal levers would weaken. His one shot would have to come in the first year.

This emphasis on the first year of the term as the prime opportunity for success in Congress involved two basic life cycles in the presidency. The first centers on the President's political support and is called the cycle of decreasing influence. Whatever his success early on, Reagan could expect to lose party seats in the midterm elections. It is a pattern that has held since Roosevelt's second term. Ford lost 48 fellow partisans in 1974, Carter 16 in 1978.

Reagan could also expect to lose public approval over the term. Ford lost 30 points in the polls during his first three months of office alone; Carter lost 33 points over four years; Reagan lost 10 points in two years. Moreover, recent Presidents have started their terms at much lower approval ratings than ever before. Whereas Truman began his term at an 87 percent rating, Carter started at 66 percent and Reagan at 51 percent. Presidents start the term with a specific

---

[5] In Jack Valenti, *A Very Human President* (New York: Norton, 1975), p. 144.
[6] The *Washington Post*, December 14, 1980, p. C1.

amount of political support, and it declines over time. Though they can slow the decline, whether through foreign crises or dramatic speeches, it still exists.

There is some dispute over why the cycle of decreasing influence exists and whether it can be broken.[7] Some observers believe that the last few Presidents have just been unlucky. If they had faced different events, public approval might have remained high. Vietnam, Watergate, and the Iranian hostage crisis were bad luck. Other observers suggest that the last few Presidents have simply been poorly prepared. Entering office with little national experience, they could only make mistakes. Public approval drops even when the President makes minor decisions. The American public expects too much and will always be disappointed.

What matters here is the widespread belief within the Reagan White House that the cycle did exist, that there could be a GOP economic Dunkirk, that there would be a public backlash against the budget cuts. Moreover, regardless of the reasons for the decline, the cycle of decreasing influence suggested an obvious strategy for Reagan: *move it or lose it*. As former Vice President Walter Mondale once noted, a President "starts out with a bank full of good will and slowly checks are drawn on that, and it's very rare that it's replenished. It's a one-time deposit." Indeed, even if the President asks for nothing, the deposits will dwindle anyway, slowly evaporating as Congress moves ahead on its own. In short, the President's credit is good for only a very short time.

Yet there is a second cycle in the presidency—one that involves knowledge and expertise. Because Presidents and their staffs learn over time, they experience a cycle of increasing effectiveness. Presidents have less public support, but they learn what to do with it. Carter clearly became a better legislative President over his term. He learned how to deal with Congress, how to stroke reluctant legislators, how to draft bills from the ground up. Following his early problems in Congress, Carter instituted a White House agenda-setting process to win passage of the Panama Canal treaties and Civil Service reform. However, by the time Carter learned how the system worked, he had lost much of his public support. The early mistakes continued to haunt him on Capitol Hill, creating a lasting impression of ineptness.

The cycle of increasing effectiveness suggested a second obvious strategy for Reagan: *be prepared*. If Presidents do not want to wait, they must enter office with at least some basic knowledge of and expertise in national politics. That means advance planning during the campaign; that means learning before the election, not after. That also means the recruitment of experienced aides, not just political hacks. Reagan, for example, was willing to hire people with considerable Washington experience, thus building White House information and expertise.

Yet even with advance planning and experienced aides, Reagan faced a

---

[7]See in particular Samuel Kernell's summary of these issues in "The Presidency and the People: The Modern Paradox," in Michael Nelson, editor, *The Presidency and the Political System* (Washington, D.C.: Congressional Quarterly Press, 1984), pp. 233–263.

dilemma. How could he move it (not lose it) without making major mistakes? The answer often was that he could not. It takes time to build careful legislation, to learn how each Congress works, to form working relations both inside and outside the White House. In the Reagan administration, for example, the mistakes came in drafting the budget package, not in the legislative liaison. Reagan's staff was skilled at passing programs but not necessarily at building them. As Stockman later admitted, his biggest mistake came from one simple phrase he repeated over and over in early 1981: "Hey, we have to get a program out fast."[8]

The cycle of increasing effectiveness also means that some White House staffers have more influence in the first months of a term simply because they have had more experience. Stockman, for example, had prepared fifty policy papers outlining cuts in domestic spending even before Reagan's inauguration. As one observer concluded, "Stockman was anxious to win fast approval for them, before the new Cabinet officers were fully familiar with their departments and prepared to defend their bureaucracies." The cycle of increasing effectiveness means that there will be vacuums at the start of a term, areas where information and expertise are thin. The advisers who can fill those vacuums will have more influence than those who must first learn their jobs. Over time, however, information and expertise will even out; initial advantages will disappear. Thus by 1983, Stockman's understanding of the budget no longer gave him an edge. "You've got Cabinet members who have a good understanding and strong views about their programs," a White House aide commented. "That means Dave Stockman has less leverage now."

A NO-WIN PRESIDENCY?

The problem for Reagan was that the cycle of decreasing influence was stronger than ever by the start of his term. The 1984 presidential campaign would start earlier; public approval would begin lower and drop faster; congressional resistance would appear sooner. With changes in Congress, Reagan was well advised to move as fast as possible, even if that meant major mistakes in his legislation. As one Carter aide remarked, "This has become a no-win job. It involves a series of obstacles, one hurdle after another. Each problem is followed by a second, more difficult problem."

For Reagan, of course, stalemate was enough in 1982–1983. With his budget and tax cuts in place, all he needed to do was protect against Democratic counterattacks. The veto power was sufficient to hold the line on his economic package, and the second and third years of the tax cut were implemented easily. But there were issues where stalemate was not enough. Reagan needed support on his proposed sale of AWAC planes to Saudi Arabia (he won); Reagan needed support on his veto of a $12-billion supplemental appropria-

---

[8]William Greider, "The Education of David Stockman," *The Atlantic*, 248 (December 1981), p. 54.

tions bill in the summer of 1982 (he lost); Reagan needed support on U.S. Marines in Lebanon (he won); Reagan needed support on social security.

CONCLUSION

These cycles suggested one strategy on social security: leadership would have to come early in the Reagan term or not at all. Without major action by the end of the first year, Reagan would have little to say to Congress. His public approval would be down, and the coming midterm elections would spell further trouble. But because of the structure of Congress and the presidency, the potential for compromise would only decline over time. Reagan already planned to spend a great deal of his political capital on the budget and might be left with little to devote to social security. By the end of the first year, Reagan would still have the formal tools of leadership, but he might not have the political fuel. The danger was that Reagan would move it *and* lose it, forcing a leaderless Congress to make the choices.

PART TWO

The Obstacles

4

A Social Security Primer

Social security hit bottom in 1982. On November 5, the social security trust fund borrowed $581 million from its companion funds to pay benefit checks on time; on December 7, the fund borrowed another $3.4 billion; on December 31, the fund borrowed $13.5 billion to cover the first six months of 1983. Already $17 billion in debt, social security would run out of money on the third day of July 1983. Benefit checks would be delayed.

The borrowing prompted the first real debate about social security since its inception. Conservatives said the program was little more than a con game; liberals said the program was fine and blamed the trouble on Reagan. Both sides had plenty of support. One particularly critical study concluded that the "social security system as it exists today is fundamentally flawed," while former Social Security Commissioner Robert Ball called the funding crisis only "modest and temporary." Political cartoonists had a field day.

In the span of a few short years, this once sacred cow had become the subject of widespread public debate. Social security was now part of an annual contest over scarce budget dollars, a source of deficit savings. Yet this debate did not occur in a vacuum. This was not a new program, subject to neutral analysis and rational change. This was not a small program, subject to policy experiments with little social cost. This was not a flexible program, easily subject to benefit cuts or tax increases. This was a program with a long public history and considerable, if often murky, social and economic impact.

Social security itself touched most of the elderly and was one of the few government programs where the public got something tangible in return for their taxes. Moreover, the program was a cornerstone of federal policy for the aged. By 1981, it accounted for the bulk of federal spending on the elderly. It provided at least half of the retirement income for two-thirds of the aged population and was the sole source of retirement income for almost one-fifth.

Over 70 percent of the elderly reported at least some personal contact with the Social Security Administration (SSA). During its forty-year existence, the social security program had grown beyond a mere symbol of the New Deal and Franklin Roosevelt. Virtually all American workers had a nine-digit number both as a permanent reminder of the social security program and as a promise of future rewards.

THE PROGRAM

The history of social security is one of slow but steady expansion, a classic example of the incremental growth of government programs. Enacted in 1935, social security eventually grew to become the single largest domestic program in the federal budget. In 1982, the system collected almost $190 billion in taxes and spent almost $200 billion in benefits. Those benefits covered three separate programs: social security, disability, and Medicare. Of the three, social security was the largest, totaling $140 billion.[1]

Because of its size, of course, social security was an attractive target for budget cutters. The problem was that the public felt entitled to benefits. After paying a lifetime of taxes into the system, they expected some reward. This was a solemn government contract—not welfare, but an earned right—and people counted on the retirement income.

The key to the contract was the payroll tax. At least prior to 1983, almost all social security funds came from a single source: the FICA, or Federal Insurance Contribution Act, tax. Workers could see the money being taken out of their payroll checks each week and were promised that the money would come back after retirement. And the amounts were not small. In 1983, the payroll tax was 6.7 percent on employees and employers each and was collected on the first $35,700 of each worker's income. (As a result of that $35,700 ceiling, the maximum such workers could pay in 1983 was $2,391. However, the ceiling was indexed to rise with wage growth each year. By 1984, the ceiling had moved up to $37,800, increasing the maximum these workers could pay to $2,533.)

Once the taxes were collected by the Internal Revenue Service, they went into one of three "dedicated" trust funds: the Old Age and Survivors Insurance fund (OASI, more commonly called social security), the Disability Insurance fund (DI, more commonly known as disability), and the Hospital Insurance fund (HI, more commonly labeled Medicare). Because the money was dedicated to the three trust funds, it could not be spent on other government programs. Any cuts in social security would only make the budget *look* smaller. The savings would stay in the trust fund and could not be used to pay for defense, foreign aid, food stamps, and so on.

---

[1]Most of the figures in this book are taken from technical memoranda to the National Commission on Social Security Reform. A complete list of the memoranda can be found in the commission report, January 15, 1983, Appendix F.

Good Intentions

Before looking at the basic characteristics of the social security program, it is important to emphasize one lesson from social security history: it is almost impossible to tell whether the drafters ever expected the program to grow so large.[2] Although SSA's actuaries correctly predicted the eventual size of the program in percentage terms, they certainly could not have predicted the dollars that would eventually be involved. A $140-billion-a-year social security budget was as far from the imagination in the 1930s as space shuttles and personal computers.

Conservatives argue that social security was meant to be small, part of a three-legged stool composed of social security, private pensions, and personal savings. They also say it was meant to be funded only by the payroll tax, with no support from general income tax revenues. Liberals, in contrast, argue that social security was meant to be the primary source of support for lower- and middle-income retirees. They also say it was meant to be funded one-third from employees, one-third from employers, and one-third from general revenues.

Unfortunately, it is difficult to tell who is right. There were at least fifteen major changes in the social security program between 1935 and 1980, each reflecting the ebb and flow of political power in the American system of government. Changes made by Democrats in 1939 support the liberal view of history; changes made by Republicans in 1950 support the conservative view. The original benefit formula, for example, was half as generous as it was in 1980; it expanded in small jumps, usually just before an election. Even if history provided some clear answers, what has always mattered in Congress is the *here and now.* Members had to consider the breadth and scope of the social security system today, not back in 1935, 1939, or 1950. Congress and the President could not go back to the less generous days of the 1950s even if they wanted to. The program had taken on a life of its own.

Nor could the debate over original intentions help solve the crisis. History could tell President Reagan and Speaker O'Neill how the social security program got to be so large but not how to solve a crisis that was not anticipated by the original drafters. Moreover, if the founders of social security shared any goal, it was that the program be allowed to grow and prosper. And that it did. Indeed, according to one of those present at the creation of the system, "Social Security will always be a goal, never a finished thing, because human aspirations are infinitely expandable . . . just as human nature is infinitely perfectable."[3]

Unfortunately, as social security struggled to meet the new challenges of the 1980s, it faced its own inertia. Indeed, there were four characteristics of the

---

[2]The most detailed history of the politics of social security can be found in Martha Derthick's award-winning book *Policymaking for Social Security* (Washington, D.C.: The Brookings Institution, 1979); a detailed history and explanation of the program and its benefits can be found in Robert Myers, *Social Security,* 4th ed. (Homewood, Ill.: Richard D. Irwin, Inc., 1993).
[3]Derthick, *Policymaking for Social Security,* p. 17.

program that made it very difficult to change: (1) it was old, (2) it was large, (3) it was funded pay-as-you-go, and (4) it balanced two incompatible goals.

An Old Program

The social security program was a survivor. Through three wars, nine Presidents, countless turnovers in Congress, friendly and hostile administrators, and the Reagan revolution, the program lived on unscathed. Its age was a powerful source of its legitimacy and its continuing public support. "We have to realize that social security is as American as mom and apple pie," one Reagan aide said. "It might not be the best retirement program, but it's the one the people know."

Yet if age was an ally, it was an enemy, too. When a retirement program first starts, it has many workers and few beneficiaries. In such an *immature* system, it is easy to have large benefits and low taxes. In the social security system, the early ratio of workers to beneficiaries was almost 9 to 1. Taxes were low (1 percent on employees and employers each); potentials for growth were high. Unfortunately, as the program aged, the ratio of workers to beneficiaries dropped. As more and more of the original workers grew old and retired, taxes had to rise to cover the benefit checks. By 1980, the ratio of workers to beneficiaries had dropped to 5 to 1; by 2020, without a new baby boom, the ratio would fall to just over 2 to 1. In such a *mature* program, there is little room for larger benefits without higher taxes.

From a relative standpoint, much larger benefits could be paid to those retiring early in the life of the system. The problem for Congress and the President was how to cut benefits once they had been set. By their nature, politicians like to give, not cut. The danger in a mature system, however, is that giving will outstrip receiving. And that is just what happened in the mid-1970s. Because of huge benefit increases from 1969 to 1972 and automatic cost-of-living adjustments (COLAs) starting in 1975, social security was in trouble by 1977. Social security benefit checks were going up faster than the government's ability to pay for them. As the economy continued to drag, social security entered another crisis as Ronald Reagan took office.

A Large Program

By virtually any measure, social security was a very large program. In 1982, the system paid benefits of one kind or another to over 35 million people in an average month and collected taxes from 115 million more. Social security covered close to 90 percent of all workers and collected taxes on almost $1.5 trillion in wages.

The program had grown in a series of small, incremental steps, punctuated by occasional major breakthroughs. (Even with passage of the rescue bill in April 1983, the social security system expanded somewhat, with higher taxes and coverage for federal employees. Still, 1983 was the first time Congress and the President had ever openly cut benefits affecting all current beneficiaries.)

Prior to the rescue bill, there were eight major breakthroughs, each adding to the system's girth. The first came with passage of the original program in 1935. Benefits would start in 1942, but only for those over the age of 65. The second came in 1939, only four years later: benefits would now start in 1940, with a new formula that guaranteed larger retirement checks in the short run. The third came in 1950, with a 77 percent benefit boost and easier eligibility. The fourth came in 1956 with the creation of the social security disability program, as well as an early retirement option for women at age 62 (the provision was granted to men in 1961). The fifth came in 1965 with passage of Medicare, a major goal of the founders, plus still more social security increases. The sixth, seventh, and eighth came from 1969 to 1972, with a total 45 percent (52 percent with compounding) benefit increase and an annual cost-of-living adjustment— the ultimate automatic pilot.

When coupled with the smaller adjustments every year or two, these breakthroughs produced a massive social program. According to Derthick, the founders ended up with an "extremely appealing" program: "First, the program was intrinsically incremental, which meant that costs would start low and grow gradually. Second, it promised taxpayers specific benefits in return for their taxes, which both eased their willingness to pay taxes and alleviated whatever stigma was attached to getting the benefits. Third, it contained many compromises and ambiguities that enabled diverse interests to coalesce in support of it." In short, social security started with a small price tag, a large return on taxes, and enough confusion to keep opponents off guard.[4]

The sheer magnitude of the social security program had several consequences for change. On the one hand, it created sizable constituency groups on all sides of the debate. With so many individuals already receiving benefits and so many more paying taxes into a promised retirement, Congress and the President faced instant opposition to most alternatives. On the other hand, the size of the program made it an attractive morsel for beleaguered budget cutters. With the defense budget off-limits, substantial savings could come only from the domestic arena. In any attempt to balance a rapidly failing budget, social security presented a target of opportunity. Moreover, the size of the program guaranteed that it would have major social and economic impacts, even if they were difficult to measure.

A Pay-As-You-Go Program

In technical terms, social security was an "intergenerational transfer tax." Translated, the program took most of its money from the young and transferred it to the old, shifting billions of dollars from workers to beneficiaries. In this pay-as-you-go program, taxes were spent immediately on benefits. There were no passbook savings accounts at SSA headquarters in Baltimore, Maryland. Indeed, SSA did not even keep records of taxes paid. Benefits were based on records of yearly earnings. Thus despite public fears, the social security system could never go bankrupt. Social security benefits never depended on money in some individually labeled account; they depended on the power to tax.

That is the essence of a pay-as-you-go program, even one that maintained a small reserve balance as social security did. Instead of saving the trillions of dollars that it would take to pay everyone's future benefits, social security simply took the money from one generation to pay another. Moreover, it is not clear whether social security should have done otherwise. If social security was to save up every last penny needed to pay future benefits, the government would eventually accumulate such massive amounts of cash that it might just end up controlling most of the nation's economy.

A pay-as-you-go program has one feature, however, that affects politics: it can get into trouble very fast. When the economy is poor, it does not take very long for social security to face an emergency. It is a simple cash-flow problem. More unemployment means fewer workers paying taxes into the system; more inflation means higher benefit checks for retirees. If both unemployment and inflation exist at the same time—something once thought impossible by economists but now known as "stagflation"—social security will pay out much more in benefits than it receives in taxes. Moreover, if the system has small margins of safety, even brief economic storms can create a serious shortfall. If benefits go up too fast or taxes come in too slowly, a pay-as-you-go system can sink quickly.

There are ways to prevent such rapid deterioration. One way is to save for emergencies. When social security first started paying benefits in the 1940s, it operated with at least some level of reserve, a pad of funds against trouble. The savings, usually called the "reserve ratio," offer protection in bad times. A *100* percent reserve ratio, for instance, means the system can cover twelve months of benefits even if absolutely no taxes come in during the year. A *zero* reserve ratio means that there is no hedge against any kind of bad economic performance. Enough money has to come in at the start of each month to cover benefits. A *negative* reserve means that the trust fund is empty and that the system either has to borrow money (but only with congressional action) or must delay benefit checks until the taxes arrive. Benefits will still be paid, but later and later each month.

In the early years of the program, social security reserves were very high, reaching 1,156 percent (or 11.56 years of protection for then-current retirees) in 1950. This reserve was a simple by-product of social security's youth. There were many more workers in 1950 than beneficiaries, and their taxes overwhelmed the $961 million spent that year on outgo. To reach a fund ratio of 1,156 percent in 1982 would have required a fund balance of almost $1.9 *trillion,* an amount almost three times as large as the total federal budget that year. Yet if 1,156 was much too high, zero was much too low. Experts were recommending a reserve of between 75 and 100 percent—that is, less than a year of safety.

A second way to protect against hard times is to build automatic stabilizers and fail-safes into the system. If the economy does poorly, the benefit COLA might be reduced. If the system is sinking fast, taxes might be increased. Most of these devices would come into play only under very poor economic conditions. If the reserve ratio falls to, say, 15 percent in any given year, benefits might be cut. Such a stabilizer or fail-safe might be sound from a commonsense standpoint, but it has high political costs. Who would decide whether taxes should go up or benefits go down? Once in place, however, such devices would offer considerable political protection. With benefit cuts and tax increases on automatic pilot, Congress would not have to make tough choices every year.

Incompatible Goals

Social security was originally designed to meet two competing goals.[5] First, under the so-called equity principle, benefits were supposed to bear some relationship to the amount of taxes paid. The more you pay in, the more you get out. It was only fair to have a link between taxes and benefits. Second, under the "adequacy" principle, benefits were also supposed to protect the less fortunate against poverty. Because the rich could always take care of themselves if worst came to worst, the benefit formula was designed to give more help to lower-income workers. Ultimately, these two goals are incompatible. Equity will always favor the rich, whereas adequacy will always help the poor. Nevertheless, the two goals were mixed together in the benefit formula.

In absolute terms, of course, upper-income workers will always get a higher benefit check. But their total benefits will always be less generous in proportional terms. In 1982, lower-income retirees received social security benefits roughly equal to 53 percent of their preretirement wages, whereas higher-income retirees received only 27 percent. Conservatives often call the difference "welfare," since the benefit formula is clearly weighted to help the poor, whereas liberals call it "adequacy." Yet whatever it is called, the benefit formula helps some more than others. In this sense, the benefit formula is always in conflict with one of the incompatible goals.

Under the formula, many retirees get more money back in benefits than they have "earned" in taxes paid. Because of the adequacy principle, lower-income retirees receive large "unearned" returns. The original idea was to protect the elderly against the stigma of welfare. Believing that older Americans would rather starve than accept welfare, the drafters decided to hide an income floor in the benefit formula. Since most Americans would have paid at least some token social security taxes in their lifetimes, they would feel entitled to benefits. It was a way of providing dignity to the elderly poor.

THE IMPACTS

Any program as large and old as social security has to have some impact, whether positive or negative. The problem is finding the evidence. Social

[5]See in particular Derthick, *Policymaking for Social Security*, Chapter 10.

security leaves many tracks on the economy and social fabric, but it is hard to establish proof. At least in the first forty years, social security seems to have had four different impacts.

First, social security reduced *poverty* among the elderly. Because the benefit formula was designed to provide an ever-rising income floor, poverty declined over time. In 1959, 35 percent of the elderly had incomes below the federal poverty line. By 1970, that figure had dropped to 25 percent. By 1980, it was down to 15 percent, about the same level as that for the rest of the public.

The fact that the total rate dropped, however, does not mean that poverty had disappeared among the elderly. Minorities and women remained particularly vulnerable in old age. In 1981, 39 percent of elderly blacks fell below the poverty line. For elderly women as a whole, the figure was 19 percent; for elderly black women, it was 44 percent. An elderly woman was almost twice as likely as an elderly man to live in poverty; and 25 percent of people over 65 had an income either just above or just below the poverty line. Yet bad as the rates were for some groups, social security had helped everyone.

The relative success of social security in lowering poverty rates became a major selling point in the early 1980s. Liberals used the figures to defend the program against benefit cuts, lest the trends be reversed. Indeed, the Save Our Security (SOS) group, a loose coalition of over 100 interest groups opposed to any cuts, called social security "our most successful anti-poverty program, keeping some 14 to 15 million persons out of poverty." It was a powerful argument. Because of the huge benefit increases in the early 1970s, elderly incomes had gone up much faster than the rate of general inflation, thereby pushing poverty down.

Second, social security influenced the *economy* in some way. In response to liberal claims about poverty, conservatives often argued that social security taxes had hurt the national economy, affecting the future of everyone, young or old. Any tax program has to have some impact on the economy, reducing the amount of money people spend or save. One computer simulation suggested that the 1980 social security tax increase had cost the economy 500,000 jobs. Still, any benefit program also has to affect the economy, increasing the amount of money people spend or save. Since social security taxes go directly out in benefits, it may be that the economic impacts cancel out, resulting in less saving and spending among one group but more among another.

Though social security had to affect the economy in some way, it was hard to find proof. According to Henry Aaron, a liberal economist and former Carter administration aide, researchers could "provide relatively little good evidence to the policymaker who is trying to decide whether and how to alter the social security system regarding the effects that social security has had on economic behavior."[6] In short, no one knew if or how social security shaped the economy. As a result, conservatives had little firm evidence to attack the program.

Third, social security affected the federal *budget deficit.* Prior to 1969, social

[6]Henry J. Aaron, *Economic Effects of Social Security* (Washington, D.C.: The Brookings Institution, 1982), p. 82.

security had no overall deficit impact, because it was not included in the so-called unified federal budget. Because social security trust funds could not be spent for any other purpose, budget makers had originally decided not to add those funds into the annual surplus or deficit. If social security was running as surplus, it would make the total budget look better than it actually was and would just mislead Congress and the President; if social security was running a deficit, it would merely draw down its own trust fund reserve but would still make the overall budget look worse than it truly was, again misleading policymakers. Far better to leave it out of the totals. Such was the original logic.

In 1967, however, a presidential commission recommended a unified federal budget, with social security in the bottom line. Whether Lyndon Johnson agreed as a way to hide the true cost of the Vietnam War or merely wanted to make sense of an increasingly complex budget is unknown. Regardless, the unified-budget deficit improved immediately with social security in the total. Without the new unified budget, the 1969 budget surplus (the first in twenty years) would have been a very slight deficit. But it was not long before social security's problems began to make the total deficits look worse. Each year from 1975 to 1982, social security only increased the deficits. In 1981, social security added $10 billion to the already massive Reagan deficit, even though the program was merely drawing down its own reserve at that point.

Fourth, the sheer size of the social security program created an *administrative monster*. Any program that pays benefits to 35 million people has to have a large bureaucratic heart. Though its overhead was low in percentage terms—running at about 2 percent a year—SSA spent almost $3 billion on administrative costs in 1982, covering just over 75,000 employees, 1,344 full-time field offices, and 10 regional headquarters. According to one count, there were fifty miles of computer tape stored in the Baltimore facility, with millions of pounds of paper in hand-carried case files. Even with so many employees in so many locations, SSA had an amazing service record. In 1982, SSA delivered most new social security numbers within ten days, processed most benefit claims within thirty days, and had 96 percent payment accuracy.[7] But even with such a strong payment record, small mistakes could affect large numbers of people. Because social security was so large, even a 1 percent error would touch almost 360,000 beneficiaries, generating countless newspaper stories of administrative incompetence.

INERTIA

Whatever the impacts, social security was not an easy program to change. The program affected too many people. Years of small adjustments had created layers of complicated rules and bureaucratic procedures. Because the benefit

[7]Social Security Administration, *Monthly Workload Trend Report Quarterly Summary*, September 1982.

checks had to go out each month, Congress and the President could not start from scratch. Because people planned for their retirement years in advance, any changes would have to come with decades of advance warning. Once in motion, social security was very difficult to stop. What had grown incrementally would have to shrink incrementally. Moreover, SSA was facing its own bureaucratic crisis in the early 1980s.

First, despite a $500-million modernization program, SSA still had a severe computer crisis. Part of the problem involved the age of the equipment. Computers from the 1960s and early 1970s still did most of the work at SSA in the 1980s and were far behind the state of the art. Part of the problem involved the nature of SSA's job. Computers were asked to issue accurate benefit checks, find possible cheaters, keep track of the living and dead, perform economic and demographic forecasts, and "notice" potential problems. Moreover, with all of the social security data stored on thousands of separate computer tapes, each had to be mounted, analyzed, and removed before the next. And the computer problems were complicated by outside requests for help. Along with paying social security benefits, SSA took food stamp applications, checked for welfare fraud, and even helped on draft registration.

The computer crisis had an important impact on the congressional debate: it set the deadline for the social security compromise. Since 1974, the annual COLA had been paid at the start of July. Because of the aged equipment, programmers had to start work in April. Each check had to be recalculated; each tape remounted, analyzed, and removed again. Thus if the social security rescue bill was going to include any changes in the COLA, it had to be negotiated before April 1983. Otherwise, SSA's computers could not do the job.

Second, SSA had a leadership crisis. As the program got older, so did the leadership. All of the social security founders save Robert Myers (then deputy commissioner, shortly to be the executive director of Ronald Reagan's National Commission on Social Security Reform) were gone from SSA by the 1980s. In 1970, for example, the average length of service on the SSA top staff was thirty-two years; by 1980, it had dropped to seventeen years. Though many of the old leaders were still in Washington, most were not involved in the 1980–1983 debate. They had to be replaced by a new generation of younger leaders, most without the experience to handle the new crisis.

Whereas there had once been great stability in the leadership of SSA, the decade leading up to the 1983 compromise was characterized by remarkable turnover in the upper echelons at the administration's Baltimore headquarters. Over the first thirty-six years of social security, there were only six commissioners. And of the six, two held the chief executive's office for more than two-thirds of that time. In contrast, there were nine commissioners (five full and four acting) between 1973 and 1983, and the job actually remained vacant during much of 1983. This turnover infected other levels at SSA. There were only two chief actuaries between 1937 and 1970 but four in the next decade. Since the actuary's office was the source of all economic and demographic forecasts, the turnover became a problem in providing fast technical advice.

The aging and turnover in the top SSA posts had a number of effects. It created an image of "revolving-door commissioners" in the media and clearly disrupted administrative continuity. It also affected the computer problem. With each new commissioner, the computer updating was pushed back a year or two. The turnover also affected staff morale. In the words of one former SSA official: "Nine commissioners or acting commissioners in less than ten years is more change than any staff, no matter how well disposed to accept change, can readily get enthusiastic about or rationalize."

Thus SSA endured three major reorganizations between 1973 and 1983, with Democrats reversing Republicans and vice versa. Each produced more confusion and less coordination. As one official put it: "New commissioners tend to want their own organizational arrangements, but recent ones have not stayed long enough on the job to justify the change. Commissioners leave, but they sometimes leave behind, generally in high positions, many of the staff they have brought in or advanced to the top. Confidence that high performance will be recognized is undermined. Employees' pride in the importance of the work for which they are responsible is diminished. Satisfaction from doing a job well and achieving a satisfactory outcome is reduced." And when the commissioners changed, so did their policies.

The turnovers and reorganizations eventually broke the old notion of an "intimate family" of social security experts. With occasional exceptions, the key participants in the social security debate came from outside SSA. Gone were the days when a handful of old social security experts would sit down with a small Ways and Means Committee and work out a legislative compromise. The social security staff was so fragmented and disorganized in the late 1970s that it could not mount a common front either inside the executive branch or on Capitol Hill. Whereas Congress and the President once relied on SSA to provide a clear position on the program, they now had to move forward without firm guidance. SSA had always been good at telling the politicians how to expand the program but could not agree on how to answer the crisis.[8]

CONCLUSION

The impact of social security on poverty, the economy, budget deficits, and the bureaucracy led to one simple conclusion: social security would be hard to change. The program's success in reducing poverty made it difficult to attack; its slow administrative apparatus made it difficult to amend. Yet the program's impact on budget deficits made it an important part of any discussion about the economy. Thus Congress and the President faced a program that demanded their respect. It was huge, old, and loaded with bureaucratic inertia.

The problem was that it was designed during a different time and for a different society. The challenge was to change the program to adapt to a new time and a new society, while remaining sensitive to its impacts on an ever-growing aging population.

---

[8]For an excellent analysis of SSA's organizational crisis, see Martha Derthick, *Agency under Stress: The Social Security Administration in American Government* (Washington, D.C.: The Brookings Institution, 1990).

5

The Politics of Assumptions

Every government decision involves assumptions about how the world works today and how it will work tomorrow. Assumptions help Congress and the President interpret the past, understand the present, and, most important, predict the future. They help policymakers define the size of the problems and the impact of solutions. If the assumptions are accurate, they can form the basis for careful, almost rational decisions. If they are clouded, they can become the target for political sabotage and manipulation.

Unfortunately, over the last decade, the assumptions used for social security have been more often wrong than right. In 1977, for example, Carter and Congress based a social security rescue bill on what quickly proved to be overly optimistic economic assumptions. At that point in history, there was little reason to expect the double-digit inflation and economic stagflation that came just two years later. At the time, the assumptions were neither too optimistic nor too pessimistic; they were the best guesses available. Looking back, they simply failed to anticipate the depth of the 1979–1980 economic crisis. Carter was not wrong to claim that his rescue bill would keep the system solvent for fifty years, at least not if he was reading the SSA's intermediate estimate. The problem was that his image of the future never came true.

ON AUTOMATIC PILOT

Those mistakes would not have mattered but for the indexing of benefits to inflation enacted in 1972. Because benefits grew automatically each year, the only way for Carter and Congress to tell if their repairs would work was to read the crystal ball. And it was wrong. If benefits had not been indexed, there would have been no need to predict the future. Congress would have retained its discretion over benefit increases. Ironically, Republicans had pushed for indexing as a way to keep costs down but later led the fight to cut the COLA because costs had grown too fast.

With social security on automatic pilot, it became increasingly important to build accurate predictions of the future. Legislators could make the "right" choices only if they knew what was coming far down the road. Moreover, because there was so little room for error in the trust fund reserves, accurate assumptions were critical for keeping the system afloat during lean years. Nevertheless, as the demand for accuracy grew, the world became more uncertain. As one Congressional Budget Office aide lamented in 1982, "We don't know who'll be in office in 1984. We don't know whether the Federal Reserve Board will give into pressure to expand the money supply. We don't know if the Middle East will blow up."

Nevertheless, Congress and the President needed some way to make decisions on social security. It was not enough simply to admit that the future was cloudy. Yet instead of giving a single "best guess" of the future, SSA provided multiple estimates. From 1976 to 1980, SSA provided three different estimates. In 1981, SSA was forced to create five! And in 1982 and 1983, the critical years for congressional debate, SSA offered four different scenarios of the future: the first was optimistic (labeled Alternative I), the next mildly optimistic (Alternative II-A), the next mildly pessimistic (Alternative II-B), and the last very pessimistic (Alternative III). The choice of scenario could change both the size of the coming social security crisis and the savings from specific solutions. By simply changing the assumptions, problems could be made to appear and disappear at will.

Separately, all of the assumptions were predictions of future events or conditions. What would unemployment be in the year 2015? What would inflation be in the year 2033? What would happen to birth rates in the next four decades? The major difference between social security assumptions and other assumptions is the time frame. Whereas most economic forecasts cover only the next five years or so, social security assumptions cover the next seventy-five years. The program is so large that changes must come slowly and far in advance. That means decades of lead time.

Together, economic and demographic assumptions create a picture of the future that can be used to predict how a program such as social security will fare over time. Some assumptions, particularly about inflation, predict how much social security will spend in future benefits. Other assumptions, particularly about unemployment and wage growth, predict how much social security will raise in taxes. Still other assumptions, particularly about fertility, predict how many workers will be supporting how many retirees. When merged together in a computer, these different assumptions generate a specific forecast of social security income and outgo years into the future. Small changes in one or more of the underlying assumptions could mean big changes in a 75-year forecast.

Since Congress rarely asks about the specific assumptions, the forecasting process can be a tempting target for political manipulation. Members are much more concerned about the bottom estimate/forecast than the initial assumptions.

THE WORLD ACCORDING TO SSA

By the early 1980s, assumptions had emerged as one key for setting the social security agenda. As an OMB official noted after the social security compromise was signed and sealed in 1983, "Only a handful of people know how important the economic assumptions really are. If you can get your opponents to accept your data, then the rest of the argument will be on your terms. You become the one who says what works and what doesn't. A change of a percentage point here and there can have tremendous impact. It's like stacking a deck in a card game."

Despite a host of public and private sources for most economic assumptions (in part because declining accuracy meant no one had a special gift), SSA still had a monopoly over the social security estimates at the start of the 1980s. That was not to say that SSA had some magic in predicting the future. Rather, most other forecasters were unwilling to put their reputations or energy into such long-term predictions, preferring to stay closer to the present. Unfortunately, despite their impeccable credentials in actuarial science, most SSA actuaries were not well trained in the intricacies of long-term economic forecasting models. Further, until indexing, the actuaries had never had to predict the future. They had merely held the economy constant into the future. None of the key economic indicators had changed from year to year.

With the change to indexing in 1972, the actuaries had to switch from static to dynamic assumptions. Benefits were going to increase automatically every year into the future. To keep the system going, the actuaries had to start predicting the future, anticipating economic booms and busts. To make estimates of outgo, they had to predict inflation; to make estimates of income, they had to predict wage growth and unemployment. Because the system was now on automatic pilot, they had to pinpoint any coming crisis. Then they would have to tell Congress and the President what to do. The question, of course, was whether they were right. Their reputation for accuracy would determine whether anybody listened.

Views of the World

That reputation was based on four basic views of the world. First, all of the economic forecasts at SSA showed a world that always got better. No matter how bad inflation or unemployment was at the start of a forecast, the future always improved. This optimism may have been a fact of human nature. After all, no one wants to predict that the world will collapse tomorrow. Indeed, SSA actuaries sometimes argue that optimistic forecasts have a self-fulfilling quality, as if simply wishing for a healthy economy would make it come true. Though these same actuaries admitted that overly optimistic forecasts led legislators astray on Carter's rescue bill, they still believed in the power of positive thinking.

Second, the forecasts showed a world without economic cycles. The actuaries acknowledged the presence of such cycles, but they still based the forecasts on steady trends over time. They simply assumed that the economic shocks would balance over the decades. However, at least in the short term, it made a great deal of difference whether the boom came first or second. If the boom came before the bust, the social security trust fund would be able to lay in a margin of safety for the bad times; if the bust came before the boom, the program might not even make it to the good days ahead. The timing of economic cycles had become critical in figuring how much to raise and when to do it.

Third, the forecasts showed a world that could be understood and predicted. The underlying belief that the world can be known far into the future is essential for building long-range forecasts. Though the estimates were never advertised as anything more than sketches of what *might* happen, they were often used as the final word on what *would* happen. And the forecasts were partially to blame. Instead of giving ballpark figures, the SSA forecasts contained precise numbers far into the future. As one Treasury Department aide remarked, "Sometimes I look at the estimates and wonder how they picked a 1.7 percent growth figure for 2015 instead of a 1.5 or a 2.3. How do they know? The answer is that they don't and they can't. But they have to build something in. It's an artificial forecast."

Fourth, despite the actuaries' optimism, the forecasts had begun to show a world in deep trouble by the early 1980s. All of the estimates started from lower economic performance each year. "Each new forecast substitutes what was thought to be a good year with another bad one," a Treasury Department staffer noted. "The performance of the economy has been so bad that even the bad estimates are good. So when you take that good year and replace it with a bad year, you lose a little more of the trust fund balance. . . . We've been stumbling from one crisis to another."

These four patterns added up to a world that would steadily improve from an ever-worsening crisis. Each year's forecast was always worse than the last but showed an eventual upturn. Each cloud had a silver lining. It might be called a form of pessimistic optimism.

The Reality

It was not particularly difficult to check the actuaries' predictions against reality: one had simply to look at actual economic performance. For the most part, the recent predictions were very wrong. From the mid-1970s to the early 1980s, they underestimated inflation, overestimated wage growth, and underestimated unemployment. To be fair, the actuaries struggled mightily against an increasingly uncertain world, one buffeted by global economic forces unheard of only a decade before. They deserve credit for their efforts to anticipate crisis and draw reasonable portraits of alternative futures. However, even given the range of guesses between Alternatives I and III, the forecasts were much too optimistic.

In theory, of course, the optimistic estimate was designed to give a rosy view of the world. If that was the goal, Alternative I did the job. Not once in past years had true economic performance come close to the optimistic prediction. In theory, the intermediate estimate, called Alternative II, was designed to be the actuaries' best guess of what would happen, the most likely prediction of the future. If that was the goal, Alternative II did not succeed. Except for 1976, the intermediate estimate was far too optimistic. Moreover, in theory, the pessimistic estimate was designed to give an overly gloomy view of the world. If that was the goal, Alternative III did not work either. Even the most pessimistic estimates were too optimistic!

The actuaries had several responses to their declining accuracy. First, their reports became longer, offering more explanations as a defense against error. Between 1976 and 1983, the annual forecast report doubled in size, from 58 pages to 120 pages. Second, and more important, the actuaries began to spread their assumptions over a larger range of possibilities. Slowly, the distance between optimism and pessimism increased. The distance between the optimistic and pessimistic assumptions about inflation, for example, doubled over a five-year period. As an SSA aide acknowledged, "We've learned the hard way to have significant variation among the estimates. Starting in the mid-1970s, we have built greater distance between the alternatives. It's a way of creating greater accuracy." In short, the actuaries expanded their predictions to cover more numbers on the economic roulette wheel. Only in 1981 and 1982 did actual economic performance fall within the range of the SSA predictions—for the first time in nearly five years of forecasting—landing between Alternatives II-B and III. This success was almost entirely the result of the greater spreads. The actuaries bet more numbers and finally won.

Unfortunately, the errors had already affected two crucial turning points in the 1970s, leading to serious legislative mistakes. The first came in 1972, with indexing of social security to inflation. SSA's best guess showed 15 percent inflation and 12 percent real wage growth for the 1973–1977 period. The actual experience was 41 percent inflation and 1 percent real wage growth. Looking at the predictions, Republicans had seen the automatic COLA as a way of controlling costs. They had been misled by the assumptions.

The second turning point came in 1977, with passage of Carter's rescue bill. SSA's best guess showed 28 percent inflation and 13 percent real wage growth for the 1978–1982 period. The actual experience was 60 percent inflation and a *negative* 7 percent real wage growth. Looking at the predictions, Democrats had thought a series of tax increases would be more than enough to take the system into the next century. Once again, Congress had been misled by the forecasts.

Were the mistakes important? The answer is clearly yes. Once benefits were tied to inflation, accurate assumptions became critical for making legislative decisions. In this large, old program, tiny mistakes in assumptions could create massive deficits. With the social security trust fund skating from check to check with barely one month's reserve, seemingly trivial errors in inflation or wage estimates could lead to a major crisis in very short order. And that is exactly what happened in 1980.

The Sources of Error

There were four sources of potential error in the social security assumptions. If they could be corrected, the predictions would improve, lending greater confidence to the occasional repairs. If they could not be corrected, Congress and the President would face more surprises.

The most important source of potential error was the world itself. No one predicted the high rates of inflation and low rates of growth that occurred in the 1970s; not SSA, OMB, or the private forecasters. "If I had made those kinds of predictions," an SSA actuary argued, "I would have been practicing in an asylum." The social security assumptions of the 1970s were simply not far out of line with the then-conventional wisdom about the future. And because the past is the starting point for any forecast, the process works only if history repeats itself. Unfortunately, as Stockman reported, "I'm beginning to believe that history is a lot shakier than I ever thought it was. . . . In other words, I think there are more random elements, less determinism, and more discretion in the course of history than I ever believed before."[1]

Most of the errors involved unknowns—whether election-year benefit increases, wars, economic busts, oil embargoes, medical breakthroughs, or whatever. The actuaries could not predict a 1973 Arab oil embargo that no one else foresaw. They could not predict a 1979 economic bust that no one else forecast. It was difficult to criticize SSA for errors that were beyond predictive experience. Indeed, as one top SSA actuary noted, "The long and the short of it is that I can't predict the future. No one can. We know that any specific estimate we make will be wrong."[2] Looking back over the first decades of social security, however, these were exactly the kinds of problems that provided both the growth and crisis in the program.

A second source of possible error was technique. There were several problems with the methods used in forecasting the future at SSA. One rested on the world-without-cycles view mentioned earlier. Because the assumptions did not allow for boom or bust, the forecasts were most vulnerable at the start and finish of an economic cycle. At the end of a recovery, for example, the actuaries were likely to be overly optimistic about the next few years, even though the economy might be slipping into a recession. At the end of a recession, they were likely to be overly pessimistic, even though recovery might be just around the corner.

The actuaries were quite aware of the problem and were experimenting

---

[1]William Greider, "The Education of David Stockman," *The Atlantic*, 248 (December 1981), p. 39.
[2]Francisco R. Bayo, deputy chief actuary for long-range program estimates, quoted in the *National Journal*, June 23, 1984, p. 1216.

with cyclical forecasts by the early 1980s. The problems with cyclical forecasting involved more than simple econometrics—that is, how to predict just how long a particular boom or bust will last. Presidents and their staffs are supportive of cyclical forecasting only when the predicted economic downturns come into someone else's administration. According to one actuary, "We had a very bad year in 1982. Everything dragged down. The Treasury Department guys wanted us to build a slow recovery as far out as possible [into the future]. What we wanted to do was put in an explicit cycle, with a recession somewhere out in 1986 or 1987. They obviously won." When that recession actually arrived in 1989, the Reagan administration was long gone, of course.

A third source of potential error arose from possible weaknesses in the SSA econometric model. As one OMB aide argued, "A lot of results surprise the actuaries because they don't know what's happening in their own models. What they do is set each number independently of the others. They do inflation one place; tax rates another; benefit increases still another. The problem is that all the variables interact. They load all this stuff into a computer and get some numbers, but they don't have any meaning."

A final source of potential error in the SSA estimates came from something called assumption drag.[3] "The problem with all of these estimates," a Health and Human Services Department official said, "is that they're out of date almost as soon as the ink is dry." Because the SSA forecasts were prepared in the spring but published in June, they were out of date by the following winter. At best, SSA had data only from the final quarter of the preceding year in drafting its forecast. But the economy has demonstrated a remarkable ability to change quickly in recent years, leading to serious gaps between the initial forecasts, final publication of the reports, and actual use on Capitol Hill. In order to draft more timely assumptions, however, SSA needed a more predictable world.

A Clouded Crystal Ball

Some of these sources of potential error could be controlled; others could not. Because the world was likely to change, it was impossible to predict very far into the future. Even with highly sophisticated econometric models, some with thousands of equations and dozens of separate indicators, private forecasters did not do very well at forecasting even the coming year or two, let alone seventy-five years. The SSA actuaries did not stand a much better chance, even if they had new computers, new models, or a cyclical methodology. "Our inability to predict the economy for one year," Stockman reluctantly concluded in 1983, "should be evident after the experience that we've gone through."[4]

The volatility of the social security forecasts in the late 1970s had serious impacts on Congress and the President. Certainly, no one could use the estimates as objective predictions of reality. No one could build a rescue bill

[3]See William Ascher, *Forecasting* (Baltimore: The Johns Hopkins University Press, 1978).
[4]David Stockman, "Face the Nation," February 6, 1983.

based on a single set of assumptions. Though some were more inaccurate than others, none could be trusted from year to year. Because it was impossible to choose assumptions on the basis of a reliable future record, politics began to play a greater role in defining the future. Rational analysis was impossible without accurate tools. The actuaries were doing the very best they could in a remarkably unstable forecasting environment.

THE POLITICS OF ASSUMPTIONS

As the economy grew increasingly unpredictable toward the end of the 1970s, the social security forecasts became the target of efforts at political manipulation.[5] The logic of this new politics of assumptions was simple. Since no one could predict the future in this volatile economy, and, therefore, since no one could challenge even the most outrageous of assumptions, why not use the forecasting process to sell the President's program? That is certainly what some of the President's top advisers wanted to do. If, as Stockman argued, "none of us really understands what's going on with all these numbers," why not manufacture a set of economic assumptions to fit the President's short-term political needs? And if, as Stockman also argued, "all the conventional estimates just wind up as mud . . . as absurdities," why not cast them in the President's image of the world? Much as SSA's actuaries resisted, their forecasting process had become a new battleground for partisan politics. Presidents had increasing incentives to shape the underlying forecasts, for in doing so, they could change the shape of the problems.

This new politics of assumptions was particularly visible early when Stockman offered his proposals for solving the emerging social security crisis in 1981. Bluntly put, he used optimistic economic assumptions in selling the President's budget package on Capitol Hill but pessimistic assumptions to press for deep social security savings. Senator Bill Bradley spotted the differ-

---

[5]It is fair to say that the following pages drew the most controversy in the first edition of this book, prompting a particularly critical response from Robert Myers, a former chief actuary of SSA and a participant in some of the discussions cited below. See Myers, "An Unwarranted Attack on the Integrity of Actuarial Estimates for Social Security," *Public Administration Review*, 46 (May–June 1986), pp. 256–260, and my response, "Politics Is the Issue: A Response to Robert Myers," in the same issue, pp. 261–266. As Dwight Bartlett III, chief actuary of SSA from 1979 to 1981, later wrote of that exchange, the arguments between Myers and me could be reduced to two fundamental questions:

1. Did and will the politicians, particularly members of the incumbent administration, attempt to influence the projections and to interpret the projections to serve their political purposes? I believe the answer is a resounding yes. . . .
2. Do the actuaries have adequate independence to resist these attempts? I believe the answer is a qualified yes, although more can be done. [Bartlett, "Letter to the Editor," *Public Administration Review*, 46 (November–December 1986), pp. 682–683.]

In response to the debate, I have edited this section to try to make clear that the political pressure on the SSA actuaries came from the White House and that the actuaries made every effort possible to protect the integrity of their work.

ence in a hearing on the social security plan: "We have two sets of books in which there are different sets of economic assumptions. One of the sets is the budget of this administration upon which all the spending cuts are based. . . . That set says there will be unemployment of 6.6 percent. . . . Then we have the pessimistic assumptions for the social security trust fund. . . . That set says the unemployment will be 9.7 percent in 1983, not 6.6 percent. So this is your classic case of where you can't have it both ways." Economic assumptions were being drafted by the President and his budget director less to give an honest portrait of the future and much more to sell the White House priorities. The problem for social security policy was that those same overly optimistic forecasts were then being forced on SSA as the basis for the intermediate, or best guess, set of projections. As to Senator Bradley's notion that a President can't have it both ways, that is precisely how the President had it. Few members of Congress understood this new politics.

Given the impact of assumptions on the size of the social security crisis and the dollar-for-dollar returns on each solution, the actuaries often had to bargain with Congress and the President over competing views of the world. Even small changes in fertility and real wage growth could have very large impacts on the short- and long-term social security deficits. And since the economy was changing on an almost daily basis, there was some confusion over which estimates (optimistic to pessimistic) to use and when to update them. In dealing with the White House, much of the conflict focused on the first years of the forecasts. "The first couple of years are the toughest," an actuary explained. "The politicos want to have the best picture on the short term. If you've got a budget before Congress, you don't want those old actuaries to come in and show your figures to be wrong. So those first years are where most of the battles come. . . . Let's say those estimates are often plausible but not probable." Yet those estimates are the key for setting the short-term targets.

Points of Pressure

Consider two recent examples of political influence in the social security forecasting process, one from the Democrats, the other from the Republicans.

The first came in the Carter administration with a change in the 1977 fertility assumption. Fertility remains the single most important factor for predicting far into the future. In 1974, after a decade of steep declines in the birthrate, SSA had lowered the fertility assumption to 1.9 births per woman. That meant there would be fewer "assumed" children to support parents in the next century, increasing the size of the predicted social security crisis. When Carter came into office in 1977, the fertility assumption was pushed back up to 2.1 births, even though actual rates hit their lowest point in recent history that year at 1.77 births. The reason? The higher fertility assumption created the image of a smaller social security crisis—there would be more "assumed" children to support parents. Democrats would not have to cut benefits to solve the coming deficits. Though the change was only two-tenths of a percent, it had a dramatic impact on the social security forecasts.

According to Dwight Bartlett, chief actuary of SSA from 1979 to 1981, the Carter administration also oversold the effects of the 1977 rescue:

> The Reagan administration was not the first administration to be guilty of attempting to use projections to serve their own political purposes. Shortly after I became Chief Actuary in 1979, I became aware of the fact that members of the Carter administration were making statements to the effect that the 1977 Amendments to the Social Security Act guaranteed that the OASDI program was soundly financed into the twenty-first century. The then SSA Commissioner Stanford Ross was one of the most outspoken with these statements. I attempted, on several occasions, to point out to Mr. Ross that the projections in the 1978 Trustees' Report raised serious questions about the validity of that statement, but to no avail. By the time the 1979 Trustees' Report became public, the projections based on the pessimistic assumptions showed that the OASDI Trust Fund would be exhausted in several years.[6]

The second came in the Reagan administration—with a series of changes in the 1981 economic assumptions, the most important factor for predicting the immediate future. Most of the political pressure centered on Stockman's 1981 budget forecast, designed to sell the President's program on Capitol Hill. Traditionally, SSA had used the President's annual economic forecasts as the basis for the intermediate social security projections. After all, the President's forecast was supposed to be the best guess of the future. In 1981, however, Stockman's forecast was seen as so rosy that SSA decided to use it for the optimistic social security projections.

The White House was incensed at the decision. SSA would merely confirm what the Democrats were saying: that the budget forecast promised far more than it could deliver. According to Bartlett, who was chief actuary at the time, "The assumptions basically are set by the Trustees of Social Security, and that's not right. The trustees have to advocate the programs of the Administration. That puts them in a difficult position when they're setting economic assumptions. They've got a conflict of interest."[7] As he later remembered the events surrounding the 1981 projections,

> most of the controversy centered around the short-range economic assumptions and most of the difficulties were with the staff of Treasury, which had the primary responsibility in the administration for the development of economic policy. The problems became so intense that by 1981, shortly after the Reagan administration came into office, it was no longer possible to find a compromise set of economic assumptions for the intermediate set . . . which would satisfy Treasury and with which I could live. I do not recall who came up with the idea of two alternative intermediate projections as a way out of the dilemma, although I suspect it was Mr. Myers [then deputy commissioner of SSA and a former chief actuary himself].[8]

---

[6]Bartlett, "Letter to the Editor," p. 682.
[7]Quoted in *The New York Times,* January 5, 1983, p. D20.
[8]Ibid.

In the negotiations that followed the actuaries finally worked out a compromise: they would prepare a worst-case forecast if the White House would allow two intermediate estimates. The President's budget would be labeled Alternative II-A, while the actuaries' best guess would be labeled Alternative II-B. Only then would the actuaries add a worst-case estimate.

It was a good bargain for SSA. "We had always wanted a way to get around the President's budget forecast anyway," an SSA participant noted, "and this was the perfect way to do it. Presidential budgets have been getting more unrealistic over the past few years; we didn't want to throw out the baby with the bath water."

Thus the 1981 report contained five different estimates of the social security future: Alternative I (more optimistic than normal to fit the President's budget in II-A), Alternative II-A (the President's budget), Alternative II-B (the actuaries' most realistic scenario), Alternative III, and finally, the new worst-case forecast. Although each projection had its reason, it is little wonder if some members of Congress were confused.

Playing Politics

Because there were multiple forecasts in 1981, somebody had to make a choice on which one to use. And the choice had to be made again and again as the economy changed. Optimistic assumptions could make the social security problem appear much better than it actually was; pessimistic ones could make it seem much worse. Optimistic assumptions could make cost-of-living cuts look much smaller than they were; pessimistic ones could make them seem larger. Under the Alternative III forecast in 1982, for example, a three-month COLA delay would save about $60 billion. Under Alternative II-B, it would only save $20 billion. The reason? Inflation was much higher under the pessimistic forecast. A COLA cut would appear to save more money.

The choice of one set of assumptions over another often rests on what each side wants to do. As Bartlett recalls the politics of assumptions during his tenure at SSA,

> I do not believe that my experiences, given the situation at the time, should be seen as surprising. Members of the administration must be loyal to the President and his policies. They must advocate his proposed policies as being effective in producing the intended results. The party out of power, on the other hand, if they are resisting policy proposals, properly highlight what they see as the negative outcomes of policy proposals. Therefore, politicians are not the appropriate people to be setting assumptions for the financial analysis of a social insurance program such as Social Security.[9]

In short, where one stands on the assumptions depends on where one sits on the solutions. On social security in the early 1980s, conservatives were on the *offensive*, looking for major benefit cuts. They used pessimistic assumptions to define the size of the coming crisis. The larger the problem, the greater the

---

[9]Bartlett, "Letter to the Editor," p. 683.

TABLE 1. The Patterns of Assumption

	Offense: *Attack* *Social Security*	Defense: *Defend* *Social Security*
For defining the problem	Use PESSIMISTIC	Use OPTIMISTIC
For selling/attacking the solution	Use OPTIMISTIC	Use PESSIMISTIC

need for some benefit cuts. Yet conservatives also used optimistic assumptions to define the impact of benefit cuts on the elderly. The smaller the impact, the greater the potential for congressional passage. Further, if conservatives could define the size of the problem with one set of assumptions but the range of solutions with another, they might win deeper benefit cuts from liberals. Whereas tax revenues did not change under pessimistic or optimistic assumptions, the impact of COLA cuts varied widely with the assumptions used.

Liberals, in contrast, used optimistic assumptions to define the size of the problem but pessimistic assumptions to attack the proposed benefit cuts. Since liberals were on the *defensive,* trying to protect their program against cuts, they needed a small problem to stop or delay congressional action. If the crisis was modest and temporary, why panic? Yet liberals also used pessimistic assumptions to show how deep the benefit cuts might go.

These patterns of offense and defense are summarized in Table 1.

The problem in the battle over assumptions was that liberals and conservatives often switched back and forth between optimism and pessimism, depending on their political needs. Both sides also moved back and forth in time, picking older or newer estimates to support their legislative positions. In early 1983, for example, liberals continued to use the year-old 1982 forecasts because the figures made their concessions on benefit cuts look bigger. Conservatives, of course, used the newer estimates because the figures made those concessions look smaller. The use of different assumptions by the same side could only heighten public confusion about social security. Overly pessimistic assumptions about impending bankruptcy created unnecessary fears about collapse, while overly optimistic assumptions about long-lasting repairs created lower confidence when the rescues did not work.

As predictive accuracy dropped, the political games increased. Without any way to predict the future but with so much pressure to adopt some kind of assumptions, Congress and the President began to select their estimates on the basis of political payoffs, not accuracy.

II-B OR NOT II-B

Clearly, no one had a monopoly on truth in the 1970s and early 1980s. The crystal balls were all clouded, adding another obstacle to change. Without accurate forecasts, Congress and the President had to add a new step to the debate. Before they could even talk about problems and solutions, they had to agree on baseline assumptions. This assumption-building process became a key opportunity for stalemate. Not only was it too complicated for the public to understand, it was beyond the grasp of many legislators. The challenge of technical analysis created a new chance for delay and confusion as each side fought to defend its vision of the future.

If no one could predict the future, how could Congress and the President make the right choices on social security? One answer was to put the program on a diet of stabilizers and fail-safes; that is, to build in mechanisms to protect the social security system from adverse economic conditions. Change the COLAs, build in automatic triggers for emergency transfers of general revenues or taxes, and so forth. A second answer was simply to *unindex* the program; that is, return the discretion over benefit increases to Congress and the President. Because these two answers were politically expensive and technically question-able, the legislative builders had to decide whether to plan for the best or the worst that could happen—whether to put social security on a pessimistic footing or let the program move forward on a less severe outlook. Even here, however, it was a political issue. "The reason no one uses truly pessimistic forecasts," an SSA aide argued, "is because we don't know we could get Congress to commit the kinds of funds or cuts to answer pessimistic forecasts. Think about the tax rates and benefit cuts needed to insulate that program against really bad economic performance."

Thus one reason even the pessimistic forecasts are often optimistic is that government simply cannot plan for the worst that might happen. Indeed, planning for the worst case might actually make it happen. Imagine raising payroll taxes high enough to cover the poorest economic performance; then imagine how many jobs might be lost and how many businesses might close. It could be a self-fulfilling prophecy. Yet the risks of not planning for the worst were obvious: the program could collapse, and public confidence could sink even further. As a result, most legislators were willing to plan for something less than the best, but not the absolute worst.

6

Public Opinion, Ready or Not

Most everyone realizes that the National Commission on Social Security Reform was set up to clobber social security—another of Pres. Reagan's devices to "rob the needy to pay the greedy." He simply wants to force elderly people to eat out of garbage cans and sleep in the gutter. He should be impeached!!! Please do not clobber social security. It is not a charity. American workers have been forced to pay into it for years, and they count on its benefits when they retire. To reduce it is as criminal as robbing someone's home.

Letter to the National Commission
on Social Security Reform
November 1982

The letter was typical of the thousands that were sent to members of the National Commission. Over three-quarters of the letters that eventually crossed Representative Conable's desk in Congress were handwritten, and 90 percent came from people either close to retirement or already on social security. Over half opposed some option—whether benefit cuts, tax increases, or a retirement age increase—but few offered support for any alternatives. Many letters simply asked the commissioners to save social security.[1] Another 25 percent expressed fear about whether benefits would be paid in the future. The letters clearly followed the four major trends in public opinion on social security: (1) support for the program, (2) a lack of knowledge, (3) declining confidence, and (4) opposition to most of the major options.

Despite conservative arguments to the contrary, the public still supported the program. People were frightened by the escalating political rhetoric and images of bankruptcy. They did not understand how the system worked, and they had lost confidence that the program would continue to pay benefits into the future. Most important, they continued to oppose most of the major

[1]These figures reflect my rough coding of the 1,000 or so letters that Conable received.

solutions. Government was caught in a no-win situation: the public wanted to save the program but opposed any change.

Congress and the President obviously cared about the opinions. In theory, there was nothing wrong with watching the polls. They are one element of representation. But it was never quite clear whether the public knew what was happening. Interest groups and political parties exploited public fears to raise money and recruit membership; opponents played on public confusion to win battles large and small in Congress; proponents wrapped solutions in complex packages to take advantage of public ignorance. For public opinion to have a meaningful impact on the policy process, it had to be informed, not manipulated.

There was, however, no doubt that the public was frightened about social security. Without a firm understanding of the program, the public was unable to grasp the full dimensions of the coming crisis or the range of possible solutions. This was not an easy program to understand. Its size had created a complicated system. The lack of public knowledge created not only ever-falling confidence in the program but an almost reflexive opposition to any major reforms.

SUPPORT

Whatever else the public said or did, there was considerable support for the program. People wanted their social security.

That support was clear in virtually every opinion poll between 1977 and 1983. There was an intense majority in favor of a rescue. When asked to list the advantages and disadvantages of social security, for example, the public could think of plenty of positives but few negatives. In one survey, 93 percent could list at least one *advantage* of social security; 59 percent said the elderly needed help, and another 10 percent said older Americans could not survive without it.[2] In contrast, over 22 percent could not list at least one *disadvantage* of the program. And of those who could, 37 percent said that benefits were too low—hardly the kind of disadvantage that erodes public support.

Much of this support came from stereotypes about aging in America. Not knowing much about old age, most Americans assumed the worst. Because it was seen as lonely and unhappy, the elderly had to be protected. That image was amply illustrated in a 1981 Harris poll. Splitting his sample of respondents into two age groups, Harris asked people *under* 65 whether crime, loneliness, transportation, and so forth, were very serious problems for the elderly. Harris then asked people *over* 65 whether those were very serious problems, personally.[3] Table 2 shows the answers.

[2]Peter D. Hart Research Associates, *A Nationwide Survey of Attitudes toward Social Security, 1979.* This survey was conducted for the 1979–1981 National Commission on Social Security.
[3]Louis Harris and Associates, *Aging in the Eighties,* a report prepared for the National Council on Aging, 1981.

TABLE 2. Views of Aging in America, 1981

Problem	Problem "Very Serious" for All People over 65			Problem "Very Serious" Personally
	18–54	55–64	65+	65+ Only
Not having enough money to live on	70%	62%	50%	17%
Poor health	48	43	40	21
Loneliness	68	53	45	13
Poor housing	45	37	30	5
Fear of crime	76	69	58	25
Not enough job opportunities	44	38	24	4
Not enough medical care	47	39	34	9
High cost of energy	82	78	72	42
Getting transportation	59	52	43	14

Source: Louis Harris and Associates, 1981. Total interviews equaled 3,428: 1,098 people aged 18–54, 492 people aged 55–64, and 1,837 people aged 65+.

Questions: "Now I'm going to read you some problems that other people have mentioned to us. For each, would you tell me whether it is a very serious problem, a somewhat serious problem, or hardly a problem at all for you *personally.*"

"And how serious a problem would you say (READ EACH ITEM) is for most people over 65 these days—a very serious problem, a somewhat serious problem, or hardly a problem at all for most people over 65?"

The table shows very serious myths about aging in America, myths that created public support for social security and other programs. Younger people saw old age as a very unpleasant experience, fraught with crime, isolation, illness, danger, and depression. No wonder they supported social security. Though older people saw their lives as personally better, they still viewed aging as an unpleasant experience for their peers. Whereas only 13 percent saw loneliness as a very serious problem for themselves, personally, 45 percent saw it as a very serious problem for other people over age 65. Getting old clearly had a bad reputation for all generations. And no one wanted old people hurt.

There are, of course, other reasons why the public supported the program. Having paid taxes over a lifetime, most Americans expected some return. Social security was one of the few government programs where people received something back for their taxes. The use of the word "insurance" to describe social security, for example, was designed to foster public support. According to Derthick, "Taxes became 'premiums' or 'contributions.' Workers had 'old age insurance accounts' in Baltimore. They were 'paying' for their own protection, building up insurance for their 'old age.' To challenge the insurance analogy or resist using the term was to show oneself an enemy of the program."[4]

KNOWLEDGE

The American Constitution does not require the public to be informed. Indeed, the founders designed Congress and the presidency with clear safeguards against public ignorance. The Senate would be appointed to protect the nation against the impulses of an elected House; an electoral college would protect the presidency against the voters. If public opinion was based on little more than fragments of information, there was no constitutional provision against that. If, in turn, major legislative decisions were based on those shreds of confusion, there was no constitutional injunction against that either. Unfortunately, public opinion on social security was often based on confusion rather than understanding.

Not that the public was completely baffled. People did know a great deal about benefits.[5] A 1979 survey by Hart Research Associates showed that the public knew that employees and employers both pay into the social security system (62 percent correct), that benefits are based on past earnings (59 percent), that social security pays benefits to the families of deceased workers (87 percent), that the program requires no proof of need for benefits (74 percent), and that payroll taxes also pay for Medicare (69 percent) and disability insurance (86 percent). Further, most would make a guess at the level of benefits (63 percent)—and a remarkable 40 percent of the guesses came within $100 of the average amount.

The question is, How much information was enough? If 62 percent knew that employers paid taxes, 38 percent did not know; if 59 percent knew that benefits were linked to past earnings, 41 percent did not know. It is impossible to say just how much information the public needed to form responsible opinions on social security and whether the government was to blame for the absence of understanding. Maybe the public only needed to know that social security was in trouble. Maybe people only needed some abstract sense that social security ought to be saved. Yet Congress and the presidency had no way of knowing which opinions were based on knowledge and which were based on ignorance.

Consider the following areas of confusion. Only 37 percent of the public knew that the federal employees did not pay into social security; 59 percent believed that social security taxes also paid for food stamps (perhaps because

---

[4]Martha Derthick, *Policymaking for Social Security* (Washington, D.C.: The Brookings Institution, 1979), p. 199.
[5]The following figures are from Peter D. Hart Research Associates, *A Nationwide Survey of Attitudes toward Social Security, 1979.*

SSA supplied food stamp applications in local offices); only 45 percent knew that social security benefits rise automatically with a cost-of-living adjustment. Moreover, whereas over 60 percent of the public would guess at the size of benefit checks, only 40 percent would guess at the size of social security taxes. Even though workers see the FICA contributions on their paychecks, of those who would guess at taxes, only a quarter could come within a percent of the actual rate. Table 3 summarizes these patterns of knowledge by five different age groups: new arrivals to the workforce (18- to 24-year-olds), the now working (25- to 34-year-olds), the middle-aged (35- to 54-year-olds), the near-retired (55- to 64-year-olds), and the elderly (over 65-year-olds). The percentages are *correct* answers only.

Generation Gaps

These patterns of knowledge are related to both age and education. As people grow older, they are likely to learn more about social security, mainly from personal experience with taxes and benefits. They are also likely to have greater interest in the subject as they approach their own retirement and start adding up their sources of income. Thus knowledge about *benefits* should grow with age. However, some concepts are too difficult to learn from simple experience. As people become more educated, they are more likely to understand such basic issues as the pay-as-you-go nature of social security funding and the relative returns of benefit formulas. Thus knowledge about the *mechanics* of the system should grow with education.

Both patterns are confirmed in the polling data. Knowledge about actual benefits increased with age. The elderly, for example, knew a great deal about social security benefits. They knew about Medicare (87 percent) and disability (92 percent), they knew about the annual benefit COLA (65 percent), they understood that there was no "needs" test to get benefits (77 percent), and they knew that employees and employers both paid into the system (72 percent). As a group, the elderly were the most informed about social security benefits, chiefly because they had the most experience with actual payments. But they were the least informed about the mechanics of the system. Over half of the elderly believed that "social security tax money collected from an individual is set aside specifically for his or her retirement benefits." No wonder they were frightened by headlines about bankruptcy. Many must have believed that their social security money was being held in individual accounts in Baltimore. Further, only 25 percent of the elderly knew social security did not pay for food stamps. If social security could be used for food stamps, perhaps it was also being used for defense, foreign aid, and so forth.

In contrast, younger Americans were confused about basic benefits. Though most of the now working (25–34) knew about the disability program, 2 in 5 did not know about Medicare; over 40 percent did not know that employee taxes are matched by employers; almost 70 percent thought federal workers were already covered by social security; less than half knew social security did not pay for food stamps; and a remarkable 70 percent did not know

TABLE 3. Knowledge about Social Security, by Age Group, 1979

True-False Question	Percentage of Correct Answers					
	New Arrivals 18–24	Now Working 25–34	Middle-Aged 35–54	Near-Retired 55–64	Retired 65+	Total
All federal employees pay into social security (FALSE)	17%	30%	42%	51%	41%	37%
An employee's social security taxes are matched by the same amount paid by the employer (TRUE)	39	56	67	73	72	62
Social security benefits are computed without regard to levels of previous wages or salary (FALSE)	53	57	63	66	55	59
Only those who can prove they are in need of income are eligible for social security benefits (FALSE)	66	76	78	70	77	74
The social security tax money collected from an individual is set aside specifically for his or her retirement benefits (FALSE)	61	69	72	58	47	62
Social security pays for the food stamp program (FALSE)	47	48	46	34	25	41
Social security taxes pay for hospital care benefits (Medicare) for the elderly (TRUE)	59	60	68	70	87	69
Social security benefits go up automatically to match the rise in the cost of living (TRUE)	42	30	38	58	65	45
Social security pays benefits to workers who become disabled (TRUE)	82	86	87	84	92	86

Source: Hart Research Associates, 1979. Total interviews equaled 1,529.

about the automatic benefit COLA. Yet as a group, the young knew more about the pay-as-you-go nature of social security, reflecting greater education. They were more informed about the mechanics of the system. But they were the least informed about social security benefits.

Among young people, perhaps the least informed were new arrivals to the workforce: 83 percent did not know federal employees were not covered by social security, only 39 percent knew that employees and employers pay into the system equally, and 41 percent did not know about Medicare. Even here, there are interesting pockets of knowledge. Over 40 percent of the new arrivals knew about the COLA. It is not clear why they knew about that single feature of social security when they knew so little about the rest.

A Little Knowledge

The overall patterns of knowledge on social security suggest two basic trends. First, the knowledge that most people did have contributed to support for the social security program. They knew something about social security benefits and had a sense that the money was well spent. Second, much of the knowledge that most people did *not* have also contributed to support for the system. The public did not know federal workers were not covered by social security; they did not know how much they paid in total taxes; the retired did not know about the pay-as-you-go funding.

Interestingly, some of the missing knowledge might have increased support. If younger workers had known that social security was indexed to inflation, whereas most private pensions are not, they might have been even more supportive of the program; if they had also known that employers match their social security taxes dollar for dollar, they might have been more confident about future benefits; if all knew that social security taxes did not pay for food stamps, they would not have worried about social security funds being spent for defense. Here, it is not clear what the knowledge about the pay-as-you-go nature of social security would have done to the elderly. If they knew there were no individual retirement accounts in Baltimore, they might have been less anxious about bankruptcy. Yet, if they knew that the system was on such a fragile month-to-month footing, they could not find much comfort.

These patterns of knowledge may also explain why the public never rebelled against higher social security taxes. One reason is that social security taxpayers were and are an unorganized mass, unable to come together to fight taxes. A second explanation is simply that no one knew what they were paying. Without that knowledge, how could there be a revolt? There was, of course, a general impression that taxes had gone up. Almost half of the public (49 percent) reported in 1979 that the social security tax had increased greatly over the *past* ten years. But almost the same number said they did not object "at all" to the tax "considering what we receive." Over half said they expected the tax to increase greatly over the *next* ten years, but 48 percent said the rate was "about right" considering the benefits. Although there must be some limit to the level of taxation the public will tolerate, it is not clear where that level is.

The public may have become so accustomed to increases that they no longer knew when taxes went up. How could they fight something they could not see?

Nor did the public appear to learn much from the debate surrounding the social security crisis and the attending media exposure. In 1979 and again in the summer of 1981, people were asked whether social security taxes are set aside for future retirement (FALSE) or used to pay benefits of those already retired (TRUE). In 1979, 71 percent of the public picked the correct answer. In 1981, following Reagan's social security proposals and extensive news coverage, the number of correct answers had risen only to 75 percent. It was not a significant improvement and could have been a statistical error. Further, most of the improvement came among younger people. For those over age 65, there was virtually no change in knowledge about how the system worked between 1979 and 1981: 2 out of 5 picked the wrong answer in both surveys.

The basic issue is whether greater knowledge would have made any difference anyway. Certainly, the lack of information made it more difficult for Congress and the President to explain tough choices back home. If the public did not know about the benefit COLA, how could Republicans justify the need for reform? If the public already thought federal workers were covered, how could Democrats show just how far they had compromised? An informed public would have been less responsive to interest group rhetoric. As it was, the public became little more than a political pawn in the social security debate, moved to and fro by all sides.

CONFIDENCE

Confidence in future benefits was also important in the social security debate. When members of Congress talked about the need for action, they inevitably talked about declining public confidence. It was perceived as the most important feature of public opinion. It affected the public's support for higher taxes, lower benefits, a later retirement age, and the final compromise. It affected the public's willingness to accept some short-term pain in return for some long-term gain. If workers did not believe they would ever see a penny in benefits, why would they accept higher payroll taxes or longer working lives? Liberals worried that younger workers would turn toward private pensions and away from social security.

It was clear that public confidence had dropped by the early 1980s. Whereas 18 percent of the public had expressed "complete confidence" in 1979 that social security would have the money to pay benefits on their retirement, only 8 percent were of this opinion in November 1982. The number who said they had "only a little confidence" or "no confidence" jumped from 48 percent in 1979 to 75 percent in 1982. Clearly, a large portion of the public had serious doubts about the future of the program. However, some worried more than others. Table 4 shows the results of the November 1982 survey.

The poll suggests several important gaps among the generations. Of all the age groups, the retired were the most confident about the future. If members of

TABLE 4. **Confidence in Social Security, by Age Group, 1982**

Confidence	New Arrivals 18–24	Now Working 25–34	Middle-Aged 35–49	Near-Retired 50–64	Retired 65+
Complete	3%	3%	5%	13%	21%
A great deal	11	8	10	22	34
Only a little	45	44	44	41	29
No confidence	38	45	39	21	7

Source: NBC News/Associated Press poll, November 1982. Total interviews equaled 1,583.

Question: "How much confidence do you have that the Social Security system will have the funds to provide retirement benefits to you or your spouse upon retirement . . . complete confidence, a great deal of confidence, only a little confidence, or no confidence?"

Congress were worried about elderly confidence, they were wrong. There are four possible explanations for the surprising figures. First, perhaps the elderly did not understand the program well enough to know how close it was to failure. Second, while the elderly might not have understood the technical aspects of social security *policy*, they did know a little about social security *politics*. Perhaps they understood that Congress and the President would never let the program fail. Third, many retirees had already been through a first social security crisis in 1977. Having watched Congress and the President patch up the program once, perhaps they understood that politics would eventually subside and calmer heads would prevail. Fourth, perhaps most of the elderly understood that social security would not have to last much longer to meet their needs. Problems in the year 2015 had little relevance to an 80-year-old in 1982.

Yet the higher levels of confidence among the elderly did not suggest they were calm. There was more than enough politics to make older Americans frightened. Confidence among the elderly had dropped between 1979 and 1982, falling from 74 percent ("complete" or "a great deal") to 55 percent, a substantial loss. Moreover, it was the elderly who wrote most of the letters to Congress, who attended the protest meetings, who rallied in Washington. Although 55 percent were still confident about benefits, 36 percent had little or no confidence at all. That was more than enough fear to mobilize the elderly to fight. Even though the elderly were more confident than younger groups, they also saw the problems on the horizon. In March 1982, a Gallup poll found that less than 5 percent of older Americans expected social security to have trouble within a year. By December 1982, only nine months later, another Gallup poll found that four times as many now expected a crisis within a year.

The near-retired were also confident about the future. Though they shared much of the elderly's confusion about the program, there was also some wishful thinking among the near-retired. Faced with a dearth of alternatives to social security and being only a few years from retirement, the near-retired may have been more confident that simply wishing would make benefits come true. What choice did the near-retired have at that point in their lives? "When you get close to retirement," as one social security expert noted, "you've already made your major economic decisions. . . . If you didn't save enough, if you bought a house in the wrong neighborhood, if you smoked all your life and have bad health, you don't have as much time to make changes. You're not as nimble."

Younger groups—the new arrivals and the now working—were the least confident about the future. Their lack of confidence reflected knowledge about the pay-as-you-go financing of the program and the long years until retirement. They knew why the program was in trouble, and they did not believe it could last another fifty years. Further, it was hard to imagine anything being the same in 2020 as it was in 1982. A large number of people under age 21 already believed that there would be a nuclear war in their lifetime—not the kind of opinion that contributes to confidence in social security.

Despite the lack of confidence, the young did not appear concerned about their own retirements. There was still time to find other alternatives. However, there was considerable fear for their parents, creating formidable opposition to any benefit cuts. A Republican Senatorial Campaign Committee aide pointed to simple demographics as the source of fear. People aged between 25 and 40 were the most likely to have children at home and parents on social security. And the fear was greatest for the high-school educated: "They're absolutely petrified about the economy. They're the ones who have mortgages to pay. They're the ones working up the job ladder. They're stretched to the limit in their budgets. And they've usually got parents on social security. If social security goes down, they'll have to take care of them, too. They know the value of social security because they've thought about what it will cost if mom and dad move in with them."

But falling levels of confidence among younger groups did not spell a mass desire to leave the social security program. There was very little intergenerational warfare on social security. In 1979, a Hart survey showed that only 19 percent of the public would leave social security if given the chance, and the bulk of these answers came from upper-income respondents. Among the young, the figures in favor of exit were somewhat higher, ranging from 22 percent of the new arrivals up to 30 percent of the now working. Asked whether the social security program should be "ended," however, only 1 in 10 strongly favored the option, with 7 in 10 strongly opposed. Low levels of confidence clearly did not translate into support for "opting out" of the program. In the 1979 Hart survey, for example, only 11 percent of the now working age group had "complete" or "a great deal" of confidence in the promise of future payments. Yet 65 percent said they would rather "be in the social security system and pay taxes" even if given the chance to get out.

Instead of talking about conflict between the young and the old, it was more appropriate to think of growing disagreement between educated professionals and blue-collar workers. In 1979, 39 percent of people with at least some college would have left social security if given a choice, compared with 5 percent of people with less than a high-school education. Even here, the two groups still supported the social security program for current retirees. There was near-unanimous opposition among both groups to any attempt to reduce benefits for people who were already retired. Further, when asked to choose between higher payroll taxes and lower benefits as a solution to the funding crisis, both education groups were almost equally opposed to lower benefits. Finally, when asked to rate Reagan's handling of the social security issue, both groups were strongly disapproving.

Ultimately, the question was whether anyone's opinions made a difference to Congress and the President. The likely answer was that politicians listen to the public that votes. Even if the young had been firmly in favor of drastic cuts, their low levels of turnout in elections made their opinions of less value when compared with those of the elderly. As one Republican Senatorial Campaign Committee aide noted, "The 18- to 29-year-olds were very negative toward Reagan on social security, but we figured two things: One, they don't vote at a very high rate so they can't hurt us much. Two, the elderly folks do vote at a very high rate and can swing an election, particularly in the off-years." Indeed, in 1978, the last year that Census Bureau figures were available, 56 percent of people over 65 went to the polls, surpassed only by the 59 percent turnout among the near-retired, those aged 45–64. In sharp contrast, only 20 percent of the 18–21 age group and 26 percent of the 21–24 age group voted in 1978.

OPPOSITION

Along with the fear of impending bankruptcy and the desire to save social security, the public consistently opposed most of the major funding options. The public wanted the system repaired but did not know how it should be done. Thus any list of the various social security solutions produced far more opposition than support. Table 5 summarizes the results from a set of three polls conducted in November 1982.

Unfortunately for members of Congress who wanted some public guidance, the results were loaded with inconsistencies. Whereas 68 percent in the *Los Angeles Times* survey said they supported taxing "the social security benefits of the wealthy," 53 percent in the Harris poll said they opposed giving "benefits only to elderly people who can prove they have little or no other income"; whereas 40 percent in the *Times* survey said they supported making the program "voluntary," only 16 percent in the NBC poll favored phasing "out social security altogether and instead have people rely on their own private retirement plans."

These polls, coming as the National Commission on Social Security Reform worked on a compromise, offered little encouragement for any solution. The only alternative with strong public support was coverage of federal workers. But the option was opposed by the AFL-CIO and the public employee unions, and it could provide only a small portion of the total savings needed to repair the social security system. In order to patch the system, Congress and the President would have to combine tax increases and benefit cuts. But 49 percent of the public opposed tax increases, and 75 percent opposed benefit reductions.

TABLE 5. Support for and Opposition to the Solutions, November 1982

Option and Poll	In Favor	Opposed
Require workers who do not pay social security taxes now—for example, employees of the federal government—to pay those taxes (Harris).	75%	23%
Base cost-of-living adjustments on increases in either wages or prices, whichever is lower (Harris).	68	26
Tax the social security benefits of the wealthy *(Times)*.	68	28
Use federal monies such as income taxes to pay for part of social security (Harris).	60	36
Support social security by using general tax revenues *(Times)*.	59	28
Keep social security benefits as they are now, even if it means having to raise social security taxes (Harris).	55	42
Bring government workers and employees of nonprofit organizations under social security coverage *(Times)*.	54	36
Reduce benefits paid to people who retire early, before age 65 (NBC-AP).	52	39
Include social security benefits in taxable income so that persons who have substantial amounts of other income after they retire would have to pay taxes on their social security benefits (NBC-AP).	47	44
Raise social security payroll taxes *(Times)*.	46	49
Give social security benefits only to elderly people who can prove they have little or no other income (Harris).	46	53
Gradually increase the retirement age for social security benefits *(Times)*.	45	52
Increase the age at which people can retire with full social security benefits (NBC-AP).	44	50
Gradually raise the retirement age for full social security benefits from 65 to 68 (Harris).	41	58
Make social security voluntary *(Times)*.	40	51
Cut back or delay social security cost-of-living increases *(Times)*.	40	54
Eliminate benefits for minor children of retired workers (Harris).	36	60
Go back to the less generous benefit formulas of the 1950s and 1960s *(Times)*.	31	51
Reduce benefits only for people who retire in the future (Harris).	22	75
Phase out social security altogether and instead have people rely only on their own private retirement plans (NBC-AP).	16	78
Reduce benefits for people already retired (Harris).	11	86

Source: National Journal, January 1, 1983. All three polls were conducted in November 1982. Reprinted by permission of National Journal, Inc. © 1983.

And these patterns of support and opposition did not vary much by age group. The elderly and the young were equally opposed to benefit changes and tax increases, to a new retirement age, and to a needs test.

Pollsters had seen these kinds of responses before. In the abstract, the American public supports any number of noble goals and programs. They support the basic notions of civil rights, balanced budgets, quality education, and so on. When pushed on specifics, however, the public rarely agrees on what to do. Everyone wants a balanced budget, but no one wants his or her program cut. Moreover, at least for social security, the public did not want either the young or the old to suffer. The elderly understood that higher taxes might hurt their children; young workers understood that benefit cuts might hurt their parents. It was not surprising that the public supported federal coverage: most (63 percent) already thought federal workers were covered. The only other option with support was the use of other funding sources "such as income taxes to pay for part of social security." But when asked by Gallup whether they approved of an increase in "federal income taxes so that social security benefits could be paid out of general revenues," only 24 percent said yes. If there was any guidance at all, it was that the public seemed to want tax increases over benefit cuts. When asked to choose between the two options in 1979, 63 percent selected tax increases, whereas only 15 percent picked benefit cuts. Moreover, 52 percent strongly opposed lowering benefits instead of raising taxes.

In the final analysis, politicians on both sides of the aisle were inevitably drawn to one conclusion about public opinion: most of the options were painful. Social security was indeed the "third rail of a subway," as one White House aide said, "loaded with high voltage." Democrats could benefit at the ballot box for a year or two, but they would have to pass a package of painful solutions at some point. Republicans could duck the issue for a year or two, but any delays of benefit checks would be blamed on their party. Both parties could delay the final compromise, but confidence would continue to fall.

POLLSTERS

Pollsters played a critical role in the social security debate, translating public opinion to Congress and the President. If they asked the wrong questions or the wrong people, the government could hardly represent the public faithfully. For members of Congress who believed in representing public opinion to the letter, polling errors would be crucial.

Yet pollsters often confused questions about social security solutions. "I don't think we have the slightest idea of what short-term pain the public will bear. The questions are inadequate," one critic noted. "The questions generally begin 'Do you favor cuts in social security?' or something like that. As far as I know, no one has proposed cuts in social security. That is not the issue. The question is the *rate of increase* in social security benefits. This isn't just playing with words. It is a critical conceptual matter. The survey research community hasn't posed it well."[6]

In their defense, pollsters were under great pressure to simplify their questions. At best, most polls lasted fifteen or twenty minutes, covered a wide range of subjects, and were over the telephone. There was not enough time for a detailed explanation of a program such as social security; only enough for a series of quick questions about highly complex solutions: do you favor benefit cuts? tax increases? the use of general revenues? The best questions on social security were the ones that forced the public to make the same kinds of calculations that Congress had to make: benefits or taxes? retirement age or taxes? taxes or cost-of-living adjustments? or some combination of solutions? Not only did these kinds of questions help policymakers understand public opinion in an era of tough choices, but they helped the public understand the policymakers. Unfortunately, they were also the longest questions.

Further, pollsters rarely asked how much the public understood. Questions about COLAs, federal employees, and the use of general revenues, for example, assumed that the respondents knew at least something about the social security system. As noted above, however, the public did not know about COLAs, did not know that federal employees were exempt from social security, did not know how general revenue financing would work. Indeed, there should have been some doubt about whether the public even knew what general revenues were. In making blind assumptions about public knowledge, pollsters misled Congress on the levels of public opposition and support. It would have been far more valuable if the pollsters had reported that the public did not understand the system very well and, as a consequence, did not know what to do about the problem. How could the public possibly know whether a COLA based on the lesser of wage increases or price increases was better than one based on the general Consumer Price Index? How could they possibly grasp the implications of a shift to general revenue financing? The answer is that most could not.

Finally, pollsters rarely paid attention to the impact of question wording and question order. By changing a word or two, pollsters could swing large numbers of answers. The use of the word "cut" in a question about benefits, instead of a phrase about "reducing the rate of growth," could have increased the number of opponents; the use of the word "elderly" instead of "retirees" could have had some impact, too. The issue is not whether one word is better than another but whether the choice of words had some unmeasured influence on answers.

The order of questions also could have affected the social security polls. Asking a question about support for tax increases *before* asking about support for benefit cuts could have affected the answers. Respondents might have been thinking less about the plight of the elderly and more about their paychecks. Asking about confidence *before* asking about specific solutions for the funding

---

[6]Everett Carll Ladd, quoted in *Public Opinion*, August/September 1982, p. 6.

crisis also could have shaped the answers. When people were confronted by a bleak menu of solutions for the crisis first, they might have recognized the "damned if you do/damned if you don't" nature of social security and felt even less confidence about the future.

Pollsters obviously make mistakes. The question is whether the mistakes constitute a serious breakdown in their role as translators of public opinion. In perhaps the clearest example of one such breakdown, a November 1982 Harris poll reported that public confidence in social security had actually gone up in 1982. It was a remarkable report. How could confidence go up at the very height of the crisis? According to the Harris poll, "Americans are evenly divided, 49–49 percent, on the question of how viable the Social Security system is. But this is a change since last year, when a 54–33 percent majority said they had 'hardly any confidence' in the long-term soundness of the system." After a year of screaming headlines, Harris had discovered a 16 percent gain in confidence! The change was almost entirely due, however, to a change in question wording. In 1981, Harris had asked the confidence question as follows:

> How much confidence do you have that the present Social Security system will be able to pay you benefits when you retire—a great deal, some, or hardly any confidence at all?

In 1982, Harris changed the question to:

> How much confidence do you have that the present Social Security system will be able to pay you benefits when you retire or will continue to pay you benefits if you are now retired—a great deal, some, or hardly any confidence at all?

The simple addition of the phrase "or will continue to pay you benefits if you are now retired" allowed the elderly to answer the question in 1982, whereas almost half of the group did not answer the question in 1981. Technically, the 1981 question did not permit any answers from the retired, but half still volunteered an answer. Since the elderly are the most confident that social security will continue to pay benefits, keeping many of them out of the 1981 question meant the confidence was underestimated and that the 1981 poll was wrong. When the retired were allowed to answer in 1982, the confidence figures moved up to the right level.

CONCLUSION

As Congress and the President looked over the range of support, knowledge, confidence, and opposition in the polls, they faced a simple choice: either spend years educating the public on the basic issues, or hide from the public spotlight; either guide the public to the tough decisions, or take advantage of the public confusion. The answer was dictated by the crisis. There was simply not enough time to bring the public to a full understanding of the social security issue or to show them how difficult it was to make the system work. It had taken almost fifty years to confuse the social security issue; it could not be reversed in a span of months.

Thus the public would remain an obstacle as long as Congress and the President cared about reelection. Unfortunately, the crisis left little time for public education. The pressure to move quickly was in conflict with the need to inform the public. The best answer seemed to involve further confusion. Congress and the President would have no opportunity to open a national debate on social security. They would try to repair the program and hope it made it through the coming decades.

There was one ray of hope for the future among the polls: as young people grew older, they would keep their knowledge about the mechanics of the system while gaining more information about benefits. By the turn of the century, they would be quite prepared to form careful opinions on social security. That, of course, could not help Congress and the President in the early 1980s.

7

The Hired Guns

It was impossible to count the total number of interest groups involved in social security in 1983. There were at least a dozen coalitions roaming Capitol Hill and perhaps four times as many private lobbyists working the issue. At least 200 other groups testified before the House and Senate on the rescue bill; another 200 hired professional firms.

Among the list of hired guns were the heavy hitters: such huge, multipurpose organizations as the AFL-CIO, the American Association of Retired Persons, the National Council of Senior Citizens, the Chamber of Commerce, the National Federation of Independent Business, and the National Association of Manufacturers. There were small fries, too: such highly specialized organizations as the American Foundation for the Blind, the National Lottery Association (for a national lottery as a new funding mechanism for social security), the National Child Safety Council (against coverage for nonprofit organizations), the Bowling Proprietors Association of America (against higher payroll taxes), the Communist Party of the United States (for a greatly expanded social security system), and the Liberty Lobby (against social security in general).

A Delicate Choice

There were two problems with the hired guns. First, the list had grown since the early 1970s. Along with the rest of the interest group community, the "social security lobby" had exploded, both in total numbers of organizations and in membership. There were more groups involved on social security in the early 1980s than ever before, and they represented more people and businesses. As government began to cut back on the budget, new groups sprang up to join the fight, representing smaller and smaller fragments of society. Since most were quite skilled at using the American system of separate powers, they presented serious obstacles to movement.

Second, the list was increasingly populated by single-interest groups. Unlike the large umbrella organizations, single-interest lobbies had little incentive to compromise on social security. For some, it was the only issue that mattered, their only reason for existence. They would not trade social security in return for something else. Unlike organized labor or the large business groups, the single-interest organizations were willing to accept stalemate as the price for victory on social security. They were willing to stop government on other issues if that guaranteed success on their one position. They proved to be tenacious in their zest for victory, using every angle to stop benefit cuts or tax increases.

Nevertheless, all the groups, whether large or small, multipurpose or single-interest, would face a delicate choice if Congress and the President agreed on a rescue package: they could either support the social security compromise or try to break it apart and start again from scratch. In short, take it or fight it. If they supported the agreement, the groups might alienate their own members, many of whom expected nothing less than complete opposition. If they opposed the compromise, the groups might end up with something much worse and might so anger Congress that they would lose access and influence on future issues.

THE REPRESENTED

Among the huge number of groups that testified in Congress, the elderly and small-business groups were the most active. The elderly groups cared for an obvious reason: their constituents would be affected by any changes in social security benefits. This was an elderly issue, and the two major aging groups, the American Association of Retired Persons and the National Council of Senior Citizens, had to be involved. The small-business lobbies cared for a less obvious reason: social security taxes seemed to affect their members much more than they did big businesses. This was a profit issue for many small companies and mom-and-pop firms, and the two major small-business groups, the Chamber of Commerce and the National Federation of Independent Business, had to be involved.

There were important similarities among the four groups that shaped their influence on Capitol Hill. All four were in business more than simply to win on the social security bill. They also wanted to survive and build their membership. There were important differences, too.

The "Gray" Lobbies

The growth of the elderly groups was a recent phenomenon. Before the mid-1960s, the elderly did not have any interest group representation. Passage of social security in 1935 and Medicare thirty years later reflected lobbying by labor unions, not elderly groups. The unions saw the legislation as part of improving the lot of workers in the future. As part of the 1970s boom in interest group activity, however, the elderly became the subject of intense competition between the American Association and the National Council. It was less that the elderly were looking for representation and much more that the American Association and the National Council were looking for members.

Of the two groups, the American Association was the larger. Started in 1958, the American Association claimed a membership of 14 million in 1982. Mail traffic was so heavy that the Washington office had its own zip code. There is little question that size made a difference on Capitol Hill. "Most of the young staffers up there have mothers and fathers who belong to the American Association of Retired Persons," one staffer noted. "You think that doesn't make a difference?" Further, the association's $41 million budget included a complete team of lobbyists. By March 1983, the American Association had seven full-time legislative specialists, two outside hired lobbyists, and a liaison budget of well over $1 million.

Yet size also created problems. First, the association had grown because it offered services to its members. Among the benefits in 1982 were a cut-rate mail pharmacy, a motor club, a monthly magazine, group health insurance, and even a money market fund. Indeed, by early 1983, the money market fund had reached $3 billion in total assets. When the American Association asked its own members in 1982 about the advantages of joining, 22 percent mentioned the publications, 8 percent the health/drug benefits, 7 percent the insurance, 5 percent the travel club, and 3 percent the money fund. Only 17 percent replied that they joined because the American Association cared about and helped the elderly. The members obviously cared more about the benefits than any legislative issues.

Second, the American Association often had trouble finding positions that would appeal to a majority of the huge membership. To keep its members satisfied, it often adopted the least controversial position. In some cases, it could not take any position at all. Given the low levels of knowledge about social security among older Americans in general and the high levels of opposition to most solutions, the American Association spent a great deal of organizational energy merely trying to second-guess its 14 million members.

Thus the membership was not necessarily committed to the legislative goals of the leadership. Indeed, between 1980 and 1982, the number of members who listed legislative positions as an advantage of American Association membership actually fell from 14 to 10 percent. Though the association's membership was huge, competing groups could easily claim that the support was, in the words of one National Council staffer, "a mile wide and an inch deep."

If the American Association started out as little more than a service lobby, the National Council of Senior Citizens started out as an organization for old union members. The group was originally created by the AFL-CIO in the mid-1960s to help campaign for Medicare, and it remained firmly linked to labor into the 1980s. "Old unionists don't die," a labor official said, "they join the NCSC." Indeed, the National Council drew most of its leadership from the ranks of former union officials. The same union leaders who had lobbied for social security in the 1930s eventually grew old and formed the National Council. Because the organization was set up for one group of people, the National Council was not as large as the American Association. Estimates placed the total membership at 4 million in 1982. But despite its smaller numbers, the National Council was better equipped to generate more mail from its membership than the American Association. The reason was that the National Council was organized around 4,000 active local clubs. Unlike the American Association, which was organized from the national level down, the council relied on the basic concept of "locals" to build up a national organization.

At the federal level, the National Council did not have a particularly large staff or budget. At the height of the social security debate, the council had only two full-time lobbyists. However, it did have access to the full lobbying strength of the AFL-CIO. Moreover, the National Council had no trouble deciding how to form alliances with other liberal groups. Because of its smaller size and the shared background of its members, the National Council leaders had no doubts about the organization's political agenda.

That certainty of purpose meant that the National Council had more lobbying weapons than the American Association. Because it knew where it stood on the key issues, the National Council could publish voting records on Congress, listing each member on specific roll calls. The American Association could not. Because it had strong links to organized labor and a long record on Capitol Hill as a lobbying group, the National Council could build alliances with other "gray lobbies," pooling its membership into large coalitions. The American Association could not, in part because few groups are willing to join coalitions unless they know what the other organizations want. The National Council had that strong sense of direction. The American Association did not. "There was never any doubt about whether you could trust the Council," a House Rules Committee aide reported. "They would not break an agreement. We were not as sure about the American Association."

Further, the National Council could get more out of its 4 million members than the American Association from its 14 million. National Council members had agreement of purpose, making them more intense constituents. The American Association was able to stimulate mail, but it often lacked the kind of strength that makes congressional staffers take notice. Finally, the National Council had more flexibility than the American Association in negotiating with Congress. Split by internal conflict in its Washington headquarters, the association's staff was indecisive on rapidly changing issues. All of these differences meant that the National Council often came to represent the elderly by default, even given its much smaller size.

The Small-Business Lobbies

By 1980, there were five major groups representing American business in Washington: the American Business Conference, the Business Roundtable, the

National Association of Manufacturers, the National Federation of Independent Business, and the Chamber of Commerce. Though many corporations had their own lobbyists or retained high-priced liaison firms, the five umbrella groups offered considerable influence on major legislative issues. Individual companies often used their own people for narrow self-interests and one or more of the five broad-gauge groups for the big tax and spending issues. As one industry lobbyist remarked, "You try to lay your money on the most options. You've got to join up with one of the big groups to make sure they don't hurt you and to build your clout. But most of your own work is on things that matter back home—better trade provisions, that kind of thing."

Of the five groups, only two spent much time working with small-business issues: the Chamber and the National Federation. Of the two, the Chamber was larger. According to one estimate, there were somewhere over 250,000 members of the Chamber nationwide by 1982. Of the quarter-million, the Chamber estimated that approximately 90 percent were small businesses. Yet in an organization of that size, it is difficult to represent any specific kind of business. If 90 percent of the Chamber's total membership were small businesses, another 25,000 companies were large. And in terms of total corporate income or number of employees, big businesses were more important to the Chamber. The 225,000 small businesses generated only a small fraction of the total corporate earnings of the 25,000 big businesses.

Although the Chamber encouraged small-business participation in major policy decisions, the larger corporations were more likely to gain influence inside the organization. The Chamber operated through a sixty-five-member policy board composed of business leaders. The board was inevitably dominated by the big companies, in part because small businesses did not have the resources to come to Washington for policy meetings, in part because of the image of big businesses as more important for winning congressional support.

Like the American Association, the Chamber faced serious problems based on its large size. First, it was hard to gain internal agreement on legislative positions. As one official noted, "If you're looking here for a legislative operation that can turn around on a dime, you're looking in the wrong place. We just don't work that way. We're a big organization and we only get involved in big issues common to us all."

Second, the Chamber had a problem whenever taxes were concerned: it generally ended up alienating at least some portion of its membership whenever it took a position. Small businesses were particularly threatened by payroll tax increases. Since they could not pass the increases on to consumers in the form of higher prices, they had to swallow smaller profits. Big businesses were less concerned about payroll taxes, concentrating on corporate taxes and other issues. "Why should a mom-and-pop firm care about how to write off $100 million in new equipment?" one lobbyist asked. "They care about how they're going to make it month to month." Given the Chamber's broad membership, there was frequent internal conflict over tax issues. The Chamber had to choose between representing its small businesses on payroll issues and reserving its influence for other contests.

In contrast, the National Federation of Independent Business did not face any indecision on taxes. Because its only members were small businesses, the group had no internal problems opposing tax increases. Indeed, anything less than outright opposition would have alienated the group's only constituency. Like the National Council of Senior Citizens, the National Federation had a number of weapons at its disposal simply because it was smaller and more focused. It could form stronger coalitions with other groups and stimulate intensity among its members. It could bargain with Congress on short notice and outmaneuver the Chamber. And the National Federation was not constrained by a large policymaking board. Though the Chamber had invested $4 million in a new communications system to speed information back and forth between Washington and the locals, the National Federation was always faster on small-business issues. "We knew what to do without asking," a Federation spokesman concluded.

THE UNREPRESENTED

The fact that the National Council and the National Federation ended up as the leading groups on social security had several important effects on the legislative debate. Both groups were surely opposed to key social security solutions. Whereas the American Association advocated a three-month cost-of-living delay, the National Council was firmly opposed to any cuts, however disguised. Whereas the Chamber was often confused on tax increases, the National Federation was absolutely opposed.

Nevertheless, the National Council and the National Federation were willing to bargain toward a solution. Both groups operated from a position of solid support from their members. The National Council and the National Federation were able to lead their memberships, not simply follow. Yet because both groups were small, they needed allies to build their influence. Both needed to form coalitions with other interest groups.

Even given the competition between interest groups to represent the elderly and small business, it is important to ask whether anyone was *not* represented. Unfortunately, the answers involve a good deal of conjecture. A 1982 survey by the American Association of Retired Persons suggested that roughly 35 percent of people over the age of 55 belonged to the group. Of the membership, 40 percent were over age 70, 45 percent had some college education, 72 percent made more than $8,000 a year, 60 percent owned their own homes, 97 percent were white, and 73 percent were glad they had retired.

But what about the people with less education, income, and so forth? What about the people who were unhappy that they had retired? Did the American Association appeal to them? Were they represented?

Consider the following figures on name recognition.[1] In 1982, 61 percent of people over age 55 recognized the National Council when presented with a list

---

[1] These figures come from surveys conducted for the American Association of Retired Persons by William R. Hamilton and Staff, Inc.

of elderly groups, and 77 percent recognized the American Association. But a large number of elderly could not name the groups. The recognition rates varied by income, education, and occupation. Over half of the upper-income white-collar respondents did not recognize the National Council, whereas only 9 percent did not know the American Association. At the lower income and education levels, however, roughly one-third of older Americans did not recognize either the National Council or the American Association.

There appeared to be a group of people who simply did not know about any possible interest representation. Indeed, of the over-55 age group, only 13 percent of nonwhites, 17 percent of those earning under $4,000, and 20 percent of those with less than a high-school education belonged to the American Association. Though the figures are very likely to be higher for the National Council, given the labor connection, there were large numbers of elderly people who did not belong to any group at all.

Simple guesses suggest other unrepresented groups. Nonunionized workers, many of the self-employed, domestic workers, the poor, and the young could find little representation in Washington. The poor did not have the money to join groups; others did not have the information; domestic workers, illegal immigrants, and nonunionized employees had other priorities, including merely making it from day to day.

All of these unrepresented groups relied on the kindness of Congress to represent their basic interests. Though there were at least two elderly groups to represent blacks and Hispanics (the National Caucus on the Black Aged and the Asociacion Nacional Pro Personas Mayores), neither had attracted widespread minority membership. Nor were minorities likely to join the American Association and the National Council. "Who's going to form an organization of the disadvantaged?" one interest group observer asked. "What's going to be their leverage and over whom? In order to have power, you've got to be able to swing elections, and the elderly poor bloc just can't do that."[2] Thus if policy-makers wanted to balance social security on the backs of future generations, who was there to stop them? If they forgot about the elderly poor, who was there to remind them?

THE COALITIONS

One lesson from the American Association and Chamber of Commerce experiences was that bigger is not always better, especially for building a strong interest group. Too many different interests *within* a group can lead to stalemate on the major legislative issues. The group may end up spending more time fighting controversies inside its organization than winning battles on Capitol Hill. All large, multipurpose groups face the problem to one extent or another. It is one reason for the rise of so many single-issue groups in

[2]Robert H. Binstock, quoted in *National Journal*, November 2, 1976, p. 1388.

Washington. Between 1968 and 1980, the total number of such groups jumped 40 percent, to somewhere over 10,000.

Yet if bigger is not necessarily better inside a group, it does matter in the legislative world. Members of Congress have only so much time in the day to meet with lobbyists and individual constituents. Size makes a difference in gaining access and building influence. As one former American Association legislative aide argued, "Some of our most dismal failures come when the two mass membership organizations are at odds and there is no clear articulation of needs from the other groups. To the extent that we can articulate a common elderly objective, and to the extent that we can work together to achieve that objective, our power increases. And to the extent that the elderly can present a united front with other human resource groups, our power increases even more. It will be a continuing struggle to get the aging groups to realize that we are part of a broader brotherhood."

Thus there has been a recent, little-noticed trend involving the rise of temporary coalitions of organizations. The coalitions come together on a specific issue, fall apart after victory or defeat, and come back together the next time the issue arises. In this way, single-issue groups can survive as organizations while generating much greater influence than they could ever build on their own. Midsized organizations such as the National Council or the National Federation can also benefit. By joining with other groups, they supplement their lobbying strength, improve their reputations in the Washington community, and compete against even larger groups. Though the largest groups often join the coalitions too, it is not clear that they gain much from the shared enterprise. Since they are already large enough on their own, they often maintain considerable distance from the coalitions.

During the social security debate, this trend toward coalitions involved three groups: the Save Our Security coalition (SOS), the Fund for Assuring an Independent Retirement (FAIR), and the Carlton group.

SOS

SOS was the largest of the three coalitions, having formed in early 1979 to fight Carter's proposed cutbacks in several small social security programs. As one SOS official noted, "After we beat Carter, we went into mothballs until Reagan announced his cuts. Then we came alive again. I suppose we'll go under after this is all done, too." By 1982, SOS had approximately 125 groups covering 35 to 40 million members. There were several very large groups in the coalition, including the AFL-CIO, the American Association of Retired Persons, the Communications Workers of America, the International Machinists Union, the United Auto Workers, the National Educational Association, and the National Farmers Union. And there were many small groups, including the National Council of Catholic Women; the Union Club of Cottonwood/Verde Valley, Arizona; the Association for Retarded Citizens; the Advocates of the Handicapped; Monmouth (N.Y.) County Office of the Handicapped; and the Gray Panthers.

The large groups in SOS were concentrated in two major issue areas: aging and labor. The latter, of course, reflected the long-standing labor interest in social security plus the National Council's role in organizing SOS. But the sheer number of groups in SOS made it, in the words of a leader, "an unwieldy coalition. We've never had everyone in one place at the same time; some have joined just to be on the list so they can say they helped if we win. We never had any rules about who could join, but you wouldn't expect business to hop on."

Though SOS provided strength in its numbers, there were problems gaining consensus among the diverse elements of the coalition. SOS came together only to fight government decisions, in part because it could never agree on any positive agenda of its own. According to one of the organizers, "SOS has to have positions with complete agreement from all the members. That's one of the basic ground rules. The only issue where we've had any basic agreement is on benefit cuts. We couldn't support coverage of federal workers because of the National Association of Retired Federal Employees and the AFL-CIO. We couldn't support any kind of taxing of benefits because AARP was opposed. We couldn't support raising the retirement age because of the UAW and the rest of labor. All we had was opposition."

Even though the American Association belonged to SOS, it was not particularly enthusiastic about the coalition. The American Association often moved on its own without consulting SOS or any of the other organizations. Other SOS members had their own difficulties. The AFL-CIO leadership council, for example, was split on a number of basic social security issues. Its federal employees opposed mandatory federal coverage, but the manufacturing unions did not. Its postal workers opposed coverage, but the trade unions did not. Thus as long as SOS opposed benefit cuts, it could develop a united front. The moment it switched to any positive program, it was unable to move. When it came time either to endorse or to oppose any social security compromise, SOS would be stalemated.

FAIR

Like SOS, the Fund for Assuring an Independent Retirement (FAIR) was an on-again, off-again coalition. It was first pulled together in 1977 to fight coverage of federal workers in the Carter rescue bill, and it returned in 1979 and 1982. Some of the same groups that joined SOS also belonged to FAIR, including the National Association of Retired Federal Employees. FAIR had a simple mission: to keep federal workers out of social security.

Once again, the coalition revolved around opposition. Once again, there was little common ground for a positive solution. FAIR's main approach was to badger Congress into a separate vote on its single issue, regardless of the impact on the rest of a compromise. Indeed, because federal workers were not covered by social security, FAIR had no interest in passing a rescue bill at all. This was very much a "single-interest" coalition. Even if FAIR had wanted to adopt positive positions, however, the long history of infighting among the unions and retirement groups would have prevented much agreement. FAIR included unions that had hardly talked to each other for decades. The National Association of Letter Carriers and the American Postal Union, for example, had been bitter competitors for the scarce number of postal employees and had to swallow hard just to agree on stopping mandatory coverage.

The Carlton Group

The Carlton group was first formed in 1975 by a small number of business organizations. The group met regularly at Washington's Sheraton-Carlton Hotel; hence, the name. By 1981, the group included representatives of the Chamber of Commerce, the National Association of Manufacturers (NAM), the National Federation of Independent Business, the American Council for Capital Formation, the Committee for Effective Capital Recovery, the American Business Conference, and the Business Roundtable. "In the 1960s and 1970s, business people in Washington just sat around wringing their hands and moaning: 'Nobody understands us. Labor has all the votes. Congress is anti-business,'" one business leader said. "In the late '70s, we finally saw that we do have a constituency we can call on: employees, suppliers, community leaders, shareholders. We started making efforts at working together, but it was negative—to stop things like labor law reform or a federal consumer protection agency. Now we're in a new mode. We're able to go affirmative."

Like other groups of business representatives (known by such names as the Tuesday Twelve or the Big Littles), the Carlton group was more an information exchange than a formal coalition. Despite the newfound belief that the Carlton group could go affirmative, it seemed much better equipped to stop government proposals than to build a full legislative agenda. The members of the group were simply too broad to guarantee action: the Committee for Effective Capital Recovery represented more than 500 corporations interested in changing the depreciation rates, while the American Business Conference represented chief executives of 100 or so "growth" companies. Even on Reagan's budget and tax cut plans, the Carlton group was more a tool of the White House than an independent force for change.

On an issue such as social security, there might be opposition to higher taxes, but little more. There were natural divisions between big and small firms, labor-intensive and capital-intensive firms, manufacturing and service firms. Whether NAM would react with the same intensity to higher payroll taxes as the small-business groups was clearly in doubt. Indeed, as one labor consultant suggested, "When business lobbyists are in favor of a package, such as the President's budget, or opposed to a program, such as labor law reform, they can pull together and really control Capitol Hill. But when it comes to compromise, they have great difficulty. Give them a little time and they'll be fighting like a pack of wolves." Nevertheless, the mere thought that business groups might somehow coalesce into a massive lobbying coalition frightened potential opponents. Conservatives could use that fear as an incentive for liberal compromise.

CONCLUSION

Like the public, most interest groups focused on opposition to key social security options instead of on positive support. When such groups as the American Association and the National Federation did offer suggestions, the options were far too radical for Congress and the President. The American Association advocated general revenue financing for social security, anathema to Republicans, while the National Federation supported a breakdown of benefits into welfare versus "investments," an outrage to Democrats.

Unlike the public, interest groups had access to the congressional system. Whereas Congress could confuse the public with complicated packages at the subterranean levels of government, interest groups remained firmly involved and informed at all levels of the legislative process and actually preferred the hidden channels. If Congress and the President wanted to hide a social security decision, it would have to be *outside* the normal process. Interest groups would try to break down a compromise as it was being formed, but they would find it much harder to defeat a prenegotiated package. Congress and the President were well advised to present a package as a fait accompli, giving few opportunities for lobbying. They were also encouraged to push for a closed rule in the House as a way to avoid separate votes on narrow issues. Whether they would be able to move a package through a more open Senate process was in doubt.

PART THREE The Crisis

8

The Social Security Bust

Social security faced a very simple problem in the early 1980s: it was going broke fast. More money was going out in benefits than was coming in, outstripping taxes by $10 to $15 billion a year. The reserve ratio, a measure of trust fund savings, had dropped to an all-time low and threatened to fall below zero in 1982. At the height of the crisis, social security was spending about $3,000 more per minute than it was taking in. Still, it seemed like a simple problem: just raise more revenues or cut benefits.[1]

If the crisis was the product of a poor economy, however, it might be better to solve inflation and unemployment first, and only then turn to social security taxes and benefits. If the crisis was just a temporary storm, the coming recovery might be more than enough to clear the skies. If it was the product of a long-term industrial decline and a "baby bust," waiting would only bring the future collapse closer.

Before turning to questions of cause and effect, it is important to note that the 1980–1983 crisis came suddenly. Only three years before the new crisis arrived, Carter had signed a sweeping reform measure that should have provided years of safety. Indeed, upon signing the largest peacetime tax increase in history, Carter had remarked, "This legislation will guarantee that from 1980 to the year 2030, the social security funds will be sound."

By 1980, however, the climate had changed. A new social security commission (one of four in a three-year period) warned of the impact of a worsening economy and opposed any tax cuts, elections or not. As the economy slid deeper into stagflation—a combination of inflation and poor economic growth—the crisis seemed imminent. The 1979 cost-of-living increase had been

---

[1] Again, most of the figures used are taken from technical memoranda to the National Commission on Social Security Reform.

9.9 percent, the largest ever, and the 1980 inflation rate looked even worse. At the start of the year, Carter had recommended several small changes to help the rapidly failing retirement fund. In midsummer, SSA had concluded that the program was going down again, but nothing could be done during the 1980 presidential campaigns.

THE CAUSES

The social security crisis actually fell into two time periods. The short-term crisis ran from 1980 to 1989. According to most economic forecasts, that crisis would end in 1990 with yet another tax increase from Carter's rescue legislation. Between 1990 and 2015, the program would enter two decades of good times, the "golden days" of social security. Though the elderly population would continue to grow, it would be offset by the huge baby boom generation, born in the 1950s and 1960s. With the baby boomers working and paying taxes, social security would build a substantial surplus during the golden days. Around 2015, however, the baby boomers would start to retire themselves, driving the ratio of workers to retirees down to just over 2 to 1. The program would spend the golden surpluses quickly, entering an indefinite period of crisis lasting well into the middle of the next century, as far as the projections could see.

The major cause of the continuing crisis was quite simple: the program gave more than it received. In both the short and long term, retirees got far more in benefits than they paid in taxes, receiving remarkably high rates of return on their "investments" in social security. In 1982, for example, it took just thirteen months to get enough benefits to cover all of the taxes average retirees had paid into social security over their lifetimes! Adding in employer taxes and a fair rate of interest (2 percent) on top of that, it took sixty-four months. Depending on COLA increases, some workers could actually make more in social security benefits by the second or third year of retirement than they made after taxes in full employment before.[2]

By themselves, however, rates of return do not say much about generosity. If it took five years to get a fair rate of return (taxes plus interest) and most retirees only lived four, it was hardly a generous program. Somebody would be cheated. Thus it is crucial to add in some measure of life expectancy after retirement. In 1982, for example, workers who made it to retirement could expect to live seventeen years longer, or for twelve years of "unearned" social security benefits. According to one study, 1982 retirees could expect to get approximately 170 percent more in benefits than they had "invested" in social security.

Those high rates of return were possible only in an immature social security program. As the system matured, the rates would drop. Given higher tax rates,

---

[2]"Social Security: An Analysis of Its Problems," *Federal Reserve Bank of New York Quarterly Review,* Autumn 1982, p. 8.

TABLE 6. **Rates of Return on Social Security "Investments"**

Measure of Returns	Nonmarried Retiree with Average Earnings	
	1982	2010*
Time to recover lifetime taxes paid by employee only	13 months	23 months
Time to recover lifetime taxes paid by employee *and* employer	26 months	46 months
Time to recover lifetime taxes paid by employee and employer *plus* interest	64 months	149 months

Source: Federal Reserve Bank of New York Quarterly Review, Autumn 1982.
*Figures do not include changes made in the 1983 rescue bill, which increased the amount of time to recover lifetime taxes.

which would reach 7.65 percent on employers and employees each by 1990, the generosity was bound to fall. Baby boomers would have lower rates of return because they would have paid more into the system. An increase in the retirement age would also lower their returns, because they would work longer. By 2010, it would take almost four years to get enough benefits to cover all of the taxes average retirees had paid into social security and almost thirteen years to cover the combined employer-employee taxes plus interest. By 2010, retirees could expect to get about 30 percent more than they "earned" in total taxes plus interest, a drop from the 1980s, but a good rate nonetheless. These different rates of return are summarized in Table 6.

Any conclusions about generosity must be qualified by other measures, however. It is one thing to look at percentage rates of return but quite another to look at the month-to-month dollars involved. In 1981, for example, the average monthly benefit for an unmarried retiree was $374, for a retired couple $640, and for a widow or widower $342. Even though the benefits were tax-free, they were hardly stunning. Clearly, generosity is a value judgment, not a simple calculation of benefits versus taxes. The argument that benefits were generous could not be disputed on a statistical basis, but whether that generosity was good or bad remained a political issue.

The Short-Term Bust

The steady decline of social security just three years after Carter congratulated Congress on its "judgment and political courage in restoring the system to a sound basis" prompted at least some soul-searching on Capitol Hill. After enacting a series of large tax increases in 1977, politicians wanted to know how the repairs could fail so fast.

The basic answer was the economy. Not only did inflation and unemployment exceed even the most pessimistic forecasts, but each year was worse than the last. The program might have survived one or two years of poor economic performance, but not back-to-back recessions and double-digit inflation. Even with such high inflation, the program might have squeaked by if wages had grown equally fast. The 1977 forecasts showed a five-year wage growth of 41 percent. In reality, wages grew faster than that (53 percent) but 7 percent *slower* than inflation. In short, tax revenues could not keep pace with benefit increases. The real wage rate—the difference between inflation and wages—was a critical cause of the short-term crisis, and this meant that the trust fund, already low in 1977, was quickly depleted by the early 1980s.

Yet even a 7 percent negative wage rate would not have mattered if not for three features of the social security program:

1. Benefits were automatically linked to inflation. Tired of huge benefit increases every election year, Republicans insisted on automatic indexing in 1972. "We wanted to save Congress from itself," one Republican remembered. "We thought it would end up saving much more money in the long-term than simply leaving the increases up to Congress."
2. The 1977 rescue legislation was "back-loaded." Instead of placing most of the tax increases early, the bill set the largest for 1981, 1985, and 1990. From a political standpoint, the back-loading made perfect sense. No politician wanted to be blamed for a huge tax increase in the next election. When the taxes went into effect, perhaps the representative or senator would be gone anyway, or better still, perhaps the public would have forgotten who was responsible. Thus, when the program hit another crisis in 1980, the tax increases were too far away to do much good.
3. Most important, the reserves were so low that even a slight economic disturbance would cause major problems. The 1977 rescue bill did little to provide a safety net for the social security fund. In 1975, for example, the social security reserve margin stood at 66 percent of one year's cost. In 1980, the level had dropped to 25 percent. This meant that social security had just enough savings to cover three months of benefits.

Though most experts agreed that the economy was to blame for the new crisis, there was considerable debate over whether the trouble would continue. Liberals argued that the economic problems were only temporary, hardly the kind of thing that would require major social security reforms. Former Social Security Commissioner Ball suggested that the short-term crisis was only "modest and temporary." Sooner or later, the economy would turn around. The argument contradicted the liberal position on Reaganomics, portrayed as a continuing crisis that could be solved only by a Democrat in 1984.

Conservatives had a different perspective. As one conservative Democrat argued, "The U.S. economy is suffering from a progressive disease—a spreading paralysis of those activities that raise the standard of living. . . . America's machinery for creating national wealth is slowing down. The ability of our workers to produce more each year is becoming weaker each year."[3] Indeed,

[3]Peter G. Peterson, "Social Security: The Coming Crash," *The New York Review of Books,* December 2, 1982, p. 1.

looking back to the 1950s, American productivity had slowed down, from an average growth rate of 2.5 percent a year in 1948–1967 to 1.6 percent in 1967–1973 to 0.1 percent in 1973–1981. According to conservatives, the social security crisis was the result of deeper economic woes that would continue well into the next century with or without Reagan, not the kind of problem that could be ignored in a reform package.

Clearly, the liberals wanted to protect social security from major benefit cuts, whereas conservatives wanted sweeping change. Liberals argued either that the short-term crisis did not exist or that it was minor, whereas conservatives saw the apocalypse around the corner. Indeed, one conservative paper, *Human Events,* attacked any Republican who dared consider compromise on the crisis: "With the Social Security crisis upon us, this Administration has had an historic opportunity to try and change the system. . . . By portraying the horrendous sums of taxes needed to 'preserve' the present system, Ronald Reagan could have sold the changes that need to be made, and turned the Social Security issue into a political plus for the Republicans." A conservative staffer on the National Commission on Social Security Reform agreed: "It's possible to see the short-run crisis as fortunate. Not in the sense of putting the system in jeopardy, but for getting Congress interested in some kind of serious reform. We've been expanding this program year in and year out for decades. Now the problems have come home to roost."

The Long-Term Bust

Unlike the short-term bust, which created an immediate financing crisis, the long-term crisis came so far out into the future that it was difficult to predict just what it would look like. However, given falling levels of public confidence, the long-term crisis had to be addressed. Recall that confidence in the program was lowest among the young. If Congress and the President failed to answer the long-term crisis, support for the program might continue to fall. As one member of the National Commission argued, "If our report . . . is to have any credibility with the vast majority of people who pay in the vast majority of money we pay out, we had better address that long-term problem. Otherwise, their confidence level will sink—if you can conceive of it—even lower."

Further, the long-term crisis appeared less severe because of the projected growth of huge surpluses during the golden days between 1990 and 2015. According to most forecasts, the social security funds would store up tremendous reserves by 2015, lessening the impact of the crisis. According to Ball, social security was actually "overfinanced" in the golden days, providing an acceptable margin of safety in later decades. Yet Congress might be sorely tempted to spend any golden savings on higher benefits immediately. The larger the surpluses, the greater the incentive to give benefit increases or tax cuts. Members of Congress were not likely to lose their interest in reelection, no matter how far they traveled into the future. And one way to win is to claim credit for an election-year benefit adjustment or tax cut. With huge social security reserves, who could blame Congress for giving the voters a present?

In the 1940s, for example, social security experts repeatedly asked Congress for tax increases but were turned down because the program already had a huge surplus. Despite the need for tax increases to fund future benefits, the rate was frozen for a full decade. "Congress saw the size of the fund and refused to do what was necessary," one former administrator recalled. "You think Congress is going to sit back in the 1990s, and watch billions of dollars build up in the fund and not come up with ideas on how to spend it?" Further, the public could not be expected to remain completely passive as their taxes remained high in the face of massive social security reserves. Thus the forecasts of huge reserves during the golden days gave little solace to those who worried about a long-term crisis. Such worries were based on one major cause and an important complication.

The single most important cause of the long-term crisis was the baby boom. According to one expert, the boom was the product of four demographic factors: "More women married than ever before. More women who married had children. They had their children earlier. And some had more children."[4] The boom first appeared in 1946, immediately after World War II, and it peaked during the mid-1950s. During the height of the baby boom, 4 million children were born each year. The baby boom, moving like a "pig in a python" through society, disrupted the school system in the 1960s and the labor force in the 1970s. Experts had only to look at the closed school buildings in 1982 to see what the baby boom had done to society in the 1960s.

However, the boom would not have made much difference if not for the "bust" that followed. By the 1970s, fertility rates (the number of births per woman) had plummeted to all-time lows. In 1966, for example, the fertility rate was 2.7. By 1976, it was below 1.8. If not for the fact that people were living longer, the population would have been shrinking, not growing. The absolute minimum for maintaining the current population size (zero population growth) was 2.1 births. By simply counting heads, it was clear that there would be a period in the next century when the number of retirees would grow much faster than the number of workers.

It was still too early to tell if the bust was permanent. It could be that women were simply waiting until later to have the same number of children as their mothers. But perhaps they were waiting to have fewer children or none at all. Regardless, as baby boomers began to retire early in the coming century, they would have fewer workers to support them. Since social security was a pay-as-you-go system, it worked only when there were enough workers to fund the benefits.

Among the complicating factors in the long-term bust was the "problem" of increasing longevity. The good news was that people were living longer. Longevity grew over the 1960s and 1970s by margins that were once unthinkable. Life expectancy in 1984 was 70.8 years for men and 78.2 for women.

---

[4]Louise B. Russell, *The Baby Boom Generation and the Economy* (Washington, D.C.: The Brookings Institution, 1981), p. 11.

Moreover, people who survived to retirement would live even longer. The life expectancy of those who made it to retirement was 82.

Thus the bad news was that more people would live to get social security and would stay on the rolls longer. Diseases that were once life-threatening had been rendered harmless. If longevity continued to grow, most retirees could expect to live past 90 by the turn of the century, creating higher costs for social security. And it was not clear that people would remain healthy during their longer retirements, meaning that medical costs might also soar, creating a separate crisis for Medicare.

Again, though most experts agreed that fertility and longevity were to blame for the long-term crisis, there was intense debate over the depth of the crisis. One analysis prepared by the Democrats argued that the future would be rosy because of higher long-term economic growth, higher immigration (meaning more workers), and lower longevity because "the human body has a finite capacity to function" much past 85. Liberals also portrayed the future as uncertain. By arguing that no one knows what the future holds, liberals hoped to deflect calls for long-term reform. Conservatives were more pessimistic and saw the future in no uncertain terms. Not only did they know what was coming, but they knew it was bad.

As in the debate over the short-term crisis, liberals used optimism to defend social security against serious benefit cuts. If the problem was defined in the most hopeful terms, Congress and the President would not risk major reforms. As one National Commission member remarked, "We were concerned that an overly pessimistic outlook would provide the ammunition for deeper cuts or . . . dismantling the program." Conservatives saw pessimism as the key to long-term cuts. As a White House aide said, "Unless the patient is really sick, you won't have major surgery. The worse the crisis gets, the better our chances for some radical reform."

Conservatives also saw the long term as the best opportunity for benefit cuts. Despite the apparent generosity of benefits in the 1980s, it was impossible to win deep cuts in the short term, if only because of the combined opposition of the SOS coalition and the electoral instincts of Congress and the President. But scheduling a change in the retirement age for 2020 would affect only people under the age of 18 in 1983. They would not vote in 1984; they were not represented on Capitol Hill by any interest groups.

Lost Hope?

The most important question was whether the economy would ever return to the growth rates of the 1950s and 1960s, whether social security could ever expect a decade of growth. Whereas unemployment averaged 4.5 percent a year in the 1950s, it grew to 4.7 percent in the 1960s and 6.4 percent in the 1970s. For the first three years of the 1980s, unemployment was over 8 percent. Whereas inflation averaged just 2.1 percent a year in the 1950s, it crept up to 2.8 percent in the next decade and soared to 7.9 percent the next. Finally, whereas real wages grew by double digits in the 1950s and 1960s, they fell to a negative 2 percent a year in the 1970s. Although inflation and real wages improved in the early 1980s, they still remained far outside the boom of the 1950s. No wonder the 1950s are remembered as "happy days"; no wonder there was a baby boom that decade and a baby bust twenty years later.

THE TARGETS

Ultimately, much of the debate over the short- and long-term crisis involved the question "How much is enough?" The key measure was the reserve ratio, the balance of trust fund savings versus expected spending. Recall that a 100 percent reserve means the system has enough savings to cover a full year's benefits. Even if no taxes were collected for that year, benefits could still be paid. In setting targets for the short and long term, Congress and the President had to make two decisions: How much was needed? And when? Building a large reserve in a short period would require steep tax increases and benefit cuts; building a small reserve in a long period would be much easier. Obviously, a smaller reserve had a lower political cost; but it was not clear just how small the goal could be without creating a continuing crisis in the program. A 1971 advisory council recommended a 75 percent reserve, as did a 1979 advisory council; a 1981 commission recommended 100 percent.

Once again, liberals and conservatives disagreed on the basic figures. The White House proposal produced a 36.5 percent trust fund reserve by 1988. Liberals wanted a 15 percent reserve by 1990, the minimum to get by; conservatives wanted anywhere from 20 percent to 100 percent phased in as fast as possible. Liberals sought the lower reserve balance as another way of protecting social security benefits; conservatives wanted a higher reserve as another way of cutting benefits.

Shooting for a 15 percent reserve by 1989, for example, SSA could make projections about the size of both the short- and long-term crisis. Feeding that figure into their computers in 1982, the SSA experts estimated that the short-term crisis was *between $50 and $212 billion*, depending on whether they used intermediate or pessimistic economic and demographic assumptions. They also predicted that the long-term crisis was *between 1.8 and 6.5 percent of taxable payroll*, also depending on whether they used intermediate or pessimistic projections.

The 1.8 percent figure meant, for example, that it would take an almost immediate 1.8 percent tax increase, plus all the other tax increases already set for later, to solve a crisis that would occur only after 2015. By 1990, the combined employer-employee tax rate would have to hit 17.1 percent, or 8.55 percent on each. Either that, or benefits would have to be cut by an equal amount sometime before 2015. Clearly, the choice of economic and demographic assumptions made a great deal of difference in how large the problem looked, and those assumptions were a constant source of conflict in the legislative debate.

By talking about the long-term crisis as a percentage of taxable payroll, Congress and the President never had to confront the actual dollars involved. Adjusted for inflation, the long-term deficit was somewhere around $1.5 trillion. As one congressional researcher said, this shorthand approach was a way to avoid "having to show enormous, almost incomprehensible sums of money." Indeed, unadjusted for inflation, the long-term deficit was somewhere around $5 or $6 trillion. How could Congress pass a $3 trillion tax increase? How could the President sign a $2 trillion benefit cut? It was far easier to talk about a seemingly innocent 1.8 percent-of-taxable-payroll shortfall than the true dollar figures.

The basic problem with the targets was not just that liberals and conservatives fought over the totals. Rather, it was that the crisis only got worse by waiting, particularly in the short term. The further social security went into debt, the more painful the repairs would become, the more people would have to give up in the future. Because of the automatic COLA, benefits would always grow year to year, driving the system deeper into crisis. Stalemate would only add to the trouble. Whereas stalemate still protected the public on most other issues, it was a threat on this dedistributive problem.

CONCLUSION

The social security crisis did not exist in a vacuum. It affected budget deficits, party fortunes in Congress, and presidential campaigns. "If we can solve the outstanding and immediate problem of social security financing," Conable wrote, "a great many other solutions will fall into place. It is not a budget issue, but unless we get it under control the budget difficulties will continue and become more acute. It is not a tax issue, but unless we can find a balance based on more than a payroll tax increase, all the other tax cuts will inevitably be more than gobbled up by the increased burden on labor."

Moreover, the social security crisis was only a symptom of major problems in the economy as a whole. Social security was but one of ninety federal programs that were indexed to inflation. As Congress and the President gave up their discretion over when and how much to increase benefits, social security and other federal programs became more sensitive to economic storms.

More important, social security's long-term crisis signaled major problems with the aging of American society. In 1900, only 4 percent of the public were over 65. By 1980, the figure had climbed to 11 percent; by 2030, it would be 20 percent. The steady growth in the aged population would affect more than just social security. First, the elderly population would contain a high proportion of women. Of the 52 million people over 65 by 2020, 60 percent would be women. Since women were still paid less than men, and since married women were more likely to survive into old age than their husbands, the question was how to protect them against poverty in old age. Second, there would be more people who were "old old," that is, over 80. Because of greater life expectancy, more people would live past the healthier years of retirement and into the medical problems of old age. Nursing home costs were already spiraling upward in the 1980s, and they could only grow into the twenty-first century.

With the vast expansion of the aging population, younger generations would have to adapt to an older society. Politically, older voters might have a much greater say over who got elected and what they did once in office. Socially, older Americans might have a greater say over the way the nation provided its services—whether entertainment, health care, or transportation. Economically, older citizens might have a greater say over what was produced by the economy and how. Thus the long-term social security crisis was only a portent of how things would work in an aging society.

9

Solutions for a Package of Pain

There was a time when the social security choices were all good. Benefit increases were large, tax increases small. Nobody was hurt; nobody suffered. The economy was strong, the future optimistic. Poverty among the elderly dropped. Workers could look forward to retirement with confidence. No one asked if the money would be there. And most of the crucial decisions were made by a very small group of leaders who believed in social security.

Then inflation and unemployment hit, coupled with lower fertility and higher longevity. The economy began to stagnate. Workers began to wonder if they would ever see a penny of their social security taxes. The program entered the first of two major crises. Interest groups formed huge coalitions and prepared to fight; Congress and the presidency were no longer structured for quiet negotiation. Most of the legislative decisions were now made on automatic pilot or in a cauldron of controversy. This was the new age of social security. All of the solutions were bad.

THE NEW POLITICS

Despite the need for action, there was no guarantee that Congress and the President would move. The obstacles were strong and the solutions were painful. But the program was too large to ignore. And even if people were opposed to change, they wanted the program saved.

Most of the conflict over what to do involved two sides. Democrats cared about social security because it was the flagship of the party, the great New Deal program. Republicans cared about social security for precisely the same reason, and because it was a tempting target in an era of growing budget deficits. Both parties wanted to do something about social security because of its stature and impact. Democrats wanted to save it; Republicans wanted to cut it. This was a new age in social security politics. Whereas Democrats once saw endless opportunities for expansion, they now wanted merely to protect and defend the old victories. Whereas Republicans once recoiled from direct attacks on the program, they were now on the offensive, looking for major benefit cuts and structural reform.

Yet these party differences had existed since the start of the program. Most of the time they were hidden from the public spotlight. All told, there were 138 House or Senate votes on social security between 1935 and 1982, each falling into one of four categories.[1]

1. Twenty-six votes involved efforts to reduce benefits or limit the size of increases. As a group, Republicans voted for the reductions 23 times, while Democrats voted against 24 times. In 1981, for example, a majority of House Republicans voted for Reagan's budget, which contained several social security cuts, whereas a majority of House Democrats voted against.
2. Eighty-five votes involved attempts to increase benefits or restore cuts. Here, Republicans voted for the increases/restorations 55 times, whereas Democrats voted in support 80 times. On a 1981 attempt to restore some of the Reagan cuts, a majority of Senate Republicans voted nay, while a majority of Senate Democrats voted aye.
3. Thirteen votes involved moves to increase the tax base or tax rates for social security. Republicans voted against these proposals 9 times, whereas Democrats voted in favor 12 times. On Carter's 1977 rescue bill, which contained a series of tax increases, a majority of Senate Republicans voted against, whereas a majority of Senate Democrats voted for.
4. Fourteen votes involved basic principles of the program, whether votes against exempting certain kinds of workers or votes in favor of restricting the size of the program. Republicans voted 11 times to restrict coverage, whereas Democrats voted 9 times to expand coverage.

On most of the votes, of course, Republicans were in the minority. Had they been able to win, social security would clearly have been a much smaller program, with lower benefit rates, lower taxes, and fewer covered workers. It would not have grown so generous. Of the 138 votes between 1935 and 1982, Republicans voted for *contraction* 73 times (53 percent), whereas Democrats voted for *expansion* 125 times (91 percent).

Given such clear party differences on social security, how could scholars conclude that the program was the product of an "intimate family portrait," a kind of friendly conspiracy among supporters?[2] The answer is simply that Congress was able to hide most of the conflict from the public spotlight,

---

[1]These figures are based on my coding of the specific votes. Though I may have missed a handful of votes, the categories capture what remain very distinct differences between the Democratic and Republican parties.

[2]See Martha Derthick, *Policymaking for Social Security* (Washington, D.C.: The Brookings Institution, 1979).

allowing a small group to meet. Though Republicans opposed social security expansion, such opposition came at the early stages of a debate. The congressional process allowed them to express their opposition but gave them a chance to protect their electoral stakes later. Of the 138 votes, 72 involved floor amendments or efforts to block consideration of the bill. These votes came *before* final passage. Of the 72 votes, Republicans opposed the Democrats 57 times (or 79 percent of the time). Of the 66 votes on final passage, Republicans joined the Democrats 58 times (or 88 percent of the time). Indeed, of the 58 votes, 11 were unanimous. The congressional process allowed the Republicans to get on the record against expansion but gave them a chance to rally around the final bill. Republicans were thereby able to show their opposition to social security while appealing to public opinion back home—that is, to have their cake and eat it too.

It was a technique that worked well only until the 1970s. With changes both inside and outside Congress, the party differences on social security could no longer be so easily disguised. Republicans could no longer hide their opposition in amendments or procedural votes. The interest groups would spot the maneuver and report it back to the public. Nor would it be so easy for the Democrats to agree occasionally with the Republicans on the need for the limits or cuts.

As the Ninety-seventh Congress turned to thoughts of a social security rescue package in 1981, there was no shortage of potential solutions, but no place to hide. In the two short years before Reagan's inauguration, there had already been three major study reports on the social security crisis. "The problem wasn't finding ways of solving the crisis," a House committee aide suggested. "It was finding the courage to do what had to be done. There were plenty of answers, but they were all bad." By November 1982, the fourth study commission, Reagan's National Commission on Social Security Reform, had completed a list of 103 different solutions for the short- and long-term crisis. However, no matter how long the list, the solutions involved two choices: *(a)* raising revenues or *(b)* cutting benefits.

The problem with the list was twofold. First, none of the solutions was particularly attractive at the start. Beyond coverage of federal employees, the public opposed all of the solutions. Second, all of the solutions grew more painful with waiting. Benefit cuts would have to be deeper; tax increases would have to be larger.

REVENUES

There were at least four major options on the revenue side of a social security compromise: tax increases, general revenues, coverage of federal employees, and accounting games.[3]

---

[3]The following summary is based on a special analysis of possible changes, prepared for the National Commission on Social Security Reform, November 1982, and published in the report of the commission, January 15, 1983, Appendix K.

Tax Increases

When the social security tax first went into effect in 1937, it was 1 percent on employers and employees each, levied on only the first $3,000 of yearly earnings. By 1983, the tax had grown to 6.7 percent each and was levied on the first $35,700. However, under Carter's rescue bill, it was set to move even higher in 1985 and again in 1990. Thus one attractive solution to both the short- and long-term problems involved simply moving those later tax increases to 1983 or 1984. Under this option, all or part of the 1990 tax rate (7.65 percent) would move forward, in either one jump or several. Though there were also a variety of oddball tax ideas, including an excise tax on cigarettes, this was the only serious option. Congress and the President could increase revenues by simply changing the dates of already scheduled taxes.

Acceleration had considerable political merit, if only because it allowed the politicians to solve part of the crisis without taking all of the heat. "We could always point back to Carter and say it was his tax increase," one Republican Senate aide argued. "That legislation wasn't a Republican bill to start with. All we would be doing is moving the increases up in time." Congress and the President could label the increases as acceleration and hope that the public would not notice.

Yet in order to use the taxes to solve the funding crisis, the acceleration had to go into effect *before* the 1984 presidential elections. That was a considerable political minus, and it created some incentive to hide the tax increase from the public. One way to hide the increase was through some kind of tax credit. In theory, everyone would pay higher taxes in 1984 but would receive an income tax refund for their trouble. In reality, a tax credit could even be designed so that no one would ever have to pay the increase. The Treasury could simply *pretend* the money had been paid and forward that amount to the social security trust fund. Since the credit would have to come from the Treasury, that kind of credit would be a "back-door" form of general revenue financing of social security, but it would disguise the tax increase in an election year.

The problem with tax acceleration was that it was not enough on its own to solve the problem. Under all economic assumptions, acceleration of the 1990 rate to 1984, the most extreme option, would generate only $135 billion, far short of the $200 billion needed to be absolutely sure of a short-term solution. Further, even the full acceleration would save only half of what was needed in the long term. Finally, even if the tax increases were hidden from workers by a tax credit, they could not be hidden from businesses. Their interest groups were already solidly opposed to an acceleration of payroll taxes, having fought hard against Carter's 1977 legislation. They had already won Reagan's promise of a veto of any payroll tax increases in 1981.

There was one other way to raise social security taxes: boost the rates on the self-employed, whether cabdrivers or doctors. In theory, they are both employers and employees and should pay the full employer-employee share. After all, when they retire, they are given benefits based on a full tax rate. In reality, under then-current law, they paid only three-fourths of the full employer-employee share, as a way of keeping their tax burdens low. Thus one quick way to bring in $18 billion in the short term would be to raise the self-employment rates to a full employer-employee share.

General Revenues

At the start of the social security program in the 1930s, there was some support for a triple-financing approach. One-third of the funding would come from employer taxes, one-third from employee taxes, and the last one-third mostly from general income tax revenues. The approach was never adopted, but it still held several political pluses. First, in opinion polls, the public had expressed some support for the broad idea of using "other tax revenues" for social security. Though it was not clear whether the public understood the link between using general revenues and higher income taxes, some politicians seized on the idea solely because it was popular among the voters. Second, the social security tax was *regressive* in nature—that is, it fell equally on all income levels, with no sliding scale on ability to pay. Lower- and middle-income earners paid the same flat rate on their wages as high-income earners. Indeed, upper incomes actually got a break because the tax applied only to the first portion of their earnings, $37,800 in 1984.

Liberals argued that it was an unfair tax and should be diluted by using the income tax to fund at least some of the benefits. It was not right that this great monument to the New Deal should be financed by a payroll tax. Because the income tax was *progressive* in nature—that is, it fell more heavily on upper-income earners, with no threshold such as that built into the social security tax—it appealed to liberals as a device for both solving the short-term crisis and restoring fairness to the tax system.

Yet if the idea had some merit for liberals, it generated intense conservative opposition. Any use of general revenues would disrupt the connection between taxes "invested" and benefits paid—the equity principle. Further, given the massive federal deficits in 1981–1983, it was not clear just where $200 billion of general revenues would come from. Even the most ardent supporters of the idea acknowledged the problem of the budget deficits. Even in a budget with a $150 billion deficit, general revenues for social security would be noticed.

Coverage of Federal Employees

Because the civil service retirement program came into existence 15 years before social security, it had seemed logical to leave the two systems separate in 1935. The civil service was relatively small, and its retirement system was self-contained. By 1982, however, 2.5 million federal workers were covered by civil service retirement, and almost 80 percent received some level of social security benefits anyway. By bringing *every* federal worker into social security, along with all nonprofit employees still not covered (hospital workers and ministers, for example), the system could generate almost $65 billion in revenues.

However, there were several problems with coverage of federal employees. First, it was an administrative nightmare. According to some, the civil service and social security systems could not be merged together without years of computer programming and a set of intricate benefit formulas. Second, there was some question about the health of the civil service retirement fund. It appeared that the civil service system was about to enter its own crisis in the late 1980s. Third, federal workers and retirees were opposed to the idea. Even if coverage was restricted to new workers, or so the argument went, the number of civil service retirees would slowly dwindle until only a handful were left in the next century. Because federal workers had been an attractive target for salary freezes and budget cuts in the early 1980s, they had a natural fear of losing their strength in numbers. The very last federal workers *hired* under civil service retirement in 1983 would feel very lonely when they became the very last federal workers *retired* under the program in the 2020s.

But despite the problems and opposition, coverage of federal employees was bound to happen. The public, the President, and many members of Congress supported it. "Every time I met with constituents in the 1982 campaign," said one representative, "they asked me why federal workers aren't covered. 'If it's so damn good, how come congressmen aren't on it?' It got to the point where we had to do something to make sure that the elected officials who made the decisions about taxes and benefits were also people covered by social security." The question was not *if* federal employees would be covered, but *how*. Covering all federal workers would bring in a great deal of money but generated too much opposition and was too complicated. Covering only new workers and those with less than five years of service would bring in close to $30 billion; covering just the new hires would bring in $19 billion.

Congress and the President briefly toyed with covering all state and local workers, too. That option, when coupled with coverage of all federal and nonprofit workers, would bring in $110 billion, over half the short-term deficit and almost one-third of the long-term needed. However, under the Tenth Amendment, the constitutional issues were so unclear that the state and local option was abandoned. Though state and local governments were free to join or leave social security voluntarily, mandatory coverage would be a federal tax on the states, a violation of the sovereignty so clearly guaranteed by the founding fathers. "What we didn't need was a long, drawn-out Supreme Court challenge on a major piece of the rescue bill," a Senate aide noted. "We wanted a clean bill that went into effect immediately and that would reassure the public that the crisis was over." Even though the Supreme Court never uttered a word on the option, it still had an impact on the final bill by creating congressional worries.

Yet if Congress and the President could somehow prevent state and local governments from leaving social security once they had already joined—ending so-called opting out—they could save several billion dollars. And a ban on opting out would probably pass a Supreme Court test.

Accounting Games

Beyond the major revenue options, there were a number of accounting illusions that could raise money for social security. Prior to 1982, for example, uncashed social security checks were never returned to the trust fund. They simply floated around forever. Somewhere in the great American postal system there were hundreds of thousands of uncashed benefit checks. By declaring lost checks null and void, the trust fund could raise $1 billion. By rounding benefit checks *down* to the nearest dollar, for another example, instead of giving the extra cents, the trust fund could raise another few hundred million.

By far the best accounting game involved the so-called military wage credits. When the armed services were first brought into social security in the 1950s, the Department of Defense agreed to pay extra money into the trust fund to offset the lower military salaries that come with the free food, housing, and so forth. Over a period of thirty years, the credits had mounted to between $5 and $20 billion, depending on the estimates.

If Congress and the President could just get the government to pay all the IOUs at once, it would make a large dent in the social security deficit. The problem was that the defense budget was already the largest in history. Adding $20 billion for old social security debts would make it look even worse, particularly with Congress looking for ways to cut military spending. Finding the money would have to involve some artful work.

A second major accounting game involved a new way of collecting payroll taxes. Since all benefit checks were paid on the third day of each month, the trust fund had to have at least one month's benefits in reserve at any one time. Yet payroll taxes trickled in over the entire month, depending on the size of the business involved. If social security could get all of the taxes in by the third day of the month, there would be less need for a large trust fund reserve. Such a "normalized" tax system could be created two ways: (1) by changing the tax schedule to force businesses to come up with all their money by the second day of each month, or (2) by pretending that the money had already come in. Since businesses were hardly likely to endorse a tougher collection schedule, any kind of "normalization" would have to involve very brief loans from the general treasury, a kind of monthly advance. Normalization could be sold as a technical change and would scarcely be noticed by most members of Congress. Though it would not account for any specific money, it would reduce pressure on the trust fund reserves.

A third accounting gimmick involved interfund borrowing. Because social security taxes were split into the three funds, it was always possible for one program to borrow from the other two. In 1981, both disability and Medicare were doing well. Though neither fund was large enough to cover all of social security's needs, there was some money available for loans. By allowing social security to borrow from the companion funds, Congress and the President could buy time for making the difficult choices. However, there was not enough money for more than a year or two of borrowing.

A last accounting gimmick involved pulling social security out of the unified federal budget. Though the move would not save any money, it was a way of isolating the program from continued budget conflict. The House and Senate budget committees opposed the move, since it would be a way of diluting their power over the full range of government spending; but most social security leaders hoped such a change would protect their territory from future budget squabbles. Social security would be out of harm's way.

BENEFITS

There were at least four major options on the benefit side of a social security compromise blueprint: cost-of-living adjustments, taxation of benefits, retirement age, and radical reform.

It is important to note that coverage of federal workers was also a benefit cut of sorts. Not only did it bring in more revenues in the short term, but it saved money when federal workers retired in the long term. Most federal workers qualified for social security benefits under previous or part-time work to start with. By bringing them under full social security coverage, they would lose part of the windfall from holding lower-paying jobs on the side.

Cost-of-Living Adjustments

If cost-of-living adjustments were one reason why the economy had such a powerful impact on social security, they were a logical place to consider benefit cuts. Conservatives argued that COLA cuts were not cuts at all, merely changes in the rate of growth, whereas liberals called them reductions in future benefits. Whatever they were called, whether cuts or slowdowns, at least three COLA reforms had some potential for savings:

1. Congress could simply skip three or six months of the COLA. Instead of paying the COLA on July 1, as normal, Congress and the President might push it back to October 1 (three months) or January 1 (six months). The delay might occur in one year or over several. Once the delay was over, however, the COLA could either return to the original July 1 date (a one-time-only delay) or remain at the new date (a permanent delay). The use of the word "delay" to describe a permanent change was misleading but politically helpful nonetheless.
2. Congress could cap the COLA at some specific maximum, say 3 or 4 percent, no matter how high inflation went. Obviously, that kind of device was good only if inflation was substantially higher, not lower, than the cap.
3. Congress could switch to a new COLA formula. One option was an inflation-minus-3-percent approach. In changing to this formula, social security would get the benefits of a cap through a built-in saving of at least 3 percent. Another option was a switch to a COLA based on the lesser of wage increases or price increases, guaranteeing that benefits would never

grow faster with inflation than the wages to finance them. These kinds of changes fell under the heading of "stabilizers" because they would help protect social security against poor economic performance.

The biggest COLA savings clearly came from permanent delays. Since the initial delay would compound in savings every year into the future (just as interest on a savings account compounds), one delay in 1983 could be worth billions by 1989. Yet even here, the savings all depended on the economy. If inflation was running at double-digit levels, a delay would save huge amounts of money; if it was down to just a few percent a year, a delay would save little and might not justify the high political costs.

Still, if the elderly were to participate in the sacrifice, it had to be with COLAs. The SOS coalition was firmly opposed to any COLA delays, though the American Association of Retired Persons did support a one-time-only three-month delay. The public was also opposed to major benefit cuts; but in a 1982 Harris survey, 68 percent did support a shift to a prices-or-wages COLA. Certainly, COLA changes became easier as inflation dropped, but they also became less impressive as a source of savings.

Taxation of Benefits

From 1942 on, social security benefits had been exempt from federal income taxes. However much covered employees believed their withholding taxes were investments or savings, the Internal Revenue Service ruled that social security benefits were gratuities and therefore not subject to tax. Moreover, because those employees paid income taxes on their earnings *before* social security taxes were withheld, taxation of benefits would constitute a double taxation on the same income.

Yet social security benefits are based on employer contributions, too. Because businesses usually claim their social security taxes as a corporate deduction, some part of benefits evades taxation completely. Moreover, because retirees often receive more in benefits than they have actually paid in taxes, taxation of benefits seemed like a logical way to capture some lost money for social security. There were at least three ways to tax benefits:

1. Tax only the amount of "unearned"—that is, benefits above employee-employer contributions.
2. Tax the half of benefits that employers deduct from their corporate income taxes.
3. Tax the half of benefits that employers deduct, but only for retirees who can afford to pay. That way, the income floor would not be touched.

Under all three ideas, the Treasury would simply forward the income taxes to the social security trust fund.

Though the savings from each option were quite substantial, there were serious administrative problems: What kinds of income would be included in calculating the tax on social security benefits? How would the Treasury separate the social security taxes from the other income taxes? Who would be exempt from the tax? How high should the income thresholds go?

Further, there were serious political obstacles to taxation of benefits. The Senate had already rejected the idea twice in 1981 in broadly worded resolutions, and there was little interest in the House. Thus the only way to win taxation of benefits was to add an income floor, so the tax would apply only above certain levels. The higher the floor, the lower the savings for social security.

Despite the problems, taxation of benefits had one redeeming feature: it was all things to all people. Liberals could claim it was a tax increase as well as a way to hit the rich with their fair share of the compromise; conservatives could claim it was a benefit cut. The main advantage was its chameleonlike nature. If an income threshold was set around $25,000 for a couple and was not allowed to rise automatically with inflation, taxation of benefits would eventually produce $30 billion of the short-term target and nearly one-third of the needed long-term savings.

Retirement Age

Almost from the beginning, the social security "normal" retirement age has been the clock against which Americans set their lives. Even with the great medical advances of the 1960s and 1970s—advances that granted extra years of healthy worklife—the clock remained firmly set on age 65. Thus, not only would an increase in retirement age save huge amounts of money, it made some demographic sense.

There were two basic ways to generate money from the retirement age:

1. Cut early retirement benefits. Starting in 1956 for women and 1961 for men, workers were given the option of retiring at age 62 with 80 percent of their benefits instead of waiting for age 65 and 100 percent. This early retirement option became quite attractive over the years. By 1982, it was exercised by well over half of all workers. One way to create savings from the early retirement option was simply to cut the amount retirees would receive. Instead of 80 percent, why not cut the benefit down to 75 or 70 percent? This benefit change was particularly valuable in the short term.
2. Raise the basic retirement age. Even though longevity had grown dramatically since the first years of the program, the social security retirement age was still the same, 65. (In fact, several features of social security actually penalized older Americans for staying on the job. For every $2 workers earned after 65, for one example, they lost $1 from their social security check. That earnings ceiling, called the "retirement test," did not apply after age 70, but it was a major cost of working until then.)

The most frequently mentioned targets for a new retirement age were 68 and 70. According to most estimates, a jump to 68 would cover half of the long-term deficit; a jump to 70 would solve the entire problem. Alongside most proposals for a retirement age increase were cuts in the early retirement option.

Estimates of the savings depended, however, on two critical choices: When would the new retirement age start? And how fast would it be phased in? The *earlier* the change was started, the greater the savings. If retirement age increased to 68 by the year 2000 instead of 2020, it would save more money. Also, the *faster* the change was phased in, the greater the savings. If the retirement age jumped to 68 in ten years instead of twenty, social security would get more money. For those who saw retirement age as the solution to the long-term crisis, a fast phase-in was crucial.

Questions of when and how fast also shaped political costs. Labor was opposed to any increase in retirement age because most of their workers were imprisoned in physically punishing jobs. "Most of our people can't wait for retirement," an AFL-CIO official said. "Extending the retirement age would be sentencing these people to more hard labor. Most are just trying to make it to retirement." Most liberals also opposed the idea because it was still a benefit cut, however disguised.

Yet conservatives stayed with the idea because it would stand the test of time. Changes in COLAs and benefit formulas could always be reversed in the future, but changes in the retirement age would have more permanence. Once the retirement age was changed in law, people would start thinking in the new terms. More important, private pension plans would start to change, making it very difficult to turn back later. It would be hard to back off even during the golden days of social security. If the change could be scheduled far enough into the future, perhaps liberals would not fight as hard. If the age could be kept down to say 66 or 67, perhaps labor opposition would not be so intense.

Radical Reform

Despite the wide range of options, many conservatives opposed any compromise at all. Instead, they favored radical surgery. Their preferred option was voluntary social security. Workers would be given the choice of staying in social security or "opting out." Social security would be slowly phased out of existence. As more and more workers left social security, the system would choke to death.

Several of the strongest supporters of this option actually worked in the Reagan administration, publishing books and articles on how to end social security while advising the President on how to save it. Some were openly hostile to the program. As one said, "I hope like hell the compromise package fails. I'd like to come back in a couple of years with another crisis and do something really dramatic."

But was the voluntary idea truly dramatic? Would it work? According to its supporters, private plans would give workers far higher rates of return than social security. In making the dollar-for-dollar comparisons, however, supporters used pessimistic assumptions to attack social security and optimistic ones to support the private plans. Under the same assumptions, both options looked equally good or bad. Moreover, the voluntary idea relied on an exceedingly optimistic assumption about human behavior: workers were expected to take approximately 15 percent of their take-home pay and invest it for retirement, not spend it on the here-and-now demands of housing, clothes, and food. It was a dubious assumption at best.

Finally, there was the problem of people who elected to stay in social security. Under the voluntary proposals, their benefits would be paid out of general revenues. But who would be paying the income taxes into general revenues? The answer was the same people who had left social security to start their own private retirement plans. Thus in many cases, those who took the voluntary option would be paying for *two* plans: their own plus the pay-as-you-go benefits of people who stayed on social security. Suddenly, the voluntary option did not look as good.

Beyond radical reform, both sides did toy with the notion of a "fail-safe" for social security. Such a fail-safe would trigger an automatic benefit cut or tax increase if social security got into trouble again. If and when the trust fund reserves fell below a certain minimum (usually 15 percent), the fail-safe would trigger in, prompting an immediate benefit cut or tax jump unless Congress acted within sixty days to generate more revenues. The notion of a fail-safe had considerable appeal, protecting the system against another crisis and Congress against another blueprint of pain. However, Democrats would not agree to a fail-safe based on benefit cuts, and Republicans would not agree to one based on tax increases or general revenues.

BUILDING A PACKAGE

Looking over the range of solutions, it was clear that liberals favored a compromise built on revenues, whereas conservatives favored one built on benefit cuts. Yet neither side could build a social security rescue plan based solely on its preferred blueprint. There was not enough money. The various options are summarized in Table 7.

Once the two sides decided to build a package together, they would have to make a series of calculations about the choices.

1. Was the political cost of the particular item justified by the dollar returns? Neither side wanted to waste its limited political resources on solutions that would not work. COLA caps, for example, were less attractive to conservatives because they would cost a great deal but might not work.
2. Was one side getting more (or giving up less) than the other? Here, Congress and the President had to calculate the size of the savings from each option. Neither side wanted to give up more than 50 percent of the package to the other.
3. Just how far could each side go in blaming the other for the pain? Conservatives would want to blame liberals for all of the tax increases,

TABLE 7. A List of Options

Option	Dollar Returns	Public Opinion	Groups Opposed

Tax increases	HIGH	OPPOSED	Business
			Conservatives
			American Association of
			  Retired Persons
			National Federation of
			  Independent Business

General revenues	HIGH	UNCLEAR	Business Conservatives
Federal coverage	MODERATE	FAVORED	Federal workers Labor National Council of Senior Citizens
Accounting games	LOW	UNCLEAR	Conservatives
Cost-of-living cuts	HIGH	OPPOSED	Labor Liberals American Association National Council
Taxation of benefits	HIGH	OPPOSED	Business Conservatives American Association
Retirement age	HIGH	OPPOSED	Labor Liberals National Council
Radical surgery	HIGH	OPPOSED	Labor Liberals National Council

thereby protecting their own political base. Liberals would want to blame conservatives for all of the benefit cuts. But at some point, both sides would be hit with responsibility for the full package. That was why such options as taxation of benefits had such appeal. They could be called anything.

The nature of the crisis favored liberal options in the short term. From a technical standpoint, it would be difficult to phase in benefit cuts quickly. The computers were too slow. "We need at least three months to make any simple changes in the COLA," an SSA staffer said. "Anything more complicated and you're talking about a year or more. Anything really sophisticated and that's a couple of years of pretty expensive computer work." By simply waiting until the last possible moment, liberals would be able to choose first. And because tax increases could not be scheduled overnight, liberals would probably pick general revenues and accounting games.

Yet neither side could solve the problem alone. On the one side, even with full acceleration of the 1990 tax increase to 1984, plus accounting games and limited general revenues, liberals would cover only two-thirds of the short-term deficit and half of the long-term one. Since labor opposed coverage of federal employees, liberals could not include the option in their ideal blueprint. On the other side, even with a six-month COLA delay in 1983, plus coverage of federal employees, limited taxation of benefits, and a slight cut in early retirement benefits, conservatives would cover only half of the short-term deficit and even less of the long-term one. Only with a fairly steep jump in the retirement age, phased in very early, could conservatives solve the long-term deficit without tax increases.

CONCLUSION

There was more than enough money on the total list of revenues and benefits to solve both the short- and long-term problems. But there was also more than enough political controversy to stifle the strongest demand for compromise.

All of the high-yield options—tax increases, general revenues, COLA caps and delays, taxation of benefits, retirement age—had high political costs. None would be easy to defend. Even if Congress and the President could agree to hurt any one specific group—say, federal employees or small businesses—that would not be enough. One or two groups simply could not carry the entire burden of a $200 billion short-term deficit or a $1.5 trillion long-term deficit.

In the end, each side had to decide what it could and could not accept. Each had enough power to stalemate the other. Since the American political system was well-equipped for gridlock, both sides could easily keep a compromise off the table. But at what cost to their political fortunes? "We knew in advance that this type of problem is solved by a whole series of initiatives, none of which are desirable politically," Alan Greenspan, the chairman of the National Commission, said. "Were one to take any of our solutions and put them in front of the Congress one by one, all would be voted down by very large majorities." The key would be a package that contained just enough pain to make both sides equally unhappy and just enough success to allow both sides to claim victory. Conservatives would need federal coverage and COLA cuts; liberals would need tax increases and limited general revenues.

PART FOUR

Artful Work

10

Reagan Moves It

The year 1981 started off well enough for a social security rescue. Legislation was moving through the normal process in the House. Rep. Jake Pickle, chairman of the Ways and Means Social Security Subcommittee, had a bill ready to go several weeks before Reagan's inauguration. Though there was no guarantee of eventual passage, his bill had the tacit approval of Rep. Dan Rostenkowski, the full committee chairman. When the bill finally passed the subcommittee on April 8, Pickle had reason to expect committee action and a shot at passage.

From a conservative standpoint, it was not a bad bill. Despite general revenues and accounting games in the short term, it carried a deep benefit cut in the long term. By raising the retirement age from 65 to 68, albeit phased in over time and justified by actuarial soundness, it cut the early retirement option back to a less generous level. Workers could still retire at age 62, but with much lower benefits compared with those for workers who retired under the then-current formula. It was just the kind of cut conservatives wanted. Coming from a Democratic subcommittee in a Democratic House, it was a good starting point for serious negotiation.

Just as the bill moved up to the full Ways and Means Committee, however, something happened that changed the complexion of the social security debate for the next two years, something that pollsters said ended all chances of a Republican sweep in the 1982 midterm elections, something that gave the Democrats the one great issue of the year: Reagan decided to "move it" with his own social security plan. What had started out as a normal process was suddenly transformed into a political firestorm. And the spark came from the Reagan budget.

Before blaming Reagan for everything that went wrong over the next two years, it is important to note that social security was hardly a "normal" issue.

Even if Pickle had won in the full Ways and Means Committee, he faced strong opposition in the Rules Committee and on the floor. The issue was bound to provoke intense conflict regardless of the process. Because the crisis was much too large for minor, incremental solutions, any package would have to involve an array of pain. Like most other dedistributive issues, social security could not be solved in the normal process. There was not enough protection.

THE PRESIDENT'S PLAN

Reagan's staff had drafted a social security proposal during the transition into office but dropped the idea in the drive for budget and tax cuts. Given the political costs of sweeping reform, social security was not given a very high priority in the new administration. Indeed, according to Pickle, "in 25 instances I asked them what their position was on these amendments. They always said 'We're working on it.' It's a tough political issue, and they preferred to have it considered later."[1] The Reagan White House had other issues those first months, and social security was put on hold.

Reagan was not particularly interested in the subject. "Reagan is a very quick study," one congressional ally noted. "A lazy man, but still very bright. He doesn't want to be burdened with any issue. . . . He had a real mental block on social security and didn't want to dirty his fingers with it." Reagan was also torn between the politics of the issue and his own ideology. As one observer suggested, "Reagan works in two sides of his head. One is the old lecture circuit side, with every issue simplified onto a 3-by-5 card. The other is the pragmatic side, with his image of what a President or governor has to do in order to get legislation passed." Reagan, the pragmatist, finally decided that social security was not worth the political cost.

Yet scarcely two months later, Reagan endorsed a $45 billion social security cut and was fighting to stave off a major Senate defeat. The explanation rests almost entirely on budget director David Stockman and his search for spending cuts.

The Magic Asterisk

Long before inauguration day, Stockman knew he would have to move quickly to win on his budget cuts. More than any other adviser, Stockman understood the cycle of decreasing influence. By moving fast, he would catch new cabinet officers off guard, before they could be "captured" by their departments. Congress would be caught by surprise, too.

What Stockman did not understand was the cycle of increasing effectiveness. There were dangers in moving the economic program so fast. "We were doing that whole budget-cutting exercise so frenetically," Stockman later admitted. "In other words, you were juggling details, pushing people, and going

---

[1]Quoted in *The New York Times,* June 6, 1981, p. A19.

from one session to another, trying to cut housing programs here and rural electric there, and we were doing it so fast, we didn't know where we were ending up for sure." According to Stockman, pieces of the budget were moving on independent tracks: "And it didn't quite mesh. That's what happened. But, you see, for about a month and a half we got away with that because of the novelty of all these budget reductions."[2] When all the budget cuts, tax cuts, and defense increases were fed into Stockman's OMB computers in February 1981, the results were shocking. Not only were there deficits deep into the future, but they grew larger every year. Contrary to Reagan's 1980 campaign promise, there was no "glide path" to a balanced budget by 1984. If Congress caught wind of the figures, the Reagan economic package would go down in defeat.

What was the new budget director to do? One answer was to rig the OMB computers, changing the underlying economic assumptions about how the world works. Stockman knew that more optimistic assumptions would reduce the huge deficits, if only on paper. Using a new forecast with much lower inflation and much higher economic growth, he went to Capitol Hill with his budget. It was a prime example of selling a presidential program on the basis of best-case assumptions. "The whole thing is premised on faith," Stockman said, "on a belief about how the world works." Even with the new assumptions, Stockman still faced $60 billion deficits as far as he could see.

A second answer was to promise another round of cuts tomorrow while counting the savings today. Stockman could tell Congress that more cuts were on the way, that the "check was in the mail." And that is exactly what he did. Under pressure to submit a new, more realistic budget in mid-March, Stockman added in $40 billion of "future unspecified savings." Because the promise was buried in a footnote, skeptical Republicans dubbed it the "magic asterisk." In this new form of creative budgeting, the deficits would look $40 billion smaller without any legislative action. "There was less there than met the eye," Stockman admitted. "Let's say that you and I walked outside and I waved a wand and said I've just lowered the temperature from 110 to 78. Would you believe me?" Apparently, majorities in the House and Senate did, passing the Reagan budget in midsummer. Unfortunately for Stockman, Wall Street and the financial markets did not. The expected stock market boom did not come; unemployment continued to grow; a recession was on. No matter how Stockman played with the computers or asterisks, the Reagan economic program was not going to work. By 1984, Reagan would have added more to the federal debt in his four short years than all Presidents before him.

Stockman needed savings *now*. But where? According to Stockman, "I put together a list of twenty social programs that have to be zeroed out completely, like Job Corps, Head Start, women and children's feeding programs, on and on. And another twenty-five that have to be cut by 50 percent. . . . And then huge bites that would have to be taken out of social security. I mean really fierce, blood-and-guts stuff—widows' benefits and orphans' benefits, things like that.

[2]William Greider, "The Education of David Stockman," *The Atlantic*, 248 (December 1981), pp. 39–40.

And still it didn't add up to $40 billion."[3] The exercise was designed to persuade the President that defense spending had to be cut, but Reagan would not budge.

As the weeks passed, Stockman was slowly drawn back to one answer to the budget deficit: social security. As winter turned to spring, Stockman finally concluded that blood-and-guts stuff would have to fill the magic asterisk.

Stockman's Solution

Yet Stockman was clearly unhappy with Pickle's bill. "The Pickle package was a fairly significant change in the long-run structure of the system," Stockman argued, "but I didn't like it because it didn't save any money in the next three or four years and we had these huge unidentified savings in the budget. That kind of attracted me immediately to find an alternative that had some immediate budget savings."[4] Pickle's bill contained less than $15 billion in short-term cuts, using general revenues to meet the deficit. But as Stockman knew, there were no general revenues to give. Even in the long term, the retirement age increase came far too late to help the Reagan administration. "I'm just not going to spend a lot of political capital solving some other guy's problem in 2010," Stockman remarked. "The Social Security problem is not simply one of satisfying actuaries. . . . It's one of satisfying the here-and-now of budget requirements."[5]

Nevertheless, Stockman understood the importance of seizing the moment: "If you don't do this in 1981, this system is going to land on the rocks . . . because you won't do it in '82, and by '83 you will have solvency problems coming out of your ears." Stockman also hoped that the coming crisis would "permit the politicians to make it look like they're doing something *for* the beneficiary population when they are doing something *to* it which they normally wouldn't have the courage to undertake."[6] What had been part of the "social safety net" in February and March suddenly became a source of cuts in April and May.

Because social security was part of the unified federal budget, its problems would continue to affect the deficits. If Stockman could win some quick cuts, social security would make the deficits *seem* smaller. In reality, of course, social security could only create an illusion of savings. No matter how large the social security trust fund became, the money could not be spent on other programs. Nevertheless, the bottom line of the unified budget would look better, even if the federal debt continued to swell.

Ultimately, Stockman turned to the early retirement option as his proposal. By reducing the benefits workers could receive at age 62, Stockman could cut

[3]Ibid., p. 40.
[4]Lou Cannon, *Reagan* (New York: G. P. Putnam's Sons, 1982), p. 379.
[5]Greider, "The Education of David Stockman," p. 43.
[6]Ibid., p. 45.

billions from the deficit. As one participant remembered, "Most of the decisions focused on two questions. First, how much should the option be cut? 10 percent? 15 percent? Second, how fast should it be phased in? next year? in five years? in ten years? Each of the answers came with a price tag. It became very tempting to cut the retirement option by 20 percent and phase it in immediately when you saw how much money you could save." Indeed, that is precisely what happened. Whereas Pickle's bill would have cut the early retirement option 16 percent starting in 1990, Stockman's proposal would have cut the option from 80 percent to 55 percent on January 1, 1982. It would have saved almost $20 billion, but it would have also affected 1.4 million Americans immediately. They would have no time to come up with any other options. According to congressional estimates, the proposal would have slashed benefits from $372 to $246 per month.

There was only one reason for the fast-track phase-in: the budget. "Stockman saw social security as the best way to get a balanced budget," a White House aide said. "The savings from the early retirement cuts were phenomenal. And they seemed so easy. You could get a tremendous wallop by making the cuts effective in 1982." According to another participant, "Stockman got a hold of the figures and kept asking, 'How much more can we get if we cut retirement benefits down to 70 percent? 65 percent? 60 percent?' The original idea was to reduce the incentive to retire early, but Stockman saw it as the way to save his tail on the budget." Moreover, in the pressure to turn fast savings, there was little time for Stockman to check all the details. "I was just racing against the clock," he said about the social security cuts. "All the office things I knew ought to be done by way of groundwork, advance preparation, and so forth just fell by the wayside."[7]

The early retirement cut was only one piece of the $46 billion package. The proposal also included a $4 billion cut in basic benefits and a $5 billion three-month COLA delay. The package contained enough in long-term savings to more than offset the future deficit, and it even allowed a social security tax cut in 1990. Still, early retirement was almost half of the total package, and according to a White House aide, "it was the broken vial of poison in the proposal. It was the lightning rod for opposition on Capitol Hill. Stockman, the politician, knew it was a bad idea, but Stockman, the budget director, saw only the dollar signs."

Because the cuts were so large and were phased in so quickly, almost 36 million retirees would have lost benefits immediately on the three-month COLA delay; another 18 million would have lost 10 percent of their benefits on a technical change in the basic formula; still another 7 million would have lost up to a third of their benefits under the early retirement cuts. In short, almost 60 million people were directly affected by the proposals—most of them opposed. Once again, the size of the program created a huge natural constituency against change.

[7]Ibid.

A Social Security Dunkirk

The early retirement cut was the first major break in a string of successes and became a target for liberal attack. In his haste to avoid a GOP economic Dunkirk, Stockman had created his own social security debacle. "By any calculations, the Administration has launched the most fundamental assault on the Social Security system since its inception 46 years ago," the House Aging Committee reported. "These cuts constitute a breach of contract. . . . Millions of people, who will retire in the next few years, will have their benefits slashed by 30 or 40 percent. . . . Now we find that Social Security is a punching bag, an open sesame from which to fund large tax cuts and budget deficits."[8] When the Ways and Means Committee finally held general hearings on the proposals, not one group testified in support of the early retirement cut, while over 60 testified against. The question is how such a proposal could have slipped through the President's seemingly invincible legislative machine.

The first reason is that Stockman's problems on social security were merely a symptom of a larger pattern of mistakes in the budget process. "The reason we did it wrong—not wrong, but less than the optimum—was that we said, 'Hey, we have to get a program out fast,'" Stockman recalled later. "And when you decide to put a program of this breadth and depth out fast, you can only do so much. We were working in a twenty- or twenty-five-day time frame."[9] Social security was but one of a series of technical mistakes over the year, a "blooper" according to Stockman. It was a classic result of the conflict between the two dominant policy cycles inside the White House. On the one hand, the cycle of decreasing influence told Stockman to move it or lose it. On the other, the cycle of increasing effectiveness told him to wait. Stockman decided to move quickly. As a result, the administration suffered a stunning legislative defeat.

A second reason for the mistake is that Stockman and the social security working group kept most of the key decisions to themselves. The social security package was put together with very little input from other White House advisers. Understanding the sensitivity of the issue, Stockman had tightened secrecy around his decisions, increasing the chances of disaster. The legislative staff did not see the final proposal until just three days before the formal announcement. "It was too late to stop that moving train by then," one aide said. "And few of us tried." Pickle, for example, was not informed about the Stockman proposals, nor were key Republicans on the Ways and Means Committee. There was no warning of what was to come.

A third reason for the mistake is that Stockman and Health and Human Services Secretary Richard Schweiker believed the proposals would pass. Since they were the only former members of Congress inside the White House, no one challenged them. "How do you tell a former senator that he's wrong about

---

[8]Select Committee on Aging, House of Representatives, "Impact of Administration's Social Security Proposal on Present and Future Beneficiaries," 97th Congress, 1st Session, July 1981, pp. III–IV.
[9]Greider, "The Education of David Stockman," p. 54.

the Senate?" a legislative staffer asked. "Or a former representative that he's wrong about the House? Who were we to tell Schweiker, the political animal, what to do on social security? He had to sell it on the Hill. Who were we to stop Stockman in the middle of the roll? He had been right that far." As Stockman admitted, "Those who were pushing the policy like Dick Schweiker, myself, and Marty Anderson were totally negligent in looking at the politics."[10] The social security package was never screened by the Reagan legislative strategy group, a collection of top White House aides. They simply deferred to the combined wisdom of Stockman and Schweiker.

There is no evidence, moreover, that anyone in the group raised serious political questions about the package. Stockman and Schweiker were not the only ones who were overconfident. As one aide said, "There was a euphoria in the White House back then that everything would go. We were on the top of our game. Reagan was back from the assassination attempt and was in good shape. The opinion polls were never better. We didn't have the vision to see what was going to happen once those proposals went up." Indeed, the social security package was announced just days after the White House had won a series of test votes on the 1981 budget. Stockman and Schweiker aside, the White House suffered from its own image of itself.

Despite all the mistakes, it does not appear that the March 1981 assassination attempt had much to do with the social security debacle. Though Reagan was recovering from surgery when most of the key decisions were made, he had not been involved in the details before. Whether recovering from bullet wounds or not, he would not have been involved until the very end of the process anyway. Facing little dissent from his top staff, Reagan agreed with Stockman and Schweiker, and the proposals moved forward to Congress.

REAGAN LOSES IT

The Reagan administration presented the social security proposals to Congress on May 12. In his press briefing, Schweiker said the package would "keep the system from going broke, protect the basic benefit structure and reduce the tax burden of American workers." Schweiker made the announcement to put some distance between the President and the proposals, but they still carried Reagan's stamp of approval. According to Stockman, "The President was very interested [in the reform package] and he believed it was the right thing to do. The problem is that the politicians are so wary of the social security issue per se that they wanted to keep him away from it, thinking they could somehow have an administration initiative that came out of the boondocks somewhere and the President wouldn't be tagged with it. Well, that was just pure naive nonsense."[11] Stockman, the politician, was right.

[10]Cannon, *Reagan*, p. 379.
[11]Greider, "The Education of David Stockman," p. 45.

Eight Days

On the first day after the announcement, the Democrats opened fire. Rep. Claude Pepper called the package "insidious" and "cruel"; O'Neill called it "despicable" and "a rotten thing to do," concluding that Reagan was "stone-hearted"; Ball said not only was it "a breach of contract, but it isn't even necessary"; Sen. Edward Kennedy called the package "hasty, ill-advised and devastatingly punitive." Senate Democrats promised to use "every rule in the book" to stop the package.

By the second day, the Save Our Security coalition, then composed of barely two dozen elderly groups, vowed to fight the proposals to the death and started to get calls from other groups wanting to join. Having been dormant since Carter's 1979 social security package, SOS geared up its machinery for a fight. By the end of the year, SOS had over 100 members.

By the third day, cards and letters started rolling into the White House and Congress, most opposed to cuts in early retirement benefits.

By the fourth day, the Democratic party began drafting a fund-raising letter on the Reagan plan. As one Democratic official remembered, "When the White House announced that package, I couldn't believe it. It was the first crack in a wall of solid resistance. When I finally got a copy of the plan, I knew we had a golden issue. If we hadn't jumped on the issue, we would have been declared politically non compos mentis." And so it went.

By the fifth day, the pollsters started reporting the public reaction. In April, several weeks before the package was announced, the ABC News/*Washington Post* poll had found that 70 percent of retired people approved of Reagan's performance as President. In May, just days after the social security package was announced, his rating had dropped 16 points, to 54 percent. Moreover, among all age groups, half said they would be hurt by the Reagan plan in the long run. Though most said the social security system was in bad shape, half said they disapproved of the Reagan proposals, and another 39 percent said the President had broken a campaign promise not to cut benefits. By August, the Harris poll found that 69 percent of all respondents disapproved of Reagan's handling of social security.

By the sixth day, Democrats and Republicans alike proclaimed the end of Reagan's honeymoon. "We started measuring the end with Schweiker's announcement," a Democrat said. Any chances, however slim, of a permanent shift in voter allegiance from the Democratic party to the Republican party also ended with social security. It became the battle cry for Democrats. As a Republican pollster said, "Realignment officially terminated in May of 1981 with the social security pronouncement. . . . There's not been a single breath of life in it since."

On the seventh day, the Senate did not rest. Instead, it started the debate on Reagan's package. The key battles were fought on May 20, eight days after the Schweiker announcement. Senator Moynihan, the ranking Democrat on the Finance Committee, introduced a "Sense of the Senate" resolution condemning the Reagan package. Though such House or Senate resolutions have no force of law, they do express the opinions of the bodies. And because they have to pass only in the one chamber, such resolutions are an easy way to embarrass the President or stake out a position.

Thus, not only did Moynihan's resolution call the President's proposals "precipitous and severe," it concluded that they constituted "a breach of faith with those aging Americans who have contributed to the Social Security system." Further, "Congress would never renege upon its commitment to the nation's retirees by allowing the Social Security trust funds to become insolvent." It would be "the sense of the Congress that no change in the Social Security benefit structure shall be made which would precipitously and unfairly deny those men and women approaching retirement age Social Security benefits on which they have planned and to which they are entitled."

Forty-one Democrats joined Moynihan in cosponsoring the resolution. Though the May 20 debate lasted four hours, not one Republican rose in defense of the cuts. One Republican called the resolution a "two-bit amendment" and an "exercise in demagoguery," but most conservatives kept quiet. "This was one of those times when it's better not to talk," a Republican senator recalled. "It was time to let the Democrats blow off some steam."

In the end, the Republicans were able to kill the Moynihan resolution on a 49–48 vote. By itself, it would have been a major victory. However, Senator Dole quickly introduced a second resolution. This one promised that "Congress shall not precipitously and unfairly penalize early retirees," a slap at the Reagan package; it passed 96–0. It was the death knell for the President's rescue package. "It was like a bunch of duck hunters waiting in the bushes with the ducks too high to hit," a Reagan official said. "Along came this old turkey, and that was it." Though Dole had limited the damage, the Senate still had to go on the record against the cut in the early retirement option. The Democrats already had the Republicans on the defensive.

Assessing the Damage

From a political perspective, the Democrats were well advised to take advantage of the issue. With the Senate under Republican control and the Democrats trailing far behind in fund-raising for 1982, social security became a rallying point. It helped the party unite its followers around a common theme. As the symbol of the New Deal, social security might also re-create the old Democratic coalition of labor, blacks, and liberals. Even Pickle saw the value of the Reagan mistake: "This was the first break in the clouds for the Democrats," he said. "It was the only good thing that had happened all year, and some couldn't resist the temptation to swing out. . . . That's as normal as breathing."[12]

From a public policy perspective, however, the Reagan disaster spelled the end to any serious reform in 1981. Democrats would not let the issue go. Indeed, when Pickle asked to move his bill up for full Ways and Means consideration in May, the House Democratic caucus said no. As the governing

---

[12]Quoted in *The New York Times*, June 5, 1981, p. A11.

body of the party, the caucus made it clear that social security would remain hot for a time. "The caucus knew it was a great issue for the 1982 elections," a House leadership aide remembered. "A delegation went to O'Neill in May and told him to back off on any social security legislation. It never came to a formal vote in the caucus, because that would have made the party look bad, but O'Neill got the message. He was already in enough trouble with his flock over the Reagan budget without losing another big issue." Though Pickle's subcommittee held hearings on the Reagan package in late May, the rescue would have to wait. As one White House aide later lamented, "It's amazing how good the Pickle bill looked after we got creamed. We should have just endorsed his retirement age increase and left it at that. We were naïve about what we could do. By the time we realized, it was too late."

A STRATEGIC RETREAT

Within hours of the Schweiker announcement on May 12, the White House knew there would have to be a retreat. Senate and House Republicans were demanding a rescue from the rescue plan. There was no doubt that Reagan would have to abandon the proposals. But how?

Inside the White House, Stockman would not let go. The problem was not the package, he said, but the lack of public understanding. "My view was, if you had to play this thing over, you should have the President go on TV and give a twenty-minute Fireside Chat, with some nice charts," Stockman said. "You could have created a climate in which major things could be changed."[13] Unfortunately for Stockman, no one agreed. "This was something that had to be dumped fast," one White House aide remarked. "We had to cut loose fast, get Reagan's name out of the papers and refocus public attention on something else. The longer social security remained in the headlines, the more we'd get hit."

Thus on May 21, even as Schweiker was defending the package on Capitol Hill, the President abandoned the proposals. "I am not wedded to any single solution," he wrote Congress in a letter of surrender. "This Administration welcomes the opportunity to consult with Congress and with private groups on this matter." Reagan then listed his three principles for a new repair bill. "First this nation must preserve the integrity of the Social Security Trust Fund and the basic benefit structure that protects older Americans. Second, we must hold down the tax burden on workers who support Social Security. Finally, we must eliminate all abuses in the system that can rob the elderly of their rightful legacy." Because the proposals were dead before they could be introduced in Congress, there was no need to withdraw a bill.

By June, Reagan had finally shaken free of his social security proposals. Though he had dumped his May package, he was still haunted by the social security issue. It was part of what was to be known as the "fairness" issue, the

---

[13]Greider, "The Education of David Stockman," p. 45.

image of the Reagan administration as cruel and heartless. For the time being, social security was off the congressional agenda. But it would return. Stockman had not solved his budget problem, and Congress had not solved the coming social security crisis. Stockman would continue to test the waters in search of social security savings, but Congress would find it increasingly difficult to move forward with any repairs.

This was no longer an issue for the normal legislative process, but there was no other forum. Neither party could trust the decisions to subcommittees or staffers. As Democrats recognized the political impact of social security in the coming congressional campaigns, they refused to let Ways and Means move forward with major legislation. The Speaker would determine what was to be done. As Republicans saw the public backlash, they also centralized authority on the issue. As much as he disliked the issue, Reagan would have to make the final choices. Thus, one product of the increasing conflict was centralization of the issue upward. The leaders would have to lead.

The problem was that neither the Speaker nor the President had the authority to enforce any final agreements, not in this Congress. Even if they sat down to negotiate some compromise, there was no guarantee of success in the fragmented political system. They would still have to go through subcommittees, through full committees, and onto the floor.

CONCLUSION

There was only one problem with keeping the social security issue alive and hot that summer: the system was sinking. The annual trustees' report warned that checks would be delayed as early as November 1982. There was clearly something wrong. If the Democrats continued to oppose a rescue, the program would collapse. According to Pickle, who was becoming increasingly isolated within his own party, "We should hold our fire. We can't inflame this subject. If we inflame it too much, nothing will get done, and if nothing gets done, the American people will have the right to throw us all out." Something would have to be done by the end of 1981 to prevent a crisis the following autumn. At least for a small band of social security leaders in the House and Senate, the answer was to create a deliberate crisis in the hope that Congress and the President would respond. It was a considerable risk, but it seemed to be the only option for an eventual solution.

11

Congress Sets a Deadline

Social security stayed hot into the summer of 1981. Inside the White House, Reagan openly complained about Democratic potshots and longed to take his case to the public. Outside, he admonished the press to "reduce the fears of social security recipients, fears that have been aroused by the demagoguery of those guys on the Hill."

Despite Reagan's protests, Democrats stayed on the attack. "The ball has been lofted right to us," said Rep. Tony Coehlo, the Democratic congressional campaign chairman. "We've taken it, and we're running with it. . . . We're not going to fumble it. It is without doubt our big issue today, and there's no close second."[1] Because Reagan's May proposals were now dead, however, Democrats desperately needed a new social security target.

It was soon provided in Reagan's 1981 budget. As one of 83 different cuts in domestic spending, the budget eliminated the social security minimum benefit. Under the benefit, anyone eligible for social security received a minimum starting benefit (then $122 a month, or $1,464 a year) regardless of how low his or her taxes or earnings had been. It was a way of providing a basic income floor, or benefit adequacy. Although the minimum benefit also went to some relatively well-to-do beneficiaries who had spent their worklives in employment not covered by social security, it was particularly valuable to nearly 3 million poor people, mostly elderly women, who otherwise would have received much smaller benefit checks. Whereas the other Reagan cuts affected students, the disabled, the poor, or welfare recipients, this one touched the old. Democrats quickly seized on the minimum benefit as the new issue. Social security would stay in the headlines.

---

[1]Quoted in Congressional Quarterly *Weekly Report*, August 1, 1981, p. 1379.

ANOTHER MISTAKE

The minimum benefit fight began only after Reagan had won a series of initial victories on his 1981 budget. However, because his final budget package was pasted together moments before the key House votes, it is not clear whether most members of Congress even knew what they were doing. Indeed, the copies of the Reagan budget proposal were still warm from copying when they arrived on the House floor for passage. Unfortunately for the Reagan White House, the minimum benefit cut was buried deep in the bill. Democrats could not find it to attack it; Republicans could not find it to remove it.

Once again, the White House had erred in adopting a move-it-or-lose-it strategy. Sensing an opportunity to defeat the Democrats on a key procedural vote, Stockman and the House Republicans had drafted their budget alternative overnight. Beyond technical errors and dozens of typos (including the name and phone number of a female staffer), the bill contained a number of serious political mistakes, including the minimum benefit cut. Few members of Congress, Democratic or Republican, could have known that they were cutting the program. Building a budget in less than twenty-four hours, of course, is a task fraught with mischief.

This June vote was not the end of the budget fight. There were at least two more steps en route to final enactment. Once the budget passed both chambers of Congress, a conference committee would have to iron out any differences. Acting as a one-house (or unicameral) legislature, the conference committee would have to forge a new bill somewhere between the House and Senate versions. Only then could the two bodies vote on the final product. As with all other conferences, there would be only two rules for the talks. First, if *both* houses had the same item in their bills, the conference could not abandon it. Second, if *neither* house had a given provision in its bill, the conference could not add it. Such maneuvers would be outside the "scope" of the conference. As with all other conferences, the House and the Senate would each have one vote on the final compromise.

In the House, Democrats made their move against the minimum benefit cut even before the budget conference started. "The President had just finished putting out the fires from the May package," a House Ways and Means Democrat said, "and along comes another social security cut. They could not get it into their heads that this was a killer issue for the Democrats." The initial salvo was fired on July 16, when House Majority Leader Jim Wright rushed to the floor to introduce a "Sense of the House" resolution on the minimum benefit. Wright's resolution simply stated that "the House of Representatives strongly urges that the necessary steps be taken to insure that social security benefits are not reduced for those currently receiving them."

Thinking that the Republican Senate was about to pass a bill restoring the cuts, Wright had moved to put the Democratic House on record first. He also wanted to put the Republicans on the defensive. As he would do so many times over the next two years, the eighty-two-year-old chairman of the Aging Committee, Pepper, rose to the attack. In response to Stockman's claim that the truly needy aged would receive higher welfare checks to replace the lost minimum benefit, Pepper answered: "Half a million of those on the minimum are eligible for welfare right now, but they have never applied for it. As many as 90 percent of the current minimum beneficiaries are women. . . . They have made it thus far without welfare, and they are not going to go on welfare now." Concluding to a standing ovation from his Democratic colleagues, Pepper shouted that "over two-thirds of these people are beyond the age of 70; 500,000 of them are over 80; and 100,000 of them are over 90. So you will not have to worry about them very much longer."

Once again, Republicans stayed low during the onslaught of criticism. "We just wanted the debate to end," one remembered. "Pepper really gave it to us." When the resolution came up for the final vote, House Minority Leader Robert Michel told his members to vote as they pleased, lest they be cast as the "Scrooges" on social security. Republicans broke ranks, and Wright's resolution passed 405–13.

It was a minor victory, however. Wright's resolution merely expressed a sense of the House and had no impact on the minimum benefit cut. House Republicans were confident that the Senate would reject any specific legislation. Indeed, the Senate had already rejected one effort to restore the minimum benefit on a party-line vote and soon rejected another. Moreover, any minimum benefit legislation would have to start with the Ways and Means Committee. Republicans knew the committee was far too busy with Reagan's tax cut to consider the issue soon. Further, because both the House and Senate budget contained the minimum benefit cut, any compromise to restore the program was beyond the scope of the conference. This was a throwaway vote, and Republicans voted en masse for Wright's resolution. Though all but one Republican had voted to cut the minimum benefit in the earlier budget package, all but thirteen voted for the symbolic resolution.

Once the minimum benefit was eliminated in the conference committee, the budget package returned to the House and Senate. With the conference over, the two bodies had to vote one last time. Only then would the budget move up Pennsylvania Avenue for Reagan's signature. This was the last chance. Refusing to grant a rule (or ticket) to the floor, House Rules Committee chairman Richard Bolling held the compromise budget as his hostage until the minimum benefit was restored. If Republicans did not support the legislation, they would lose their budget. It was a tactic from the days of powerful Rules chairmen who could kill legislation by denying access to the floor. A bill was quickly drafted and introduced. On the same day the House voted to pass the compromise budget, it also voted 404–20 to restore the minimum benefit. The minimum benefit had been eliminated in the budget vote, only to return in a separate bill. By holding the budget hostage, the Democrats had finally won. Such are the ways of the legislative process. Congress can move very fast when it wants to.

The question was whether the Senate would agree. As if to prove that Congress has its own internal checks, the Senate refused to restore the minimum benefit on a party-line vote. Republicans remained solid against restoration. Because the month-long August recess was about to start, Senate action on the minimum benefit would have to wait until autumn. (Eventually, Congress eliminated the minimum benefit, but only for those who became eligible after 1981.) In the meantime, Stockman started looking for more social security cuts. It was simply too tempting a target for a budget director.

A SECOND RETREAT

With Congress safely out of town, Stockman began pushing for another round of cuts immediately. The stock market boom still had not arrived, interest rates remained high, and Stockman decided to tackle social security one more time. By then, a COLA delay was the only way to get social security savings. Despite the possible firestorm, Stockman was able to persuade Reagan on a three-month freeze. This last round of budget cuts amounted to only $16 billion total, but it was sold as a crucial step for restoring business confidence in the face of mounting deficits. This was the new era of psychological economics. What mattered was the perception of lower deficits, not the reality of federal borrowing.

Once again, Reagan was warned by congressional leaders to avoid social security. Republicans had already suffered two defeats on the issue. Members were losing patience. The two Republican insect coalitions were on the rise. Another round of social security combat would only drive the Gypsy Moths further from the Yellow Jackets. The mere hint of another Reagan social security package frightened Republicans. On September 21, Republican leaders traveled to the White House to talk Reagan out of this latest offensive. "At best, it would be a difficult fight," one senator told the President. "At worst, it could be the end of the Senate majority in 1982," another added. The amount of money involved in the COLA cut was a scant $3 billion, hardly enough to justify the resulting political hammering. Reagan reluctantly agreed, and the COLA delay was removed from the package. Stockman had lost again.

Unfortunately, word had already leaked out. When O'Neill caught wind of the new proposals, he immediately replied that the Democrats would "help the President keep the promise he made during the campaign. We don't intend to let him wreck the system." Democrats were on the attack yet again. "Each time the President cooled them down," a White House liaison aide reported, "Stockman would heat them up. We had to do something to pull the whole issue off the agenda; something that would keep even Stockman quiet."

The answer was a *national commission.*

Making his second strategic retreat of the year, Reagan finally took his case to the public on September 24. Complaining that there "had been a great deal of misinformation and, for that matter, pure demagoguery on the subject of social security," Reagan blamed the Democrats for his troubles. Referring to the ill-fated May proposals, Reagan said, "We hoped [the proposals] could be a starting point for a bipartisan solution to the problem. We were ready to listen to alternatives and other ideas which might improve on or replace our proposals. But the majority leadership in the House of Representatives has refused to join in any such cooperative effort."

Endorsing restoration of the minimum benefit, Reagan called for a national commission on social security. The fifteen-member commission would be appointed by Reagan, O'Neill, and Senate Majority Leader Howard Baker and would be asked to "review all the options and come up with a plan that assures the fiscal integrity of social security and that social security recipients will continue to receive their full benefits." The commission idea was clearly designed as a way to remove the issue from the political firing line. "It was a classic cover-your-ass maneuver," a Senate aide noted. "There was absolutely no need for another commission on social security. It had been studied to death already." Conable agreed: "We do not need another study," he said. "If we don't straighten out social security this fall, the sensitivity of the political election cycle will prevent us from doing it for another four years."

The commission idea came from Baker as a way of protecting Republicans from themselves. "Republicans would be able to point to the commission when they came under fire," a Senate leadership aide said. "It would shield them from criticism. Our members could say that the issue now belonged to a bipartisan national commission." Though Republican social security leaders saw the commission as a needless delay, Republican political strategists viewed it as the only escape from the issue. If the commission produced a social security compromise, all the better.

Unfortunately for Reagan, the commission did not remove social security from the political spotlight. The public was not satisfied. On September 12, 65 percent said they disapproved of Reagan's handling of social security. On October 28, four weeks *after* his nationwide address, 68 percent disapproved. Reagan's speech did not appear to soothe the minimum benefit issue, either. The Harris poll reported that 87 percent of the public opposed the minimum benefit cut, while 48 percent said Reagan "will not be able to keep his promise that no person now receiving social security will lose any of their benefits." A CBS News/*New York Times* poll reported that almost half of the public did not trust Reagan to make the right kinds of decisions about social security. According to a Republican pollster, "The speech did not stop the damage. There wasn't much more room for slippage on social security after that. We had reached bottom." Only 25 percent of the public approved of Reagan's handling of the issue.

CREATING A CRISIS

With the President and Stockman in full retreat on social security by fall 1981, the House and Senate faced a choice: either patch up the system to limp through another year, or draft a serious short- and long-term reform package. Pickle's bill was still on the table in the House, and pieces of Reagan's May proposal remained in tattered form.

Congress had to do something. Though inflation had dropped in Reagan's first year, the 1981 COLA was still above 10 percent. The social security forecasts had grown more pessimistic, and preliminary projections for 1982 were among the worst in recent years. According to the 1981 forecast, the assets of the social security trust fund "would soon become insufficient to pay benefits when due. This would occur in the latter half of 1982 under each of the alternative sets of assumptions."

By October 1981, there was no way to deny the immediate crisis. Though Democrats and Republicans continued to debate the long-term forecasts, benefit checks would be delayed as early as October 1982 if nothing was done. Democrats still argued that the crisis was merely a passing storm, whereas Republicans said it was much more serious. However, both sides knew that something had to be done to get the system past the November 1982 elections.

WHO MOVES FIRST?

In the House, the Democratic leadership had already decided to wait. There would be no serious reform in the Ways and Means Committee, regardless of Pickle. Even before Reagan's September retreat, O'Neill met with his Democratic leadership and ordered a halt to further legislative action. The Democratic caucus would not permit full hearings, hoping to keep the issue alive without saying what ought to be done. "If anyone is going to break President Reagan's commitment not to reduce benefits," O'Neill said, "it's going to be the President. He's not going to get the Congress to do that for him." Concluding that the "system is not in disastrous condition," O'Neill would not yield. The Ways and Means Committee could work on a temporary repair but not on serious reform. Individual members could not be trusted with the golden issue, particularly if they wanted to solve it.

Most members of the House sighed in relief. A prolonged and bitter debate over social security was the last thing they needed going into an election year. "No one's going to make their political reputations on social security," House Republican leader Michel noted. "There are no Medals of Honor to be won on this one. The best one can hope for is a Purple Heart." Yet late checks would not help in an election year, either. The House would not take action on social security alone.

By October, the Senate was just starting work on the minimum benefit bill passed by the House in July. Seeing the legislation as a possible vehicle for more serious reform, Finance Committee chairman Dole hoped to take a major bill into a conference with the House and reach a quiet agreement on a short- and long-term solution. Dole's bill did not contain the early retirement cuts, but it did increase the retirement age. If he could just sit down with Pickle and Rostenkowski, Dole felt sure he could reach an agreement.

Facing charges from Moynihan that "there is no crisis in social security," Dole's rescue effort was doomed in the Senate. As one Republican aide remembered, "We got into a contest to see who would go first. The Democrats wanted us to take the bait and announce our own package. They didn't want to do anything about social security but wanted us to give them more cannon fodder." Dole eventually settled for a simple minimum benefit bill, coupled with ten years of unlimited interfund borrowing as a temporary patch. "What we have done is take the easy way out," Dole said at the end of the debate, "the cosmetic approach." Moynihan, in contrast, called it a "gracious retreat" from the Reagan proposals and "a responsible change of opinion" from the Republicans. On October 15, the Senate passed its version of the minimum benefit bill on a 95–0 vote.

There was one last attempt at serious reform in 1981. Just before the House-Senate conference, Pickle offered another package in the Ways and Means Committee. "Time is running out on us," he complained. Pickle's proposal would have raised the retirement age to 66, cut the early retirement option by 10 percent, changed the basic benefit formula, and switched the COLA to the lesser of wages or prices. The package was defeated 18–14, with Pickle aligned with the Republicans. As Conable argued, "I think it is a disgrace the way we have turned tail and run on social security, and I would include in that the Administration and everybody in the room here who did not vote to at least try to do something in the long term."

At the end of the vote, Pickle turned to Rostenkowski and asked, "Is there any point to trying further?" He already knew that the answer was no. O'Neill had concluded that there was no need to "move hog-wild" into social security before the next elections.

A Meeting of Minds

In many respects, conference committees were the very first secret negotiating groups in American history. They were not mentioned in the Constitution but quickly became the central tool for resolving House-Senate differences. Because conference committees were originally closed to all but a handful of members, they also became a device for stopping important bills and making secret deals. Though conference committees were opened to the public in 1974, they still provided rare opportunities for private negotiation. They still had closed-door caucuses and back-room meetings. At least for social security in the early 1980s, conferences offered some protection from the sunshine.

Thus, in many respects, the November minimum benefit conference was the last, best hope for some kind of social security leadership in 1981. With the President, House, and Senate unwilling to act on their own, perhaps the conference could succeed.

Unfortunately, there were two obstacles to any serious reform in the conference. First, SSA needed to have the minimum benefit bill in hand by early December, just about the time Congress would adjourn for the Christmas recess. Because the SSA computers were so slow and because the minimum benefit was now scheduled to end in March, any restoration of the lost funds would have to be programmed in early December. The House and Senate had very little time to act. Second, the two versions of the minimum benefit bill were almost identical, leaving major reform far outside the scope of the conference. The House had merely restored the cuts, while the Senate had authorized ten years of borrowing between social security and its companion funds to provide a temporary patch. As one of the Republican conference members said, "The House has taken no action on the central issue, and the other body has provided us with a measure which might keep the social security trust fund afloat for a very few years only, at best. Therefore, the hands of the conferees effectively are tied; they can do no more than provide cough syrup for a patient that is dying of chronic pneumonia."

Conable's Crisis

The conference began in earnest on November 16 and quickly engaged in a subtle debate over how to inspire congressional courage on social security. The question was how to set a deadline for future action. According to one member, if interfund borrowing was the only solution, "we are pushing ourselves right up to the edge of the cliff, and we don't have another generation of time in this program."[2]

Yet the conferees also understood that Congress could not pass a major reform bill coming into an election year. The best they could do was set a deadline for action sometime *after* the November elections. That was the only way to put future pressure on Congress. The question was not *if* the crisis would hit, but *when*. A deadline on interfund borrowing would either destroy the program or generate the needed courage to do something in time. Under pressure from Conable, the conference rejected the Senate's ten-year unlimited borrowing provision and moved toward a one-year deadline. Conable was betting on a lame-duck session of Congress as the moment for reform. "One way or the other," he warned his colleagues on the conference committee, "we are voting for a lame-duck session." Because the session would only come after the 1982 elections and would include defeated and retiring members, it might be less sensitive to political pressure. After all, it would be the furthest point from the next elections.

The risks of such a one-year limit were obvious. If the lame-duck session did not deal with social security, Congress would have to act early in 1983, just when the new Reagan budget would arrive. The potential for political conflict would be much greater. Social security would get caught up in the budget yet again. As Congress moved closer and closer to the crisis, the potential for stalemate would actually increase. "The price of each member's vote would be higher," a White House staffer concluded. "With the system on the edge of collapse, every representative and senator could demand a big trade for their support. And opponents would have the edge." Congress would be embarrassed again; the checks would be delayed; public confidence would fall even further.

The conference committee was clearly aware of the dangers. It did not have to adopt a one-year deadline. It could allow interfund borrowing for several years, giving Congress a little more time to build up its courage. Since this was the only opportunity to patch the system in 1981 or 1982, using it for a deliberate crisis would carry the ultimate risk of failure. Nevertheless, a crisis

---

[2]The following narrative is based on the transcripts of the conference.

would be an important action-forcing event to move Congress forward. Even if the leaders could not build a rescue bill, they could inspire future action.

In the end, the conference adopted Conable's deadline. "If you want my vote," Conable had told the conference, "this is my price. But maybe you don't need me?" Faced with Conable's threat not to sign the final agreement, the conferees voted to terminate the interfund borrowing privileges on December 31, 1982. Without Conable's signature on the conference report, House Republicans would not support the agreement.

To give Congress a little extra time under Conable's crisis, the conference allowed the social security trust fund to borrow not more than enough money to meet the trust fund's outgo during the first six months of 1983. As a result, the crisis would occur on July 3, 1983, at the start of the seventh month of the year. That was the day the checks would not go out. If the 1982 lame-duck session failed, the House and Senate would have just over six months to build a package, move it through the committees, get it past the floor, and have it on the President's desk. Given the computer problems in Baltimore, however, there would be even less time if COLA changes were involved—perhaps three months, at the most, to reprogram the benefit formula.

With the deadline in place, the final conference report was signed by both houses. It then passed the Senate 96–0 on December 11 and the House 412–10 five days later. Reagan signed the bill before Christmas. Conable's social security crisis was in motion.

CONCLUSION

By the end of December 1982, the social security trust fund had borrowed $17.5 billion from its companion funds. That money, plus assets on hand, plus the taxes that would come in, would last until July. After that, without some kind of action, the checks would not go out on time. A small band of social security leaders in the House and Senate had designed the perfect device for congressional pressure. Though they had not been able to draft any kind of serious reform, they had been able to do the next best thing: create an inescapable crisis. It was an important device for passing dedistributive policy. Since Congress was a crisis-activated body, the key was making sure the members knew that a crisis was coming.

Now the question was how Congress would respond. If not in the normal legislative process, perhaps a new form of government would evolve. Because of the political stakes involved, however, the issue was now firmly controlled by Reagan and O'Neill. Though the two were friendly enough outside of the political arena—"two Irishmen who love to swap stories," as one White House aide argued—they had serious disagreements on social security. In many ways, they represented the most distant points on the social security compromise. O'Neill had supported every major expansion of the program, whereas Reagan had campaigned against Medicare in the 1960s and for radical reform in the 1970s.

12

A New Form of Government

Social security was quiet the first few months of 1982. The Democratic party continued to "prospect" for money on the issue. One fund-raising letter warned potential contributors that "THE REPUBLICAN PARTY HAS RAISED MILLIONS OF DOLLARS TO PRESS FOR DEEP CUTS IN SOCIAL SECURITY. THEY PLAN TO SPEND OVER $30 MILLION TO DEFEAT DEMOCRATS WHO HAVE BLOCKED EARLIER ATTEMPTS BY REAGAN TO DESTROY SOCIAL SECURITY AND TO REELECT REPUBLICANS WILLING TO SUPPORT REAGAN EFFORTS TO MAKE OLDER AMERICANS PAY FOR REPUBLICAN PROGRAMS BENEFITING THE WEALTHY FEW." The letter proved remarkably successful, netting $1 million in a matter of weeks.

Otherwise, Congress was noticeably quiet in early 1982, girding for the coming campaigns, resting from the long 1981 congressional session. Reagan's National Commission on Social Security Reform was just starting up: hiring its staff, preparing a few working papers, setting an agenda, settling into its quarters across the street from the White House. Beyond a few stories about the commission, the issue had finally dropped from the headlines, replaced by the budget and foreign policy. For example, during May 1981, the *New York Times* had carried fifty-one stories on social security, six of them on the front page. During January and February 1982, the paper carried only half as many, none of them on the front page. And most of the stories were about what was *not* happening.

It was already clear that Congress and the President would have great difficulty passing much of anything in 1982, let alone a major social security rescue bill. As Congress moved closer to the fall elections, the chances for dedistributive action waned. Whereas members might vote for new programs, tax cuts, and pet projects right before an election, they would not tackle social security reform. Dedistributive action would have to take place at the furthest point from the elections, not the closest. Moreover, Reagan's popularity had dipped below the 50 percent mark, and the 1982 elections loomed as a referendum on the ailing economy and social security. House Democrats, still bitter about the 1981 budget and tax victories, were not in a mood for compromise.

Despite Reagan's 1981 budget and tax cut victories, the House Democrats now had the power of stalemate. There were just enough Gypsy Moths to break the conservative coalition on the floor. Meanwhile, the economy was still sinking, with unemployment moving toward the double-digit range. In the natural life cycle of the presidency, Reagan had passed the peak of his congressional influence.

Yet Reagan had the power of stalemate, too. He could veto any Democratic bill and had enough Senate support to defeat any House override. If Reagan could not pass anything in Congress, he could certainly defend his earlier gains. It was the Democratic party that would learn how hard it was to pass a bill in the new Congress and how easy it was to defeat one. If the Democrats wanted to move on their own, they would have to win four times: once in each house to pass the bill, and once in each house to override a certain Reagan veto.

There would be only one chance for any kind of compromise with Reagan in 1982: the budget. The President would have to present a budget to Congress and would have a stake in getting something passed. Otherwise, Republicans would go into the fall elections carrying the largest deficits in history. Perhaps the budget would also provide an opportunity for social security reform.

THE LOST BUDGET

Compared with Reagan's 1981 budget, the 1982 version was based on more pessimistic projections and a dose of economic reality. Whereas the 1981 budget had promised a surplus by 1984, the new budget showed a $98 billion deficit in 1983, a $92 billion deficit in 1984, and an $83 billion deficit in 1985. What had once been a glide path to surplus had become a blastoff to deficits. "That deficit is just mind-boggling to most of our people," House Minority Leader Michel remarked. "That's kind of hard for a real hidebound conservative to swallow."

Stockman had known about the impending doom for some time. Looking back over the past year, there had been at least five reasons for the growing deficits.

1. Some of the 1981 budget cuts were illusions, paper changes that held no real savings. Stockman's "magic asterisk," for example, remained in the budget long after it was clear there would be no more cuts.
2. The 1981 budget fell $70 billion short of Reagan's goal. Though Congress passed $130 billion in cuts, Reagan had originally asked for $200 billion.
3. Supply-side economics never came true. According to the theory, Reagan's three-year tax cut should have stimulated private investment, boosting productivity and increasing the supply of economic goods. Stockman had

long ago admitted that supply-side economics was an illusion, too; a "Trojan Horse" for an old-fashioned "trickle-down" tax cut. Upper-income wage earners would get the bulk of the tax cut in the hopes that they would invest it wisely. At least through 1981, they were still waiting. In reality, the Reagan tax cut had cost the federal government hundreds of billions in future revenues and had yet to produce the promised boom.

4. The Federal Reserve Board, an independent agency that controls the national money supply, failed to cooperate with Reagan. The Fed actually tightened the nation's money supply in 1981, clamping down on inflation, pushing interest rates up, and thereby stalling the economic recovery.

5. Reagan refused to accept any cuts in his $1.5 trillion defense budget. With defense off-limits, there was no way to move toward a balanced budget.

In short, the world simply refused to perform as Stockman had predicted in the 1981 budget. Because his 1981 projections had been so optimistic, the poor economic performance looked all the more stunning. Each 1 percent mistake in Stockman's unemployment forecast, for example, added $19 billion to the 1982 deficit; each 1 percent mistake in his real economic growth figure added another $8 billion; each 1 percent mistake in his interest rate projection added another $2 billion. And most of Stockman's mistakes were more than 1 percent. His unemployment forecast for 1982 was 7.2 percent; the actual figure hit 10 percent by October. People out of work meant less taxes coming in and more unemployment benefits going out.

Another Stalemate

Unlike in 1981, the prospects for passage of the new Reagan budget were slim. Reagan was no longer riding the crest of public support. Indeed, just to get down to a $98 billion deficit in 1983, Congress would have to pass almost $60 billion in additional domestic cuts, hitting welfare, food stamps, and medical care for the poor. These "blood-and-guts" cuts would have been tough in any year, let alone an election year.

Thus within a week, Congress had already said no. New budgets emerged daily in both houses. Reagan had challenged the "paid political complainers" to "put up or shut up," and they started to put up. Even Stockman invited alternatives, telling the House Budget Committee that the President would "look very carefully at a good-faith sincere effort . . . to propose something different." On defense, Stockman said there "might be room for savings." On taxes, there would be no compromise on the third year of the tax cut but some room for what Stockman euphemistically called "revenue enhancers" (tax increases). Having learned his lesson in 1981, Stockman avoided social security. Despite the pressure to draft an alternative budget, the Democrats worried about moving first, particularly if they were "all alone and subject to political attack," as one Budget Committee aide said. If the President wanted Congress to take the first step toward compromise, it would have to come from the Republicans.

A First Step

On February 23, Sen. Peter Domenici, chairman of the Budget Committee and a Republican from New Mexico, made the move. "Our situation is more than serious—it is frightening," he said. "And political leaders do all a disservice by pretending that we can swallow $100-billion deficits as though they were aspirin tablets." Domenici then offered his own budget package, including a limit on defense spending, a freeze on domestic spending for three years, a cap on Medicare, a freeze on federal pay raises in 1983, tax reform, and, most important, a one-year freeze on the social security COLA.

Though Domenici's plan contained cuts in virtually every spending program, the social security freeze became a new target for Democratic attacks. Within days of Domenici's speech, Republicans were retreating again. The Republicans had moved first, only to be hit hard. With the President's budget already dead, it looked as if Congress would be unable to pass any budget at all. Republicans would not make another move in public.

It was a remarkable change from just six months before, when Congress had marched to the tune of Reaganomics. By early March 1982, it was clear that Congress and the President would have to bargain. Reagan could not win on an up-or-down vote this time. The politics of confrontation would not work. Yet at a March 9 meeting with all 53 Senate Republicans, Reagan said he would be "glad to consider any comprehensive congressional plan" that did not raise taxes or cut defense, in effect saying no to negotiation.

Even if he wanted to compromise, the question was how. Budget negotiations could not take place in the normal legislative process, not with the television cameras on, not with every proposal subject to attack. The negotiations had to be secret, giving the President and Congress a chance to hammer out an agreement before the interest groups could move. It had to be outside normal procedures.

The answer was the "Gang of Seventeen."

THE GANG OF SEVENTEEN

The Gang of Seventeen was born in late March and was so named by Conable in a parody of China's Gang of Four then on trial for crimes against the state. The seventeen leaders who participated were Dole, Russell Long, Domenici, Fritz Hollings, and long-time Reagan friend Paul Laxalt from the Senate; James Jones, Rostenkowski, Bolling, Michel, Conable, and two other Republicans, Del Latta and Trent Lott, from the House; and Stockman, Kenneth Duberstein (congressional liaison), James Baker, Richard Darman (deputy chief of staff), and Treasury Secretary Donald Regan from the White House.

Though Republicans outnumbered Democrats twelve to five, only two people mattered: Reagan and O'Neill. The gang would have to keep the principals informed and would have to get their approval before cutting any deals. Like a House-Senate conference committee, the Gang of Seventeen was designed to resolve the differences between two positions. Unlike a conference, the gang was not bound by any formal rules or legislation. It was up to the group to define the range of problems and solutions. Thus it is important to note who was *not* present: Pepper, Sen. William Armstrong (a conservative leader on social security), Edwin Meese (another Reagan confidant and White House counselor), Rep. William Archer (a leader of the Yellow Jackets), and Rep. Jack Kemp (the prime House sponsor of supply-side economics). Though Lott also represented the Yellow Jackets, the gang was noticeably short of ideologues. It was structured to provide an opportunity for a compromise and was not accountable to any outside group beyond Reagan and O'Neill.

April

In early April, according to one of the House participants, "We all received a call from the White House telling us to gather in the driveway of the Rayburn House Office Building to be picked up by unmarked limos. The big boys themselves did not attend—Senate Majority Leader Baker, O'Neill, or the President—sending representatives whose actions they could disavow if the meetings blew up." Bolling apparently held O'Neill's vote; James Baker held Reagan's.

The first meeting was held at the Vice President's mansion. The rest of the meetings were held at Blair House, across from the White House. The gang usually arrived at the new Executive Office Building and sneaked through an alley to the back door. "The press was particularly frustrated," one gang member said. "They apparently never learned where we were being picked up. Stakeouts were put on some of the members to try to find out where the meetings were being held. Once they learned that we were meeting at the White House, the press stood guard at the gates. Thundering herds rushed from one gate to the other as it appeared that we were entering or leaving. Gamesmanship, in short, became an entertaining sidelight of our press relations."

The meetings seemed to inaugurate a new form of presidential-congressional government. The meetings were secret. There were no minutes or transcripts. All conversations were strictly off the record. The gang was free to discuss all of the options without fear of political retaliation. It became an ad hoc, month-long negotiating group, existing completely outside of the constitutional system. This was not just separate institutions sharing power; this was a new kind of government body involving a *single chamber of national leadership.*

Though there were similarities to past presidential-congressional devices, this was a distinct form of government. Unlike presidential commissions, the gang had considerable power to enforce its final decisions inside Congress. And the gang was not bound by any laws on open meetings. Unlike one of Lyndon Johnson's presidential task forces, the gang was asked to resolve serious differences between competing branches of government, not to simply endorse White House bills. This was not some presidential tactic for finding congressional cosponsors or a device for co-opting political opponents. This was far more like a House-Senate conference committee than any past presidential body. But in this modified conference committee, the President would at least have a final vote.

In order to make any agreement, however, the leadership would have to guarantee that Congress would pass the compromise. If an agreement emerged, the House and Senate leaders would have to ram it through the two bodies without any opportunity for discussion or amendment. Otherwise, it would become a target for attack and counterattack, with no chance of passage.

The Snags

The first order of business in the early meetings involved the basic economic assumptions. There were literally dozens of budget projections floating around Washington, each painting a different picture of the future. To craft an agreement on a package of solutions, the gang would have to make a preliminary compromise on the size of the problem. Using the President's initial budget forecast as a baseline, and assuming no tax increases or spending cuts, the gang concluded that the deficit would hit $182 billion in 1983, rising to $216 billion in 1984 and $233 in 1985. The figures were far worse than in the original Reagan budget.

Despite this first compromise, the Gang of Seventeen ran aground in late April: Democrats wanted Reagan to drop the third year of his tax cut, while Republicans wanted Democrats to freeze the 1983 social security COLA. Inside the gang, the COLA generated the greater controversy. Republicans decided to move on to other issues. "Before doing social security," one said, "we wanted to make damn sure the negotiations were going to work. We didn't want the gang to break down and hear the Democrats blaming it on the fact that we wanted social security cuts. We put the issue on the table for the time being."

Nevertheless, social security could not be ignored. By the end of the first week, Bolling had suggested a "social security solvency figure." The figure would involve some amount of money to be raised through future unspecified action. The figure was to be a simple "plug," another "magic asterisk" of sorts, allowing Congress and the President to claim lower deficits without having to pass a reform bill first. Republicans tabled the idea, hoping to find other areas of agreement before taking on the tough one.

It was only later that Bolling returned with a formal social security proposal. The Democrats would accept a social security COLA cap of 5 percent in 1983 and 1984. Unlike a COLA delay, such a cap would save money only if inflation exceeded 5 percent. If inflation continued its drop, falling below 5 percent in 1983 or 1984, the Democratic proposal would not save any money. (Again, it is important to note that modest COLA changes would have done almost nothing to solve either the short- or long-term social security crisis. The only reason social security was even on the gang's agenda was the budget deficit. Even though COLA changes would make the budget look better, it was only an illusion.)

It became increasingly clear that the COLA issue would have to be resolved by Reagan and O'Neill face-to-face. Bolling simply did not have the authority to bargain much further. Nor did the Republicans have the power to drop the tax cut. "In fact," according to one participant, "Baker said three times a day, to make sure that nobody would misinterpret him, that he had not been authorized to retreat in any way on the third year of the tax cut and knew the President to be absolutely locked in cement on it."

As the gang continued its work, the personal relationships remained good. According to most, there was little acrimony or backbiting. There were some suspicious leaks on the Republican side, probably coming from the Senate Budget Committee staff, that were designed to put pressure on the gang for deeper spending cuts. However, as one member reported, "We had little doubt that in an autocracy in which we were the leaders, we would be able to carve up the necessary solution and provide a balance acceptable to all, but as agents of the President and Speaker, we found our reins too tight."

In the end, neither side could agree on the social security COLA and tax issues, and they invited the President and Speaker to a final summit meeting. The remaining issues had to be settled by the two principals, not by the agents. The confrontation was set for April 28.

The Summit

With the entire gang gathered in a sweltering hearing room in the Capitol building, Republicans offered their compromise: a three-month delay in both the social security COLA and the 1983 Reagan tax cut, pushing both back from July to October. "There was quite a pause there," one member said, while Reagan mulled over the figures. "In order to get that, I agree," he said. But O'Neill refused. "I will not discuss COLA—they're off the table," the Speaker replied, later describing the three-month double delay as a trade of "an apple for an orchard." O'Neill then presented the Democratic plan: a three-month delay in the 1983 COLA in return for complete elimination of the third-year tax cut. Reagan refused. He could take some pain on his tax cut, but not that much, not in exchange for a simple three-month COLA delay. "I can crap a pineapple," the President told the Speaker, "but not a cactus."

That was it; three weeks of negotiation down the drain. The summit meeting was over; the Gang of Seventeen was finished. As Laxalt said, "It's been moved from the Gang of Seventeen to the Gang of 535."

The finger-pointing began immediately. One White House participant concluded: "We had hoped for give and take there and what we found from the other side was mostly take and very little give."[1] O'Neill said the only Reagan "concession was to allow a slight three-month pause in his program of giving billion-dollar tax cuts to the rich." In exchange, Reagan "wanted the Democratic party to become his accomplice in making more brutal cuts in programs such as social security." It was exactly the kind of political rhetoric that both sides feared most in the negotiations.

[1]James Baker III, quoted in Congressional Quarterly *Weekly Report,* May 1, 1982, p. 969.

SOME LESSONS

The gang was an important attempt to leave the normal legislative process in search of a compromise on a very difficult issue. Its failure involved practical politics and small-group dynamics.

First, the philosophical differences were simply too deep. "I rather think now, looking back, that this effort was dead in the water from the beginning," Laxalt said. "The philosophical differences were just too great to overcome."[2] For his part, Reagan was solidly opposed to any compromise on his tax cut. He had fought hard to win it and clearly wanted to keep it. That he was willing to delay the third year for even three months reflected a major ideological compromise on his part. For O'Neill's part, there would be no compromise on social security without victory on the tax cut. "I'm as firm on social security as the President is on taxes," he had said in early April. "If he's firm in cement on the third year, I'm not going to balance the budget on the backs of the elderly."

Second, there were a number of practical problems with the Gang of Seventeen. One was the size of the group. Seventeen was too large a number. If Reagan and O'Neill were the only people who mattered, why bring all seventeen budget leaders together to hammer out a compromise? The smaller the group, the greater the opportunities to talk. It would have been easier to create a sense of mission, trust, and camaraderie. "One thing we learned," a White House staffer acknowledged, "was to keep the number of players down to a minimum."

A third, more important problem with the gang was the issue of who spoke for whom. The Republicans assumed that Bolling was the Speaker's man in the negotiations but wondered if the Speaker knew what was going on. If Bolling was merely talking for Bolling, the Republicans could have little confidence that the trades would stand up in the House. If Baker and Stockman were merely representing themselves, the Democrats could have little confidence that the President would sign a final bill. There was more than enough caution to go around, and the growing doubts that Bolling and Baker could "deliver" their bosses made it more difficult to bargain in good faith.

Fourth, the gang met too close to November 1982. With the elections only months away, most members of Congress wanted to start campaigning. Both sides were sorely tempted to take their cases to the public. Moreover, the election atmosphere created even greater doubts about the prospects on the floor. According to Rostenkowski, "Democrats in an election year are the most undisciplined group of people I've ever been associated with."[3] Republicans, too, were not enthusiastic about a budget compromise. Conservative Republicans refused to support a package with such high deficits; they promised a filibuster in the Senate and endless amendments in the House. Both sides were willing to wait until after the November elections.

[2]Paul Laxalt, quoted in ibid., p. 968.
[3]Dan Rostenkowski, quoted in ibid.

These problems could not be handled in such a short period of negotiation; the result was collapse. The gang was branded a failure. Yet the effort held several important lessons for making decisions on dedistributive issues. The gang had engaged in the kinds of intense political discussions that had once occurred in the halls of Congress. Under a veil of secrecy, the leaders had been able to raise the most sensitive issues without fear of the morning papers or interest groups. Perhaps this new form of government held the potential for future negotiations on social security. After all, the Democrats had accepted a COLA cap, something once thought impossible, and Reagan had accepted a tax increase. Though most of the participants were frustrated by the outcome, there was wide agreement that the gang had been a valuable exercise in presidential-congressional compromise.

A $40 BILLION SOLVENCY PLUG

During the April negotiations, the House and Senate budget committees remained quiet, stalling for time. With both chairmen on the Gang of Seventeen, neither committee had much to do. Though the first budget deadlines were quickly approaching, the committees hoped for a compromise. "Being on the Budget Committee is not a pleasant experience," a House member said. "You have to say no to all sorts of people. If we could have gotten a compromise from the talks, it would have saved us a lot of grief." Thus when the gang collapsed, responsibility returned to the budget committees. Members pored over the remains in search of any agreements that might help build a new package.

In the House, Democrats decided to wait for a few weeks, holding out for some sign of progress, perhaps a new effort at bipartisan negotiation. Moreover, O'Neill had made it clear that the Republican Senate would have to make the first move toward compromise. The House would not take the risk.

In the Senate, there was no such reluctance. Budget Committee Chairman Domenici came back from the Gang of Seventeen determined to forge a Republican budget. He began work almost immediately and had a new budget within days.

Domenici had three strategies for passing his new budget. First, to get Reagan's budget out of the way, Domenici asked for an immediate committee vote on the morning of May 5, only eight days after the Gang of Seventeen had failed. Reagan's 1982 budget was defeated unanimously, with Domenici casting the first "nay" vote. The maneuver was designed to make room for Domenici's substitute. It was an embarrassing defeat for the White House but merely confirmed what everyone already knew: the President's budget was long dead. The move was also designed to get Stockman and the White House back to the bargaining table. After the Gang of Seventeen, Reagan had forsworn any further negotiations. The defeat might wake the President to the budget realities. He would not be able to say that his budget was still alive, that the Democrats were responsible for the stalemate.

Second, to cut the budget deficits, Domenici rescued the social security solvency figure from the Gang of Seventeen. Since Congress would have to do something by July 1983, why not add those potential savings into the bottom line of the budget? The budget deficit would look that much smaller. Because the solvency plug would not include any legislative recommendations—whether tax increases or benefit cuts—it looked like a simple play. It was only an illusion, a promise of future returns.

Using Stockman's data, Domenici finally priced the solvency figure at $40 billion. That was the minimum that Congress would have to cut from benefits or raise in taxes to save the system. The resemblance to Stockman's "magic asterisk" was no coincidence. Domenici had drafted his new budget in constant contact with the White House. The solvency figure was merely a device for making the budget look better. "It was a $40-billion sock to be filled later," one Republican said. Indeed, according to the Senate Budget Committee, it would be up to the National Commission on Social Security Reform to figure out where the $40 billion would come from.

Third, to meet budget deadlines, Domenici moved for quick committee approval the night of May 5. Domenici won passage of his new package on a straight party-line vote. It was a rare example of how fast committees can move under the hand of a skillful chairperson. Yet it was also another example of the move-it-or-lose-it approach. The next morning, Reagan pledged his full support for a budget offensive in Congress.

When the budget finally appeared in print later that afternoon, however, all hope for passage was lost. The social security solvency figure was no longer harmless. It was now the most visible item in the budget. There, in bold type, was the $40 billion figure. There, in clear terms, was an order for the Senate Finance Committee to report a social security package by December 1, 1982. There was even a new deadline for the bipartisan National Commission. It was now asked to finish by November 30, four weeks ahead of schedule.

Stockman was shocked. The Senate Budget Committee had overstepped its boundaries to instruct both Congress and the President to get moving. Not only did the budget tamper with the National Commission, it looked as though Republicans were using social security once again to cut the deficit. The Senate Finance Committee, normally a source of support on the budget, was angered about the order. The National Commission was taken by surprise. Moreover, the solvency figure was supposed to be buried in a footnote, just like the magic asterisk, merely a tool for showing a glide path in the deficits. The White House prepared for another round of attacks.

They were not long in coming. By noon, May 6, Domenici's new budget was dead, a victim of the social security plug. In the span of two short days, Reagan's budget was out and Domenici's effort had failed. There would be no budget this election year. Almost a year to the day after Reagan's disastrous 1981 proposals, the Republicans suffered another major social security defeat, this one just six months before the midterm elections. Though the problem was only a so-called solvency figure, Democrats charged that social security was being used to balance the Reagan budget. In their haste for budget savings, Domenici and the White House had repeated the same political mistakes of a year before. Only seeing the bottom line, they had miscalculated the potential fallout.

As in 1981, the attack was led by Moynihan. As in 1981, he introduced a sweeping "Sense of the Senate" resolution, condemning both the Budget Committee and the President. As in 1981, the rhetoric was hot, with the Democrats rising to the one issue that continued to hurt Reagan. The key lay in painting the $40 billion solvency figure as a $40 billion benefit cut. And Domenici supplied most of the evidence. Asked whether he considered any tax increases in drafting the plug, Domenici replied, "Certainly not." Benefit cuts could be the only way to get the $40 billion.

When the resolution came up for debate a week later, Domenici acknowledged his role in this new round of social security heat. "I take full responsibility for truth in budgeting," Domenici said. "Instead of running around here talking as though we are doing something wrong, let us be honest with ourselves. Those who do not want social security insolvency around and do not want social security on the budget just do not want a truthful budget." Domenici knew that his budget was dead and was now fighting simply to retain some Budget Committee jurisdiction over social security.

In both chambers of Congress, Republicans, not Democrats, were pushing to remove social security from the unified federal budget, stripping it out of the annual process. "We've got to take social security off-budget as it was in the pre-Johnson days," Minority Leader Michel said. "It causes the elderly anxiety, grief and apprehension, and ought not to be there. Social security has gotten so politically charged . . . that it's just muddling up everything." In the House, Representative Kemp offered an amendment to remove the program from the unified budget. In the Senate, Sen. John Heinz introduced a similar bill, arguing that removal "will not solve either the social security financing problem or the problem of budget deficits. It will, however, help to clarify the hard choices with which we are faced." Republicans were trying to save themselves from self-inflicted pain, reprimanding Stockman and Domenici for opening the old wounds. "That solvency figure was a dead fish across our face," a House Republican said. "Domenici had no business taking us down that road again, not so close to the November elections. You can't run on the bottom line."

Domenici was able to stave off this first effort to remove social security from the unified budget, and his party defeated the Moynihan resolution by a 53–45 vote. However, as in 1981, the Senate eventually passed a second resolution promising full payment of the 1982 COLA and concluding that "Congress shall not include any more than is absolutely necessary to preserve the financial integrity of the social security system." The resolution passed 91–7 and was a final effort to cool social security down before the 1982 elections. Whether the solvency figure was a thinly veiled attempt to cut benefits or an innocent act of truth in budgeting, Republicans got stung again.

CONCLUSION

Even if the Gang of Seventeen had succeeded, social security would have remained in deep trouble. All of the 1982 social security battles involved the search for very short-term budget savings. Social security could not be easily repaired, especially in the budget process. As long as it remained part of the annual process, however, it would be a tempting morsel. Perhaps that was good. Perhaps social security should have been subject to yearly contests with other programs. But given public opinion and interest group opposition, those annual contests would always produce intense conflict, with Republicans often on the losing end.

With the Gang of Seventeen and Domenici's budget effort both finished, all eyes turned to Reagan's National Commission on Social Security Reform. Congress and the President had been unable to solve the crisis through the normal legislative process. The move-it-or-lose-it approach on social security had now failed three times: in Reagan's May 1981 proposals, in Reagan's 1981 budget package, and in Domenici's 1982 budget. The National Commission was now the last chance. But the elections would come first.

13

An Election Break

The $40 billion solvency plug provided plenty of fresh ammunition for Democratic congressional candidates. With unemployment breaking the double-digit level by October, Republicans were already predicting huge losses. Not only was Reaganomics an apparent failure, it was hurting the elderly. The $40 billion solvency plug was just one more example of Republican cruelty and became part of the Democratic battle cry "It's Not Fair, It's Republican." Claude Pepper, then chairman of the House Aging Committee and himself an octogenarian, campaigned in twenty-five states. (One Democratic official called him "the sexiest man in America.")

The campaigns were particularly hard on those Republicans who favored a social security compromise. Because public knowledge was so low, Democrats could easily argue that the coming crisis was an illusion, a Republican device for cutting benefits. Conable, for example, took his hardest hits on social security. "My opponent would say, 'Conable wants to cut your benefits!' and I would shout, 'No, I don't!'" Conable remembered. "Then afterwards, the little old ladies would come up to me and say, 'Why do you want to cut my benefits?' It was just a disgusting experience." The repeated attacks led the normally unflappable Conable to accuse his fellow national commissioner, Moynihan, of "blathering" on the issue. He later apologized. According to Republican party aides, Conable's campaign was not unusual. Democrats made social security one of the top issues in the 1982 campaign.

Thus even if social security had no objective impact on the voters' choice, many members of Congress still *believed* it was important. And if they believed it was a key issue in the past, perhaps they would act differently in the future. Members of Congress scare very easily. Perhaps Republicans would finally accept some tax increases to avoid another defeat in 1984; perhaps Democrats would finally agree to some benefit cuts to settle the issue in their favor.

For the time being, however, the campaigns forced the cancellation of the October meeting of the National Commission, lest tempers boil over. The commission could not act until after the elections anyway.

THE CAMPAIGNS

Republicans were in deep trouble on social security at the start of the 1982 campaign season. Reagan's approval ratings on the issue continued to sag, hitting an all-time low in April 1982. Less than 25 percent of the public thought his handling of the issue was excellent or good; 72 percent said it was only fair or poor. Further, a February survey by the President's own pollster showed that 54 percent of the public believed Reagan had already cut social security benefits. If the election became a referendum on Reagan and social security, Republicans would lose badly.

The political problems were most pronounced among two groups. First, Republicans were in trouble with family-aged voters, people between 30 and 50 with a high-school diploma or less. "They're mostly Democrats we won over in 1980," a Republican Senatorial Campaign Committee aide said. "They provided our margin of victory in 1980. They're the ones with kids at home and parents on social security. They have the assembly-line jobs. They have a lot to lose on social security." Family-aged voters were also the most concerned about unemployment, the other tough issue for Republicans. Second, the GOP was in trouble with the near-retired, people between 50 and 65. Reagan's May 1981 proposals had taken direct aim at their benefits with the early retirement cut.

A Republican Postman

The question was how to reduce the damage among the two groups. One answer was to help the public forget Reagan's social security proposals. As the campaigns moved into May and June, it was clear the issue was still hurting the party. Democrats had stepped up their attacks and appeared to be winning public support. The Republicans desperately needed some way to remind the public that Reagan cared about the elderly, that he still supported the program. It came on July 3, with payment of the 1982 social security cost-of-living adjustment. Though the 7.4 percent COLA was automatic, it was proof that Reagan had *not* cut benefits. It was payment in full, just as he promised. The only problem was how to help the public make the connection.

That came with the postman ad.

Originally created by a Republican candidate in South Carolina, the ad caught the eye of the national party and became a centerpiece of the summer campaign. Running during the first two weeks of July, the ad featured a kindly old postman cheerfully delivering social security checks containing the full 7.4 percent COLA. "I'm probably one of the most popular people in town," the postman said, walking down the steps of a pleasant small-town home. "I'm delivering social security checks with the 7.4 percent cost-of-living raise that

President Reagan promised. He promised that raise—and he kept his promise. In spite of the sticks-in-the-mud who tried to keep him from doing what we elected him to do." Pausing for a close-up on his weathered face, the postman concluded, "President Reagan has made only a beginning. But he *has* kept his word. And it *is* a beginning. For gosh sakes, let's give the guy a chance." The commercial lasted only thirty seconds and cost only $40,000, but it became one of the most effective ads in recent campaign history.

Yet the ad was designed less to change voter opinions than to "inoculate" the public against the coming Democratic campaigns, to plant a seed of support that might survive until November. Republican campaign experts did not expect a reversal of public opinion on social security, but they did hope to freeze opposition and undermine future Democratic attacks. By telling people that Reagan was responsible for the benefit COLA in spite of those "sticks-in-the-mud" in Congress, the ad took full advantage of public ignorance. Recall that only 45 percent of the public even knew that there was a benefit COLA. They could hardly be expected to know it was automatic, that it would have been paid with or without Reagan, that the postman was not telling the truth.

The ad reached 67 percent of all U.S. households, and 35 percent of the public recalled seeing the commercial. One-third of the public agreed with the closing line "For gosh sakes, let's give the guy a chance." Moreover, the ad appeared to reverse Reagan's steady decline on social security. In June, two weeks before the commercial, the President's pollster had asked the public if it was their "impression that Ronald Reagan has increased or reduced social security benefits?" Only 17 percent said Reagan had increased benefits, while 49 percent said he had reduced benefits. Another 34 percent said there had been no change. Two weeks after the commercials, 37 percent said Reagan had increased benefits—a jump of 20 points in the President's favor—while 41 percent said he had reduced benefits. Only 17 percent still said there had been no change. The result suggested that Republicans were reaping rewards from the COLA increase, even though Reagan had tried to cut it at least twice since his inauguration. "Since when is a commercial supposed to be accurate?" a Republican National Committee official asked. "Do women really smile when they clean their ovens?"

Though the postman ad was designed for family-aged voters and the near-retired, it had its largest impact on people over 65. In June, 39 percent of the retired said they would vote Republican if the election were held that day. By July, the figure had jumped to 53 percent. In the span of a month, what had once been a 7 percent Democratic lead had turned into a 13 percent Republican edge. The retired, of course, had received the COLA on July 3 and made the connection with the postman ad.

Though the ad was less successful among the two targeted groups, it still worked a small miracle. In May, 51 percent of family-aged voters said Reagan's handling of social security was poor. By August, the figure had dropped to 40 percent, a shift of 11 points in the President's favor. If these voters were so important to Republican fortunes, the ad seemed to make a slight difference. Among the near-retired, however, the ad did not have much impact. In June,

49 percent of people between 50 and 64 said they would vote Democratic if the election were held that day. By July, the figure remained unchanged. Apparently, the postman ad had done little to calm their fears.

Democratic Scissors

Democrats were stunned by the postman ad. Not only was it misleading, it was remarkably effective. Pepper said the ad lowered "the art of deception to depths not explored since the Nixon administration," arguing that it was "nothing less than a hypocritical attempt to mislead the American people into thinking President Reagan and the Republican party are responsible for the very benefit increase which they fought so hard to postpone." O'Neill charged that the Republican party was "betting a multimillion dollar media campaign it can lie to the American people and get away with it." Even the postal unions got involved, claiming that the ads misrepresented mail carriers as Reagan supporters. "If there is a trophy for political opportunism and unmitigated gall," the Democratic National Committee said, "the Republicans and White House have retired it."

Yet the best way to fight a postman was with scissors. The Democrats needed an ad campaign of their own.

The first Democratic ad was on the air by mid-July and pictured a social security card being slowly pared down by Republican scissors. "The Republicans all say they believe in social security, a sacred contract with the American people," the commercial began. "That's what they say. Look at what they do. (Snip) In 1981 they tried to cut cost-of-living increases by $60 billion over 10 years. (Snip) In 1982 they said either increase social security taxes or cut $40 billion to help balance the budget. (Snip) When are they going to stop? (Snip) Not until it hurts. (Snip, Snip) It isn't fair . . . It's Republican."

The second Democratic ad was more complex, playing on public fears of bankruptcy and the elderly's lack of knowledge about the mechanics of the system. Opening with a shot of an old farmhouse, the ad asked, "What if the checks stopped? What if the Republicans finally won their battle against social security?" Showing an elderly woman walking slowly to her mailbox, the ad said, "All that stands in their way is a group of tough Democrats who understand and care. But the fight will continue next year and the next." Showing the woman's growing fear as she looks down the deserted highway, her mailbox empty, the commercial concluded, "It's another good reason to vote Democratic." Like the Republican ad, the second round of Democratic commercials was also misleading, creating an image of social security collapse that could not occur.

The combined impact of the two Democratic ads was impressive. A large portion of the postman gains was wiped out. Republican polls showed that the number of people who believed Reagan had reduced benefits had moved back up from 41 percent to 49 percent by October, while the number who thought he had increased benefits had dropped from 37 percent to 25 percent, thereby reversing most of the earlier Republican shift. However, if the postman ad was designed to freeze public opposition and to inoculate voters against the Democratic campaigns, it worked. Not surprisingly, the number of people who were too confused even to give an opinion about what had happened to benefits had risen from 1 percent in May to 10 percent just after the elections. Such was the impact of the competing ads.

The Postman Always Rings Twice

With the Democratic counterattack in full swing, Republicans prepared a second wave of postman ads. The new ad featured the same kindly postman, now walking down Main Street, America. "Well, I'm still delivering those social security checks," he smiled with a handful of envelopes in hand. "And they've still got the 7.4 percent cost-of-living raise President Reagan promised. To listen to some folks, though, you'd think he was gonna cut it out the day after he started it. He didn't and he won't, and folks shouldn't try to scare us like that." Handing a check to an elderly woman who looked suspiciously similar to the actress in the Democratic ad, the postman concluded, "Like I said before, President Reagan has made only a beginning. But it's a *real* beginning. And I think we should give the guy a chance."

Despite a considerable investment in production costs, the second postman ad never ran. First, the postman no longer looked as friendly. Most of the Republican staffers who viewed the ad noted a rather sinister quality in the postman's voice and demeanor. No one knows why. Second, and more important, the Republican party had committed most of its money to a new ad campaign under the banner "Stay the Course." That campaign focused on the positive and was designed to shift public attention away from the economy and social security. Things will work out in the end, the new campaign argued, if we only stick with the Reagan program. Third, campaign experts felt that any further advertising on social security would only raise the public's sensitivity. "We made some gains on the first ad," a Republican congressional campaign committee aide said, "but it was a very risky strategy. Usually, you play to your strengths and never say one word about the weaknesses."

Even with this newfound caution, the Republicans still made a critical mistake late in the campaigns. Ironically, the gaffe occurred in the mails. Throughout 1982, the Democrats had been raising money on the social security issue, sending millions of letters to potential contributors. Most of the envelopes carried the message "IMPORTANT SOCIAL SECURITY INFORMATION: CONTENTS REQUIRE IMMEDIATE ATTENTION" and looked very much like official Social Security Administration mail. The letters had been extremely successful, bringing several million dollars into the Democratic war chest.

Though Republicans were not short on campaign funds, they decided to launch their own social security fund-raising letter—mostly to see if there was "gold in them thar hills," as one party aide argued. The letter claimed that Democrats were "principally responsible for the disastrous condition of the Social Security system" and invited readers to cast one of three enclosed ballots for reform. The letter promised to send the ballots to the National Commission on Social Security Reform. Unfortunately for the party, the first two ballots read as follows:

1. MAKE SOCIAL SECURITY VOLUNTARY. This proposal would insure that those now receiving benefits would continue to do so, but would give future retirees the choice of either remaining in the system or providing for their retirement through private pensions, profit sharing, retirement funds or other retirement programs of their choosing.
2. SPLIT OFF THE WELFARE ASPECTS OF SOCIAL SECURITY INTO A SEPARATE FUND. This proposal would return the Social Security system to its original status as a retirement insurance program by offering benefits only to those who pay into the system and their survivors.

Once again, Republicans had been caught; this time, only weeks before the November elections. Pepper and O'Neill launched immediate attacks, gladly supplying copies of the first ballots as evidence of a secret Republican plan to destroy social security.

All in all, it was not the most enlightening of debates. Already confused about how social security worked and frightened about future benefits, the public could learn little from either party in the 1982 campaigns. This opportunity to educate and inform had been wasted on partisan gain. The question, of course, was whether any of the arguments had an impact on the vote. Was social security a factor in the 1982 elections?

THE RESULTS

All totaled, almost 66 million people voted in the 1982 midterm elections. The 40 percent turnout was an increase of 6 percent over the turnout for the 1978 midterm elections and reversed a decade of steady decline in off-year participation. Apparently, the parties had made the election more interesting to the public, driving up voter turnout. Of the 66 million votes, Democrats won 36 million, or 54 percent, while Republicans won 30 million, or 46 percent. Voters seemed to prefer the Democratic position on jobs and social security.

Votes into Seats

Yet congressional elections are not decided on the basis of nationwide voting. Those 66 million votes were divided into state and district contests, each with unique features. In the House, for example, the Democratic share of the national vote translated into 269 seats in the new Congress, an increase of 26 seats and a 101-seat edge over the Republicans. Here, 54 percent of the national vote equaled 62 percent of the House seats.

In the Senate, however, the Democratic share translated into 46 seats, no change from the old margin. Here, 54 percent of the national vote equaled only

46 percent of the Senate seats. However, a shift of just 43,000 votes in five states—Nevada, Rhode Island, Vermont, Missouri, and Wyoming—would have given the Democrats a new Senate majority.

The difference between national votes and actual seats was the result of many factors, including redistricting in the House, incumbency, campaign spending, and local issues. Because the Democrats controlled so many state legislatures, and because those legislatures were responsible for redrawing House districts after the 1980 census, some elections rested on the skillful manipulation of population lines. In California, for example, a highly compli-cated redistricting plan was credited with creating six new Democratic seats. According to Republican experts, as many as half the House losses came from just that kind of skillful redistricting by the Democrats.

A second important voting factor was incumbency. Because incumbents are highly visible, their opponents have to spend more money just to catch up. In the House, 90 percent of all incumbents who ran for reelection in 1982 won. It was a standard pattern for the House. In the Senate, however, 93 percent of all incumbents won. It was a surprising reversal of past trends. Recall that past Senate elections had been a fifty-fifty gamble. In contrast, only 2 out of 30 incumbents were defeated in 1982. Though many of the Republicans were returned to the Senate by the slimmest of margins—6 by less than 51 percent of the vote—incumbency appeared to make at least some difference in the Repub-lican campaigns. In contrast, 14 of the 18 successful Senate Democrats won by more than 60 percent of the vote. Because Senate campaigns involve a much greater national flavor than House contests, incumbency is often canceled out by the issues. In 1982, Democratic incumbents were helped by the issues, boosting their vote tallies, whereas Republican incumbents just squeaked by.

As with most other elections, there were a number of interesting patterns in the votes. All 39 House Boll Weevils were reelected, suggesting that they were doing something right back home; only 5 Gypsy Moths were defeated, confirming their opposition to Reaganomics and the budget cuts; only 14 of 52 Republican House freshmen were defeated; 16 of 17 senators targeted for defeat by the National Conservative Political Action Committee (NCPAC) survived; 15 of the 18 candidates endorsed by Sen. Jesse Helms and his new right Congressional Club were defeated. All in all, a very good year for incumbents.

Still, in sifting through the results, there was little evidence of a major national swing. Even though O'Neill called the elections "a disastrous defeat for the President," a 26-seat loss was hardly dramatic, particularly since the average midterm defeat for the President's party over the past seven decades has been 36 seats, and since Democrats had earlier predicted a 50- to 75-seat gain. Even though Reagan claimed that he was "very pleased" with the outcome, consider the record for the candidates he endorsed with a personal campaign appearance: for governor, 3 won, 7 lost; for senator, 7 won, 6 lost; for representative, 26 won, 12 lost. All combined, of the 61 candidates blessed with a Reagan visit, 41 percent lost. In contrast, of the 73 candidates for whom Pepper had campaigned, 54 won—a success ratio of 74 percent.

Votes and Social Security

The absence of a huge party swing did not mean that social security was unimportant. "You've got to count more than the seat switches," an aide to Speaker O'Neill said. "You've got to consider the message from the voter. For every Republican who has been beaten, there is another one who barely skated through." Indeed, one of the closest House elections came in Republican Minority Leader Michel's district in Illinois. Plagued by high unemployment at Caterpillar Tractor in Peoria, Michel was reelected with a handful of votes. "He now knows how the Gypsy Moths feel," a Republican House colleague said. "He may become a Gypsy Moth himself."

There were three ways the social security issue might have shaped the 1982 election results:

1. It might have influenced some voters directly. Asked in an October CBS News/*New York Times* poll if any single issue would affect their votes, 42 percent of the public said yes. Asked what the issue would be, 5 percent of them said social security. Asked whom they would vote for as a result, three-quarters said the Democrats. Thus on a national level, Democrats might have gained 1 percent from the issue.
2. Social security might have influenced some voters by reinforcing their party identification. Asked by CBS News/*New York Times* which party would make the right decisions on social security, 49 percent said the Democrats, 30 percent the Republicans, 4 percent both, and 3 percent neither. Clearly, social security worked in the Democrats' favor. It was second only to unemployment in helping the party.
3. Social security might have influenced some voters by creating an overall negative image of the President. Despite the postman ad, public disapproval of Reagan's handling of social security had returned to the 70 percent level by October. Among 23,000 voters interviewed by ABC News as they left polling places on election day, only 36 percent approved of Reagan's performance on the issue.

Still, it is hard to know just how much social security affected the final outcomes. Even if it had an impact on the national tallies, that impact was diluted by state and local factors. Exit polls of voters showed that Democrats had picked up support among older voters between 1978 and 1982. Among people over age 60, for example, Democrats took 56 percent of the vote in 1982—up from 53 percent in 1978. The 3 percent rise, while small, might have accounted for part of the 26-seat gain.

However, the translation of votes into seats was murky—as it often is. According to most top Democratic and Republican pollsters, if social security had a major impact, it was indirect. "It wasn't so important as a single issue," a Democratic expert concluded, "but it did add to the fairness issue. It was tied into everything else Reagan did—the tax cuts, the corporate giveaways, unemployment, budget cuts. Social security helped reinforce the traditional Democratic coalition." A Republican pollster agreed: "The issues changed 180 degrees between 1980 and 1982. In 1980, it was all size of government, taxes, those kind of things. In 1982, it was unemployment, social security, fairness; the Democratic bread-and-butter issues."

Yet Democrats could not find any mandate for their party in the 1982 elections. "The voters do not want a legislative stalemate," one top Democratic pollster warned his party. "Rather, they seek help and assistance in solving what they perceive to be very tough problems. In the end, if the Democratic answer is nothing more than a simple and thorough assault on Reagan's programs, the Democrats will suffer the same fate at the polls in 1984 that the Republicans met in 1982."[1] In short, the Democrats could not just say no.

On Capitol Hill

Whatever the objective impact, social security was widely perceived as important on Capitol Hill. Dole said it had cost his party 13 seats in the House and wondered aloud what would happen to the 19 Republican senators up for reelection in 1984; Pepper said it had brought 50 new Democrats into office.

Social security certainly had an impact on the new members of Congress, whether Democrats or Republicans. As one of the top issues in their first campaigns, social security would be remembered. Because these new members would be particularly concerned about their next election, they were more likely to follow public opinion back home. And that meant less willingness to compromise. Indeed, asked by *The New York Times* if they favored COLA cuts to solve the coming problems, 89 percent of the new members said no; asked if they favored tax increases, 78 percent said no; asked about a retirement age boost, 67 percent said no.[2] One wonders if they had any preferred alternatives at all. And compared with the rest of the House, the new members were less flexible. Like the public, they seemed to oppose everything without having any alternatives of their own. Whatever the objective impact of social security in the 1982 elections, these new members believed it had been important and were locked in against the major options.

Yet if there had been no shift in party seats, no close elections, no major change in Democratic fortunes, there was one change that truly mattered: Rules Committee Chairman Richard Bolling had retired, opening the seat for Pepper. "It may be that I can use the Rules Committee more than it's ever been used to help the cause of the elderly," Pepper said in making his decision to leave the Aging Committee. "After all, the Rules Committee can do almost anything it wants to."[3] In congressional elections it is not just how many members win or lose, but which ones return.

Though Pepper was 82 at the time, he had plenty of energy to devote to social security. Any legislation would have to go through his committee en route to the floor. By shaping the rules for the floor debate, by allowing some

---

[1] Peter D. Hart, internal memorandum.
[2] *The New York Times*, November 4, 1982, p. A18.
[3] Quoted in the *Miami Herald*, November 19, 1982, p. A1.

amendments and denying others, by limiting the order of arguments, Pepper could stop almost any bill from passing. He would have to be involved in any social security bargains. Unlike Bolling, who had shown at least some willingness to compromise on the social security COLA in the Gang of Seventeen, Pepper was not open to negotiation on benefit cuts.

Pepper's decision was particularly important in his ongoing battle with the more conservative Ways and Means Committee. "Pepper wanted a policy committee," an aide said. "When he was on Aging, all he had was a mouthpiece to raise his issue. Aging could not draft legislation. If Rosty [Rostenkowski] wanted to draft a conservative social security bill, Pepper had no way to stop it. Rosty didn't have to return his calls. On Rules, if Pepper doesn't like a bill, he can keep it off the floor. Now the mountain must come to Mohammed."

CONCLUSION

There was little doubt that Democrats had won the social security issue in 1982. It was a cornerstone of their campaign and kept Republicans on the defensive. Yet with the 1982 elections over, the question was what the Democrats would do with the issue. "Social security is—without question—the most combustible issue before us," Representative Rostenkowski said after the elections. "It carries five times the political risk of a $100-billion tax increase. 'Political football' is a pretty hackneyed phrase, but I can't think of a better way to describe the political battering social security has taken over the last year and a half. All I can say is the scrimmage ended last Tuesday. And the real game has begun."

The first plays in the game were called at the November meetings of the National Commission on Social Security Reform.

14

Commission-itis

The National Commission on Social Security Reform was created to put out a very hot political fire. It kept the issue alive for the Democrats and provided some political cover for the Republicans. Few expected it to solve the social security crisis. Even the chairman was pessimistic. "Knowing where all of you stand," Greenspan told the first meeting, "I expect to get 15 reports, maybe more."

Nevertheless, by mid-1982, the commission was the only social security game in town. After repeated failures within the normal legislative process, it became the last, best hope for compromise. Pickle had failed, only to be followed by Reagan, Dole, and Domenici. Faced with public fears and interest group opposition, Congress and the President desperately needed a place to work. Moreover, if the commission could produce a social security agreement, perhaps a similar device would work on other issues—MX missiles, budget deficits, Caribbean policy, education, and so on. Congress and the President did not seem capable of moving any other way. Soon, Washington was infected with commission-itis.

A NATIONAL COP-OUT?

Congress was hardly enthusiastic when Reagan first announced the National Commission in September 1981. Conable called the commission a "cop-out"; Dole concluded that it was "a slight reflection" on the Senate and "our ability to pass something on our own." Few members of Congress were warned in advance. It surely came as a surprise to the social security committees. As a Republican member of the commission recalled, "I first heard about it when Reagan made his TV speech. No one called me before that, probably because they knew I'd dump all over it."

There were several reasons why Congress was reluctant to endorse a national commission. Social security had already been studied at length. This was not the first national commission on the social security crisis, nor the second, nor the third. It was the fourth major study commission in less than three years. "We already knew as much as we needed to know," a Republican commissioner noted. "What we needed was action." A national commission would also eclipse Congress. A national commission would invade Ways and Means and Finance Committee turf. Further, a national commission would delay action on the crisis. Since the commission would not make a report until after the 1982 election, nothing would happen until the lame-duck session, if then.

Still, once Reagan made his announcement, Congress could do little to stop the commission. If O'Neill refused to accept Reagan's invitation, the social security crisis would be laid at his feet. "You can't walk away," O'Neill later remarked about another commission. "The one who walks away gets the blame." The President had divided the fifteen appointments equally between the House, the Senate, and himself and had even promised to name two Democrats among his five. What could be more bipartisan? O'Neill would get three appointments, the House minority two, the Senate majority three, the Senate minority two, and Reagan five. What could be more generous? The Democrats could not refuse without taking the heat for the coming crisis. They would have to join the commission.

Now the question was whether Reagan and O'Neill would pick people who could compromise. By appointing their favorite ideologues, they could easily sabotage the commission. Merely sending fifteen members to a national commission did not mean anyone would sit down and bargain.

The Appointees

For the *House Democrats,* Speaker O'Neill appointed three liberals: Pepper, former Rep. Martha Keys, and former Social Security Commissioner Robert Ball. It was a very partisan group and formed a liberal anchor on the commission. Of the three, Ball would be the Speaker's man on the commission, as well as the intellectual leader of the liberals. Pepper would be the link to elderly groups.

Rostenkowski and Pickle were conspicuous by their absence. "Keep your options open," Rostenkowski told one Ways and Means member. "You'll just come back as an advocate for something and be in a strait-jacket." If and when the National Commission failed, Rostenkowski wanted to start with a clean hand. He did not want to show his cards until the real game began. Gambling that the commission would collapse, Rostenkowski refused to play. He lost his influence over a commission package but increased his bargaining room in the House.

For the *House Republicans,* Minority Leader Michel appointed Conable and Rep. William Archer. Despite initial doubts, Conable finally agreed to join.

Conable would be part of a Republican commission majority, a pleasant change from being in the House minority. Archer was included as the ranking Republican on the Social Security Subcommittee. He was also one of the most conservative members of the House; a "bright man, a pure man, an obstructionist who believes in the absolute rightness of his cause," according to a House colleague. A Yellow Jacket who frequently disagreed with his own party leadership, he was the perfect ideological balance for Pepper.

For the *Senate Republicans*, Majority Leader Baker appointed three colleagues: Dole, Armstrong, and Heinz. The message was obvious: the Senate was sending its social security leadership to the commission. Whereas the Ways and Means majority was not present, the Finance Committee majority was well represented: the chairmen of the full committee (Dole) and of the key subcommittee (Armstrong) were both selected. Senate Republicans understood that the commission might be their one chance to influence a social security package. If the commission failed, the initiative would return to the House and the Ways and Means Committee. With Heinz, chairman of the Senate Special Aging Committee, the Republicans were leading with their social security experts.

For the *Senate Democrats*, Minority Leader Byrd appointed Senator Moynihan and AFL-CIO President Lane Kirkland. Moynihan was the ranking Democrat on the Social Security Subcommittee and was the author of Senate resolutions repudiating Reagan's May 1981 proposals and condemning the $40 billion solvency plug. Kirkland, of course, represented organized labor, and he brought a negotiator's background to the commission. In his early days at the union, he had worked in the social security division, learning both the substance of the issue and the politics of Congress.

For the *President*, the White House appointed five conservatives to the commission: Alan Greenspan as chairman, plus Robert Beck, Mary Falvey Fuller, Alexander Trowbridge, and Joe Waggoner. Greenspan had been chairman of the Council of Economic Advisers under Ford and was acceptable to both the conservative and moderate wings of the Reagan staff. Perhaps his greatest attribute as chairman of the commission would be his personal style. He was slow to anger and would keep a low-key, even-handed style in his dealings with the commission. In many respects, he was an "honest broker," someone who could be trusted to find a reasonable middle ground between the two camps on the commission.

The four other White House appointees formed a solid pro-business anchor on the commission. Two were leaders of powerful business lobbies: Robert Beck (the Business Roundtable) and Alexander Trowbridge (the National Association of Manufacturers). One was a former conservative congressman from Louisiana: Waggoner. One was vice president of a large California consumer products corporation: Fuller. Two were Democrats as promised—Trowbridge and Waggoner—but all four were solidly aligned against social security tax increases and strongly in favor of benefit cuts.

All told, the commissioners had an impressive grasp of the social security issues. Fuller had served on a 1979 commission; Conable, Archer, Pepper, Dole,

Armstrong, Heinz, and Moynihan were all legislative specialists in the area; Kirkland had received his training at the hands of some of the founders of the program; Keys was an advocate of greater women's protection in social security; Waggoner had been on Ways and Means during the years of social security expansion. Indeed, the member with the least social security experience was the chairman, Greenspan. That lack of knowledge was actually an advantage in leading the group toward a consensus on the size of the coming problem. Greenspan could easily play the honest broker.

In the end, both Reagan and O'Neill had held the number of ideologues to a minimum. The Democrats had appointed two—Pepper and Moynihan—and the Republicans two—Archer and Armstrong.[1] Though other members had strong opinions on benefit cuts and tax increases, there was room for compromise. Reagan's appointees were clearly pro-business and anti-taxes, while O'Neill's were pro-elderly and anti-cuts. Yet there was some willingness to talk. The question was whether Rostenkowski's absence would be too much to ignore. Ways and Means would have to start the legislative process once the commission was over. Without Rostenkowski on board, any package might be doomed.

Counting Heads

With the appointees in place, the commission broke along several lines. Reagan liked to talk about an eight-to-seven split between Republicans and Democrats. After all, he had appointed two Democrats. O'Neill liked to talk about a ten-to-five split between conservatives and liberals.

O'Neill was probably right. Indeed, the five congressional Democrats rarely met with the two Reagan appointees. As one commission staffer said, "We had to be very careful about the two Reagan Democrats. We never had a Democratic caucus room as such. It was called 'the Caucus Room for the Congressionally Appointed Democrats.' We never had a Republican caucus room, either. It was 'the Caucus Room for Commissioners Who Want to Meet with Alan Greenspan.' That way, Trowbridge and Waggoner always had a place to go." It was clear that the two Reagan Democrats were not welcome among the liberals.

The fact that Republicans held a numerical majority did not mean they controlled the commission. In fact, they were often divided and confused. The three congressional moderates—Conable, Dole, and Heinz—would accept limited tax increases in return for benefit cuts. The four business representatives—Beck, Fuller, Trowbridge, and Waggoner—were unsure. The two congressional conservatives—Archer and Armstrong—would not accept any tax increases, however disguised as accelerations of already scheduled rates or balanced by benefit cuts. The last Republican, Greenspan, had to keep his position open as chairman. Thus as long as the five liberals maintained a common front, they

---

[1]Up for reelection in 1982, Moynihan was particularly harsh in the campaigns. Later, however, he became an important force for consensus.

held a plurality over the ten Republican appointees. At least on this fifteen-member commission, five members could control the outcome.

Perhaps the most important split on the commission was between the seven legislators and the eight outsiders. The legislators would return to Congress when the commission was over and would have to sell any package to their colleagues. If they could fashion a final agreement in the commission, it would have a good chance of passage in Congress. Whereas previous commissions had spent considerable time thinking about the ideal world, this commission was firmly rooted in practical politics.

Moreover, because the congressional budget committees were not represented on the commission, there would be no one to protest removing social security from the annual budget process. As Senate Budget Committee chairman Domenici later complained, "This commission was not established to review budgetary treatment of social security. If it had been established for that purpose it would have been composed of somewhat different members." As it was, five of the fifteen commissioners were from the Ways and Means and Finance committees. And both committees resented any invasion of their territory. Such was one impact of the recruitment process.

Yet even the outsiders had strong political experience. Ball was a leader of the Save Our Security (SOS) coalition; Kirkland was president of the largest labor union in the nation and spoke for both federal employees and blue-collar workers; Trowbridge and Beck headed two of the largest business groups. Indeed, the commission provided a rare blend of lobbyists and legislators on the same decision-making body. The presence of such high-level interest leaders provided automatic access for all of the major pressure groups. There was no need for hearings or outside testimony. The interest group leaders were already on the commission. Nor was there any need to pressure Pepper on benefit cuts; he had been an early supporter of SOS. Nor was there any need to pressure Archer and Armstrong on tax increases; they had been early allies of the National Federation of Independent Business and the Chamber of Commerce. Such were the subtle and not-so-subtle connections between interest groups and government on the commission.

IN LIMBO

With the membership appointed and a staff in place, the first meeting of the National Commission on Social Security Reform was held on February 27, 1982, at the Washington Sheraton Hotel. The commission's executive director, Robert Myers, presented a brief paper on the history of social security; Greenspan gave a pep talk on the need for a spirit of compromise; the commissioners received a letter from Reagan wishing them success and concluding that the group was a "product of the leadership of both parties of both houses of the Congress as much as it is mine." As one commissioner concluded, "We were already starting to spread the blame."

After that first meeting, the commission settled into what Ball later called "soporific academic discussions." Reports were often read out loud, line by line. Members were sometimes seated alphabetically, sometimes at random, but always next to someone different. It was Greenspan's way of introducing the commissioners to one another.

Greenspan also tried to insulate his commission from the surrounding political conflict. But with so many legislators on the commission and the television cameras at each meeting, heat was bound to jump from the House and Senate floors to the new forum. When the Senate Budget Committee produced its $40 billion solvency figure, complete with the request for a new commission deadline, the battle broke loose.

Asking that the television lights be left on for the duration of the May 10 meeting, Pepper argued that the solvency figure had destroyed any chance for a commission agreement; Moynihan called the Budget Committee action an "order" for the commission to "report a $40-billion reduction in social security benefits over the next three years." As Greenspan struggled to stem the conflict, Armstrong charged that Moynihan had been "engaged in the most outrageous statements on the floor of the Senate," making social security "a demagoguerous issue from front to back and top to bottom." Concluding that the commission was becoming a forum for "demagoguery," Armstrong said he was "very skeptical that this task force is going to be able to produce anything that is of much use." As tempers flared in this, only the third meeting of the commission, it was clear that the group had been infected by the same political tensions as Congress and the White House.

That brief moment of conflict guaranteed a summer and fall of stalemate. With Moynihan and Pepper on the campaign trail attacking Reagan, and with Armstrong and Archer attacking O'Neill, there could be no movement until after the elections. It was already evident that the commission would need a sizable majority to sell any compromise to Congress. An eight-to-seven split would not be enough. But it was not clear how large the majority had to be. It would have to include the five liberals, if only because they voted as a block. But how many Republicans? Could Dole and Conable ignore Armstrong and Archer? Could the conservatives persuade the four business leaders to hold out? Who spoke for Reagan? Who spoke for O'Neill?

Such were the questions as the commission prepared for its November meetings. Coming a week after the elections, this would be the furthest point from the 1984 campaigns. For dedistributive issues, this was a prime opportunity to act. This was the time of lowest political sensitivity. The question was whether it was low enough. Tempers were still hot from the fall campaigns. How could Republicans forget the rhetoric with Pepper sitting across the table?

Not all was conflict, however. Behind the scenes, Myers and the commission's professional staff were busy compiling an awesome collection of material. As one memo after another poured out, the staff laid the groundwork for future debate, while offering an impressive and growing portfolio of options. When and if the commission decided to decide, this work assured a menu of alternatives from A to Z, all carefully priced out.

THE NOVEMBER COLLAPSE

The midterm congressional elections were held on Tuesday, November 1. Though the election appeared to be a wash, O'Neill appeared on network TV to say there would be no lame-duck action on social security, not with 26 new Democrats joining Congress in January. In a preelection letter to House Democrats, O'Neill had already warned that "many of our Republican colleagues will be defeated this coming week precisely because they voted to cut social security. To allow these same Members another crack at social security would be an insult not just to their constituents but to the American electorate as a whole."

The First Move

O'Neill's announcement prompted an immediate response from Republican members of the commission. With the major commission meetings now scheduled for November 11–13, Republicans feared another political disaster. This time, however, the 1984 elections would be on the line, along with the presidency. "I'm not backing into that buzz saw again, and I'm sure not walking straight into it," Dole said. The Democrats would have to make the first move. Dole even sent a telegram to the eight Republican commissioners recommending that "WE NOT ATTEMPT TO DRAFT A FINAL COMMISSION POSITION NEXT WEEK. AFTER THE VERY PARTISAN DEBATE THAT HAS SURROUNDED SOCIAL SECURITY IN RECENT WEEKS THERE SHOULD BE A COOLING OFF PERIOD AND TIME FOR REFLECTION BY THOSE WHO HAVE THE RESPONSIBILITY FOR PRESERVING THE SYSTEM. . . . I DO NOT BELIEVE THE COMMISSION MEMBERS SHOULD BE TRAPPED BY LEADING PARTISANS WHO SEEK POLITICAL GAIN RATHER THAN SOLUTIONS TO A SERIOUS SOCIAL SECURITY FINANCING PROBLEM. IF THOSE WHO HAVE BEEN DOING ALL THE TALKING HAVE A SOLUTION WE SHOULD HEAR ABOUT IT IN ADVANCE OF ANY FINAL COMMISSION REPORT."

Since Republicans favored benefit cuts, it would be far better to let the Democrats take the first step. It was already clear that tax increases could not solve the short-term crisis. Further, Dole reminded the Democrats that the House would have to produce a reform package if the commission failed. "There is no need and little value for the commission to rush forward in an attempt to reach agreement next week," Dole said. "After all, the House of Representatives has the constitutional obligation to initiate social security financing legislation." Perhaps the responsibility would sober the Democrats into some hard bargaining.

It was just this kind of sparring that led Greenspan to ask that the crucial November meetings be held at the presidential compound at Camp David, in the Catoctin Mountains of western Maryland. Camp David could provide the solitude and atmosphere for a responsible social security dialogue, just as it had for the Egyptian-Israeli summit meeting with President Carter several years before. "If it worked for Anwar Sadat and Menachem Begin," a commissioner said, "it could probably work for Bill Archer and Claude Pepper." There would be no television cameras, no public spectators, only the peace and quiet of the mountains.

There were several problems with the location, however. First, few of the commissioners wanted to spend a long weekend cloistered at Camp David, particularly if the meetings turned into partisan wrangling. A weekend together might strain relations to the breaking point. Second, some of the Democrats wanted the cameras present just in case the Republicans ganged up for deep benefit cuts. Third, the White House social staff wanted to keep Camp David for Ronald Reagan. "If the social security commission could get a few days up there," a White House aide recalled, "then why not the Commission on Private Sector Initiatives? Pretty soon, Camp David would be more of a commission spa than a presidential retreat." Fourth, and most important, Camp David would clearly link the commission to Reagan. Throughout the commission's existence, the White House staff had called it the "Bipartisan Commission" or the "Greenspan Commission," but never the "Reagan Commission." Camp David might tie failure to the President. Without a guarantee of success it was much too great a political risk. The White House said no.

With Camp David out, the commission staff scurried for a new location. Coming so late, the staff could not find facilities in downtown Washington. The meetings would be held at a hotel in Alexandria, Virginia, not far from Washington.

Thursday Morning

Meeting in a windowless hall, facing a phalanx of television cameras, a sea of reporters, and hundreds of spectators, lobbyists, old social security leaders, actuaries, and staffers, the commission finally began discussions. Because the meetings were televised live by the CSPAN cable network, the lights were always on. Some of the commission staffers wore sunglasses.[2]

The first morning was devoted to the size of the social security crisis, particularly in the short term, from 1983 to 1990. The commission looked at a range of estimates, including a special forecast from the Commerce Department. Greenspan had asked for a Commerce model as a way of providing up-to-date estimates for the commission and as a way of checking on the SSA assumptions. Under the intermediate assumptions, Commerce projected a $125 billion social security deficit by 1990. Under the pessimistic assumptions, Commerce foresaw a $228 billion shortfall.[3]

In a surprisingly quick exchange, the commission decided that the short-term problem was somewhere between $150 and $200 billion, a neat compro-

---

[2]The following narrative is based on transcripts of the meetings and personal notes.
[3]It is still not clear why Commerce, not SSA, estimates were used. Some suggested to me that the problem was in the slowness of the SSA forecasting process. Others argued that it was a political issue—that the White House trusted Commerce more than SSA. The answer may never be known.

mise of Commerce forecasts. The $150 billion end gave liberals some defense against deep benefit cuts; the $200 billion end gave conservatives a lever for something more than tax increases. "If I sense the consensus, if there is such a thing," Greenspan told the group, "I would stipulate that we've agreed to the range of $150 to $200." There was no formal vote, only the absence of protest from the two sides. "In the interest of harmony," Moynihan said, "obviously we can live in a $150-to $200-billion problem, but we get there by assuming a very, very unimpressive performance in the 1980s." By his silence, Ball signaled his agreement. As Moynihan later admitted, "There was a point when we thought you might squeeze by, but when unemployment went to 11 percent, there was no point kidding yourself."

Almost as an afterthought to that first compromise, the commission also agreed to a long-term target of 1.8 percent of taxable payroll. In return for a more pessimistic short-term forecast, liberals insisted on a moderate long-term target. Because the Commerce Department did not have a long-term forecasting model, however, the commission had to rely on SSA for the figures.

The targets were major victories for the commission. As one member said, the commission "adopted a yardstick against which people can measure the adequacy of steps to be taken by Congress. It is no longer possible for Congress to do something inadequate and then pretend the problem is solved." In short, the commission had set the congressional agenda. It had defined the size of the problem and had adopted a set of assumptions that would test the final solutions.

Although the commission also agreed on a host of smaller recommendations—to remove social security from the unified federal budget, create a stabilizer in the event of future crises, add two public members to the board of trustees that governs social security, and eliminate windfall benefits for certain beneficiaries—it was unable to reach a compromise on solving the problem. Though it tried mightily in the coming weeks to reach accommodation on a package of alternatives, its primary achievement was in setting the targets for other negotiators. This is not to denigrate the commission's work, for everything in the subsequent legislation flowed from those targets, not to mention the commission's staff work. Rather, the politics of social security reform required even greater protection from the sunshine; if not the old smoke-filled rooms, then at least the opportunity to lay all the cards on the table without public inspection.

Thursday Lunch

With the targets in hand, the two sides returned to their respective caucuses. Trowbridge and Waggoner, the two Reagan Democrats, met with Greenspan and the Republicans, while the five liberals met alone. Both sides had a very simple choice: either put forth a formal proposal or allow the commission to fail. If the members could not reach a compromise, however, they could always forward a list of possible options to Congress. As Dole remarked, "We'd send the list to Congress and say, 'Happy New Year!'"

When both sides finally met for a late lunch that Thursday, Heinz made a simple proposal: Why not split the short-term solution half-and-half between benefit cuts and tax increases? As part of the deal, each side would get to decide just what kind of pain it wanted. Republicans would have to come up with about $100 billion of self-inflicted tax increases, while Democrats would have to agree on $100 billion in self-inflicted benefit cuts. It was more of a guiding principle than a formal solution. Though commission moderates found some merit in the idea, it was rejected by both sets of ideologues. The liberals felt they could do better than just 50–50, while the conservatives refused to move on any tax increases.

Though Heinz failed, he did establish the basic operating rule for comparing the social security solutions: each proposal would be classified as a tax increase or benefit cut, then totaled up into percentages from each side. The rule held up throughout the year and became a handy tool for attacking or defending the various reform packages.

Friday

There was one last chance for an agreement the next day, when Democrats offered the first of two major reform proposals. This first package would have advanced the 1990 tax increase to 1984 ($132 billion); increased the tax on self-employed workers ($18 billion); covered all nonprofit employees ($7 billion); covered all newly hired state and local employees, despite the constitutional issues ($13 billion); covered all new federal employees and those with less than five years of service ($21 billion)—coming to a grand total of $198 billion in the short term. For the long term, the package would have raised taxes in the year 2020 by a full 1 percent, while reducing benefits by 5 percent. The package was 100 percent tax increases in the short term, but it did cover federal employees. It was 80 percent taxes in the long term, but it did contain a benefit cut.

In presenting this first package, however, the Democrats asked the President to sign *first*. Only then would they go to Speaker O'Neill. "They put the burden on us to sell it to the President," one White House aide said, "but there wasn't enough there to satisfy our own people on the commission." Because they did not want to go out on a limb alone, the Democrats needed a signal from the White House. The negotiations recessed while both sides scrambled to check with the two principals.

Even though the proposals were supposed to be secret, they quickly leaked. The two major aging groups, the American Association of Retired Persons and the National Council of Senior Citizens, both held press conferences to denounce the long-term benefit cuts. Federal employees were also fast to act, pouncing on Kirkland. He had tentatively agreed to coverage for federal workers (or at least had not opposed it); now he faced intense, well-organized opposition within his own union. Business groups were also ready, armed with statistics on how many jobs the tax increases would cost.

The speed with which the groups mobilized was surprising, and it gave all of the commissioners pause about the secrecy of their negotiations and the inevitable opposition. Apparently, merely having Ball and Pepper was not enough to silence the American Association or the National Council; having Kirkland was not enough to calm the federal employees. "To think that a package might sit out there for three or four months before Congress could act was frightening," one commissioner said. "They would pick it to shreds. Just talking about some of those options was enough to get them mad."

Saturday Morning

In a last-ditch effort to reach some kind of compromise, liberals presented their second proposal on Saturday morning. They added a three-month COLA delay ($25 billion) and dropped state and local coverage because of constitutional uncertainties. The package would still cover all new federal employees and those with less than five years of service and was worth almost $210 billion. It was now 88 percent revenues and 12 percent benefit cuts in the short term. Though still a long distance from the 50–50 split, it was a move in the Republican direction. And it had the Speaker's approval.

By late Saturday morning, however, it was clear that the commission could not agree. For the liberals, this was their last, best offer. "This wasn't a starting point," a liberal staffer said. "We couldn't use it as a basis for further agreement. You have to realize what a concession the package was. It had federal coverage despite Kirkland and the AFL-CIO; it had a three-month COLA cut despite Pepper; and it had a long-term cut in replacement rates despite Ball." For the conservatives, the liberal proposal was a step toward a possible compromise. But as a final agreement, it was not enough.

And the White House was not interested. Greenspan could not get through to the President and had to relay the idea to chief of staff James Baker. When Baker finally called back, the answer was no. Baker had concluded that the offer was too heavy on taxes.

Moreover, though the Speaker had signed off on the liberal proposal, Rostenkowski and Pickle had not. In fact, just the day before, on November 13, Rostenkowski had sent a letter to the 435 members of the new House warning them against making any commitments on social security. "The Committee on Ways and Means has the job of drafting a legislative response to this looming crisis," he wrote. "I urge you to 'keep your powder dry' until we can analyze and bring into perspective options presented by the commission and others." Promising to hold hearings on a package February 1, 1983, "with the intention of bringing a balanced bill to the floor of the House in late March," Rostenkowski argued that "we must weigh the effects of large payroll tax increases on a work force already staggering under the highest unemployment rates since the Depression." Concluding that "the political choices are up to us," Rostenkowski's letter seemed to promise a more conservative bill from the normal legislative process.

Rostenkowski's letter also seemed calculated to stop further commission movement. Even though it was addressed to House members, copies were sent to all of the commissioners. Why would either side move with the Ways and Means chairman so obviously opposed to action? Any agreement would simply twist in the wind until February. Remarkably, liberal Democrats soon realized that they might get a better deal from the commission than from their own House committee. "It began to look like we would do far better with a five-member minority in the commission than a 290-member majority in the House," a commission staffer said. "Rostenkowski would not accept the kinds of tax increases we were talking about."

When it became clear that Reagan would not sign the package without further compromises, the liberals gave up. When it became clear that Rostenkowski had no intention of allowing lame-duck action on social security, the conservatives also backed off. "We didn't want our agreements to go into Danny Rostenkowski's hip pocket," a Republican commissioner said. And without any legislative action until February, every interest group in Washington would have three months to pick the compromise apart. The only way to pass a package of painful solutions would be to move quickly through the interest group waters, before the groups could organize their attacks. Three months was much too long to wait.

LOOKING BACK

Ultimately, the National Commission effort at compromise was doomed to failure by the Speaker and the President. All the problems might have been easily resolved by the two principals. As Heinz later wrote, "Only a compromise package sanctioned by a 'summit meeting' between the president and Speaker O'Neill and their key lieutenants will enable all members of Congress, new and old, to get on board. Without this political umbrella, many members of both parties will be obligated to oppose many of the financing options that must, of necessity, appear in a comprehensive proposal." The commission could be a shield for negotiations, but only if Reagan and O'Neill agreed to meet.

Neither would move. O'Neill refused to call Reagan. He had 26 new Democrats en route to Washington for the Ninety-eighth Congress in January, a tough new Rules Committee chairman named Pepper who opposed any benefit cuts, a Ways and Means Committee that wanted a piece of the action, and a Democratic party that wanted revenge for the 1981 Reagan budget and tax cuts. If the commission failed to produce a compromise, the initiative would return to the House. At least in November, O'Neill was willing to gamble that his party could produce a rescue bill. It was Reagan's commission; let him move first.

Yet Reagan refused to call O'Neill. His MX missile plan would be the top priority in the lame-duck Congress, not social security. Further, according to the White House staff, Reagan was not interested in another summit with O'Neill, not after the Gang of Seventeen. Nor was he interested in social security. "Reagan had to be engaged in all this somehow," a staffer said. "Up to November, he was still talking about voluntary social security as an option. We had to wean him from the idea and bring him into the real world. But that takes time. He had no interest in November."

Even the White House staff was not up to speed on social security. "We hadn't met on social security for months," a White House aide said. "Somebody might have discovered that we were talking about it and used it in the campaigns. Everybody was still thinking about it, but only in their separate worlds." According to Dole, the White House had been "frightened to death about social security," leaving the issue to a very hungry Democratic party.

Whatever the reason, Reagan was not going to move. "I don't care how much they ask for it," he said, "for me to impose myself on the commission and say, hey, fellows this is the way I want you to go, I would then stand back, cock my ear and wait for the loud outcry from Capitol Hill and the same old political football would be seen going up in the air like a punt on third down." Though he never explained why any football team would punt on "third down," he did not want a repeat of the May 1981 disaster.

Ultimately, it was Reagan's move. Without his support, the National Commission collapsed. When O'Neill signaled his agreement to the liberal package, Reagan had to respond. His unwillingness to answer left the ten-member majority without any guidance. Whereas Ball spoke for O'Neill, Reagan never delegated any authority to Greenspan, or any other Republican for that matter. "The ball is in Reagan's court," a commissioner said that Saturday morning. "He's got to pick up the phone and call Tip. If he doesn't do anything, this issue is going to blow up next spring." Though the Republican commissioners continued to pressure the White House for some help, the President remained silent.

The fact that the commission even called for help from Reagan and O'Neill showed the depth of the stalemate. It also showed the basic problem with commissions as a form of government: they have no magic to solve tough issues that the principals do not want solved. Merely appointing a group of experts, giving them a year of intensive study, setting a deadline for a report, and providing some basic encouragement could not guarantee a solution. The National Commission had succeeded in delaying the key social security decisions until after the 1982 elections, the basic political goal. It had also succeeded in defining the size of the problem, a testament to the members.

THE LAST GASP

The National Commission held one more formal meeting December 10. It lasted only fifteen minutes. It was clear that the commission was stuck, that no agreement could emerge from the majority. Moreover, with the Ninety-eighth Congress quickly approaching, the liberals were already backing down from their initial proposals. They were willing to start all over in January. As Greenspan gaveled the commission to a close, the National Commission was all but dead. It might still act as a cover for other negotiations, but it would not be able to act on its own. "I see no purpose in maintaining commission deliberations beyond a point where we can be productive," he said. A Republican commissioner agreed: "The failure to report any bipartisan package of remedies should be a warning sign to both President Reagan and Speaker O'Neill. The political problems in reaching agreement are far worse than the congressional leadership or the president now realize."

After the meeting, the majority gathered for a last caucus. A White House representative asked if they saw any chance for an agreement. The answer was no, not even among themselves. With the commission set to expire on December 31, only a funeral seemed to remain.

15

The Flight of the Phoenix

With the collapse of the National Commission, lame-duck action on social security seemed impossible. Conable's gamble in the 1981 minimum benefit conference had failed.

Coming at the end of a two-year Congress, the lame-duck session had once offered an opportunity to make tough choices. As the furthest point from the next election, "a lame-duck session is the time of lowest political sensitivity," Conable noted. "The departing cannot be called to account, and those who are returning will have a full two years of insulation before they have to face the electorate again. Holiday good cheer leads the pols to think they can do pretty much what they want." The 1982 lame-duck Congress would include 81 House members who had been defeated or were retiring, "with nothing better to do than bite bullets on social security." They had little to lose by voting for deep benefit cuts or massive tax increases.

The problem with the lame-duck session would be time. Since Congress would adjourn by the end of the year, a handful of senators could block action on virtually any issue. As long as they could stall, they could win. "You're uniquely at the mercy of a few people who want to obstruct," Senate Majority Leader Baker concluded. Further, the President would have only so much time to lobby and would have to concentrate on a small list of priorities. In 1982, Reagan had the MX missile and a gasoline tax increase to worry about, leaving no time for social security.

TO THE EDGE

Nevertheless, those who pushed for lame-duck action understood one basic rule of social security reform: it would only get harder as the July 1983 deadline approached. The potential for stalemate could only increase. Indeed, Conable's crisis was quickly becoming a double-edged sword. It forced Congress and the President to confront the coming crisis, but it also increased the potential for stalemate. In the Senate, individual members could demand a higher price for their votes; threats of filibusters would take on added significance. In the House, social security could only "be a very tough vote for our new members to cut their teeth on," a representative said. "No one can blame an eager candidate for making promises, but it is difficult to change one's tune so soon after a first election." In both chambers, social security would inevitably get tangled up in the 1982 budget process. Headlines about the coming bankruptcy would only heighten the public panic. As Conable continued to warn, "It's long been my theory that if you are raising the suspicion that what you are doing to social security is designed to reduce the deficit, well, you might as well forget it."

Yet the White House remained quiet through December. "Social security has become a buzzword like busing and abortion were in the late 1960s and early 1970s," a staffer said. "It's so hot there is no right side to take in that fight. I don't think we can educate people on the issues. If we had the best solution in the world, you know what would happen the minute we put it out: we'd get burned again."

But if not in the lame-duck session, when? If not in Congress, where? "Social security is not under control as a political issue," one Republican wrote the President in mid-December, "and you must address it, regardless of other priorities facing us. It is safe to say that no other issue affected us so much in the past election or is fraught with so much political peril for the future. The issue must be addressed on the highest level now or the crisis of next spring will be another political disaster."

A CHRISTMAS PACKAGE?

As the White House surveyed the political landscape in December 1982, there were a number of incentives for trying to rescue something, anything, from the commission before the Ninety-eighth Congress convened in January.

First, the President's 1983 budget was already in trouble. Having failed to gain an agreement in 1982, he faced an even tougher fight in 1983. The budget deficits were climbing beyond $200 billion a year, and all pretense of a balanced budget was gone. It was clear that Reagan would have to consider some tax increases along with spending cuts. In the midst of the spreading panic over the deficits, social security emerged again as a solution.

Second, Reagan's approval ratings were still falling, and not just on social security. In a December 1982 Gallup poll, 50 percent of those surveyed disapproved of Reagan's overall handling of his job; only 41 percent approved. That was lower than the figure for any previous President at that point in the term. Jimmy Carter was at 51 percent approval after two years, Richard Nixon at 52 percent, John Kennedy at 76 percent, and Dwight Eisenhower at 69 percent.

Moreover, the media were increasingly critical. *The New York Times* said, "The stench of failure hangs over Ronald Reagan's White House," while the *Washington Post* heralded the "phasing out of Reaganism." Even the friendly *Wall Street Journal* warned that "the situation is steadily deteriorating and can now be salvaged only by dramatic action."

As the White House struggled late in the year, however, there was some evidence that the National Commission was still breathing. Reagan had extended the life of the commission by 15 days, to January 15, 1983, and proposals for solving the social security shortfall were circulating among some of the members. Most of the activity came from Alexander Trowbridge, one of Reagan's two Democratic appointees. As a conservative, Trowbridge felt at ease with Republicans; as a Democrat, he had some access to liberals. In all, Trowbridge offered eight successive packages. He would talk to Ball, make a few changes, then talk to Dole or Conable and make a few more. It was an informal process, with no final agreements. To his credit, Trowbridge kept some semblance of negotiation alive. Though there was no consensus for a final proposal, the Trowbridge plans were all moving in the right direction: toward that ideal 50–50 package.

What mattered most throughout this process was the percentage split between tax increases and benefit cuts. Neither side cared too much about the specific proposals as long as the percentages were breaking toward a compromise. The question was always how to sell the final package on Capitol Hill, and that meant an image of fairness as measured by sacrifices on both sides. Though none of the plans ever hit the 50–50 mark, there was steady improvement over time. In the short term, which was of primary concern to a budget-conscious White House, the splits moved from zero benefit cuts and 100 percent taxes in the very first liberal proposal in November down to 46 percent benefits and 54 percent taxes in the fifth Trowbridge package. The long-term proposals also showed similar improvement, particularly by using increases in the retirement age. According to Robert Myers, the final Trowbridge proposal actually contained two different alternatives, "one of which had $79 billion of additional taxes in 1983–89, but an ultimate retirement age of 66, and the other of which had $64 billion of additional taxes in 1983–89, and an ultimate retirement age of 67. Further, the COLA delay for 6 months (included in only one of the two alternatives—the other being a phased 9-month delay) produced $46 billion in 1983–89. . . ."[1]

Under fire on the budget and in the opinion polls, the White House took the Trowbridge plans as sure signs of movement and assumed that the liberals had signed off on each successive package. In fact, the liberals had never approved any of the Trowbridge proposals.

That did not stop Stockman from meeting with the President a week or so before Christmas. "The first step was to get the President's agreement that we ought to proceed," one of the participants said. "At the start, you really have to work with him on the political realities. He starts out with grand schemes. If he

[1] Personal correspondence to the author.

were king, we would have done something very different. The trick was to remind him that he wasn't king, only President." Stockman's agenda was short: (1) Would the final Trowbridge plan be acceptable? and (2) Should the White House initiate secret negotiations with the commission? Reagan answered yes to both.

In essence, Reagan had signed off on a plan containing billions in higher social security taxes, a COLA delay of either six or nine months, coverage of all federal employees, a retirement age increase of one or two years, and a new method of calculating the COLA. The details would have to be ironed out later, but the basic message was clear: the White House staff could make the first move toward compromise.

It was a classic Reagan decision. "He has a remarkable sense of what the best deal is," one aide argued. "He'll stonewall until he's sure he's got a good compromise. It'll look like he's set in concrete, but he knows when it's time to move."

THE GANG OF NINE

With the President finally engaged, the first question was how to get the Democrats to the negotiating table. Once again, the answer was the National Commission. Only this time, it would not be the real game. It would merely be a front, a cover for a secret gang composed of White House aides and a handful of the original commissioners. The second question was whom to invite. Pepper was too hot; Kirkland too committed on union issues; Archer too pure; Armstrong too inflexible. The White House finally decided that it had to start with the Democrats, and that Moynihan and Ball were the only ones with enough clout to make an agreement stick and enough room to maneuver.

There were personal reasons to invite Moynihan and Ball, as well. Stockman knew Moynihan from their days at Harvard University in the early 1970s. Stockman had been a divinity student at the time and had even baby-sat for the Moynihan kids. Darman knew Ball from their days at Health, Education, and Welfare under Nixon; Darman had been an assistant secretary and had worked with Ball on social security.[2]

With their personal relationships as an entrée, Stockman and Darman journeyed to Capitol Hill only days before Christmas. The first order of business was to get Moynihan and Ball to join the negotiating process. "Once you start negotiations like that, the press will find out," one of the four remarked. "If you fail, somebody will get blamed. You don't start talking without some commitment to success." The White House also needed a promise of absolute confidentiality. No one was to know that the first calls came from the White House. Since the President had repeatedly promised not to interfere with the commission, these early contacts had to be kept secret,

---

[2]The following narrative is based on memoranda to and from Conable, my personal notes, and confidential interviews with most of the key participants.

even from other commissioners. "We began a minuet to make sure the initial calls came from Moynihan and Ball," one White House staffer said. "So we told Greenspan to tell them that we would be very interested to receive a telephone call at such-and-such a time on such-and-such a date. That's how it all started."

According to the participants, Darman and Ball met only once. In the course of the three-hour discussion on Capitol Hill, Ball informed Darman that the final Trowbridge plan was still a great distance from a possible compromise and that the Democrats would need several major concessions to accept even a three-month COLA delay. It was very bad news. Without the Trowbridge plans as the starting point, the White House would be at a disadvantage. Further, Ball told Darman that the labor unions would have to have help selling any social security tax increases, preferably some kind of income tax credit. Finally, Ball said that the second liberal November package was no longer on the negotiating table. The bargaining would have to start with the first liberal plan, containing 100 percent taxes in the short term. There was a long distance to go.

In contrast, Stockman and Moynihan met often, but on a very different agenda. Avoiding specifics, they focused on the need for a spirit of compromise. They even met for a drink on Christmas Eve to muse about social security and the collapse of the American system. "They just talked about the kinds of problems we'd all face if we didn't do something about the problem," one White House aide reported. "They kept talking about the breakdown of government institutions, increased public cynicism, those kinds of things. It was all part of the conditioning that had to be involved in the bargaining. We all had to believe that the negotiations were important for something more than immediate political gain. We had to believe."

Yet Moynihan had a problem. He had to hide White House involvement in the talks. If his Democratic colleagues ever found out that Stockman had started this latest round of negotiation, any package would face quick defeat. He had to get Dole involved as soon as possible, while keeping Stockman's role quiet. In short, Moynihan needed to rewrite history. As he later explained in a *Washington Post* column, the crucial meetings now took place on January 3 in the Senate, not weeks before in the White House. "The commission was just about resigned to failure," Moynihan said, when he tapped Dole on the shoulder during Senate swearing-in ceremonies. "Are we going to let this commission die without one more try?" Moynihan asked. Dole could not say no. Moynihan, of course, had been involved in secret talks for at least two weeks by then. However, by changing history after the fact, Moynihan helped protect the final compromise from partisan attack, while sharing both the credit and the blame with the Republicans.

A Gang Is Born

Whether Dole knew about the earlier discussions or not, he met with Greenspan and Moynihan on January 4 to set the terms for secret talks. It was clear these talks would have to be held to a very small group. Once again, Armstrong, Archer, and Pepper could not be invited. They would only get in the way. Ball would attend as the Speaker's man on social security; Conable as the sole Republican from the House. Beyond these five (Ball, Conable, Dole, Greenspan, and Moynihan), no other members of the National Commission would be invited. "The group had the least interest in being pure," one said. "All of us were experienced negotiators, pragmatic. It would have been very hard for Pepper to participate. Armstrong and Archer were ruled out right away as too pure, and the Republican business types had too much organizational pressure, too. What we had left were five people who knew how to bargain." The five commissioners joined four White House staffers: Stockman, Baker, Darman, and Duberstein. All four were veterans of the Gang of Seventeen, as were Conable and Dole. But this was now the Gang of Nine.

Like the Gang of Seventeen, this new gang would operate in secrecy, with no records or transcripts. Everything would be off the record and in absolute confidence. Like the Gang of Seventeen, the new gang would have only two votes: one for Reagan and one for O'Neill. "Only two people really mattered," one participant said: "Ball and Stockman. They represented the Speaker and the President. . . . Most of the negotiations eventually involved just those two representatives, sitting across from each other at the table." But this group would be much smaller than the Gang of Seventeen, limited to a handful of key players.

The gang first met on Wednesday, January 5, 1983, at Baker's home on Foxhall Road. "Most of us were pretty familiar with the furnishings by that point," a gang member said. "We had been there off and on for the budget talks, parties, and such. No one had to tell us where the bathrooms were." The White House did not push for a formal package at the beginning. "They didn't want specifics," one said. "Just proportions; a 50–50 deal. It would be up to Congress to fill in the blanks. And the key would be how you classified each piece of the bill, as benefits or taxes."

As in November, Ball and Moynihan opposed the 50–50 idea. "Suppose Congress took the proportions and tried to draft a bill," one said. "The battle would be over how you labeled this provision or that provision. Nothing would be resolved." Further, the Democrats could do better than 50–50. After all, the White House was desperate for an agreement.

In rejecting a 50–50 split, Ball offered his own proposal: a three-month permanent COLA delay, coupled with a 4 percent COLA cap in 1983 and 1984, and three separate tax increases between 1984 and 1990. Each increase would come with a corresponding income tax credit for employees but not employers. Because inflation was already down to the 4 percent level in 1983, however, Ball's COLA cap would not save much.

Group Dynamics

After an hour of what one member called "excursions, alarms and counter-alarms, and philosophical ponderings," the first meeting adjourned. White House limos returned for a second meeting at four o'clock. The negotiations quickly settled into a pattern of give and take between Stockman and Ball.

"Every hour," a member said, "Baker would announce that he could not guarantee the President's support. And one of the Democrats would say they could not guarantee the Speaker's support. It was a ritual. The Republicans would say, 'You have to give us something we can take to the President,' and the Democrats would say, 'You have to give us something we can take to Claude Pepper.'" More important, neither side wanted to be the first to *refuse*. Every time one side offered a proposal, the other came back with a counterproposal. It was a good sign.

The Gang of Nine met again on Friday, January 7, and on Saturday, January 8. The gang took time out for the Washington Redskins–Detroit Lions football play-off Saturday afternoon. "There were natural small-group dynamics involved in all of the meetings," a White House participant said. "The Skins–Lions game was an important diversion and helped cool us off. There was already an almost self-fulfilling drive for an agreement. Things like the football game helped us reestablish our commitment after we had some pretty serious fights. We were able to get together and root for the home team."

There were also games with the media. Though the secret meetings were quickly discovered, the discussions never leaked. "This is a very open town," Conable said at the time. "Everyone knows about the meetings and wants to find out who said what. We're going to hold the meetings in different locations, try to confuse the press, and hope that nothing slips out. It's fun in a way, relieves the tension. We all like to play cops-and-robbers." Because the group was smaller, there was more secrecy. Because none of the members was allowed to bring any staff, there were fewer players who knew what was going on.

Throughout the negotiations, Stockman and Ball took the lead. The other White House representatives were noticeably quiet, as were Conable, Dole, and Moynihan. The three legislators did not want to reveal their positions before a final agreement was almost certain, and Stockman was the White House expert. Duberstein's major role, for example, was to keep Rostenkowski posted on the negotiations, giving the Ways and Means Committee chairman some occasional input.

Greenspan was not particularly active, either. "He's really a very shy man," a gang member recalled, "and not used to hard bargaining. He was great when it came time to define the problem. People trusted his judgment, and thought he was fair. But when it came time for some hardball politics, he wasn't cut out for it. Who did he represent? Stockman was the President's man. In that kind of bargaining, you've got to be a trader. You have to go eyeball to eyeball with your opponent. There's no room for talking about the ideal world, just what can be sold to the principals."

For Stockman, the Gang of Nine represented a new opportunity for social security cuts. Though he had been silenced on Capitol Hill, he had found a new forum for social security reform, far from the madding crowd. Ball also reveled in his new chance for impact. This was exactly the kind of negotiation that favored his technical expertise. "There they sat," one participant said, "the two numbers men, throwing statistics around, debating the basic formulas. It was up to them to sift through the technical bull, and up to us to make the political decisions."

Despite all the camaraderie, a shared sense of mission, and a Redskins victory in the play-offs, there were still serious differences over the substance of an agreement.

MORE POLITICS OF ASSUMPTIONS

The first hurdle in building a compromise agreement involved another fight over the economic assumptions. In defining the social security problem back in November 1982, the National Commission had used Commerce Department assumptions to set a $150 to $200 billion short-term target, but SSA assumptions to fix a 1.8 percent of taxable payroll long-term target. However, it was clear by January that the economy was improving faster than had been predicted only three months before. Inflation was coming down fast.

Though inflation did not affect the long-term target, it was critical in the short term. Stockman was especially concerned about the new figures. Warning Republican gang members that the short-term discussion was "clouded by *massively incongruent* assumptions and data sets," Stockman concluded that COLA options "produce radically different results depending on economic assumptions." A COLA delay would look much larger under a pessimistic inflation forecast than under a more realistic outlook. Ball's three-month COLA delay, for example, would save $36 billion under the pessimistic forecast but only $15 billion under Stockman's new inflation figures.

If Democrats were allowed to use the old figures, a 50–50 split would involve a much smaller COLA cut. Because tax revenues did not change much under different economic assumptions, small adjustments in the inflation forecast could produce large returns. It was in Stockman's interest to use more optimistic assumptions in debating the various *solutions* before the Gang of Nine, even though he had used pessimistic, even worst-case, figures in defining the size of the *problems* in 1981 and 1982. In contrast, it was in Ball's interest to use pessimistic assumptions in projecting the savings from COLA cuts, even though he had used optimistic assumptions in debating the targets. The debate over the numbers was still on.

As Stockman knew, the economic assumptions were an important source of power for the White House. If Ball and the Democrats did not agree to his new set, Stockman openly threatened to rig a much more pessimistic forecast when the official SSA figures came out in February. "Because we controlled those forecasts," a White House aide said, "we could inflate the estimates to make the problem look much, much larger. Even liberal Democrats would have to face up to a long-term problem in the 3 or 4 percent of taxable payroll range. Either they were going to take a more reasonable inflation figure, or we'd hit them with a very pessimistic forecast later. There are hundreds of little variables that can be manipulated. They would have to advocate some very large tax increases to cover the problem on their own, and they weren't willing to do it." This is not to argue that the SSA actuaries would have acquiesced to such manipulation without a fight. The actuaries had plenty of resources to resist such efforts to distort the integrity of their forecasts, not the least of which was Moynihan.

Nevertheless, by threatening a new battle over assumptions, and the exhaustive, even arcane, debate that would go with it, Stockman may have persuaded the Democrats to accept a more moderate—and, it turns out, a more accurate—inflation assumption. "Only by defining the problem as manageable," Moynihan later said, "can you manage it." After considerable discussion, the Democrats finally accepted the new forecast. There was no denying the improvement on inflation, particularly for 1983 and 1984. "Everyone is entitled to their own opinions," Moynihan also said, "but not to their own facts."

Stockman's memo also reminded Republicans that some options were better than others for cutting budget deficits. Because the government would have to match its employees' social security contributions, coverage of federal workers would generate $26 billion for the trust fund, but only $12 billion in budget savings. Stockman was still looking to social security as a device for trimming the budget deficit, and he even delayed the printing of the 1983 budget until the Gang of Nine finished its work. That way, Stockman could show the savings in his new budget report.

Ganging Up

With a new set of economic assumptions, the gang moved forward with the negotiations through the weekend of January 8 and 9. "It was an incremental process," a participant noted. "There were no major breakthroughs, just a bunch of small agreements that added up to a major package." Indeed, according to Conable, "It's impossible to tell who blinked first. The negotiations were back and forth for two weeks." It was clear by Saturday, January 8, that Republicans were willing to accept some tax increases while Democrats were willing to take some COLA cuts. The major question was, how much?

Saturday also brought a guest: Armstrong. Arriving from a Christmas vacation back home in Colorado, Armstrong confronted Dole in the Senate halls on Saturday morning and demanded a role in the gang. Recall that Armstrong had been deliberately excluded from the negotiations. Yet Dole had little choice but to bring Armstrong. Though Dole was angered by the breach of courtesy, he offered his subcommittee chairman a ride to the meetings anyway. Thus, the Gang of Nine briefly expanded to ten.

Yet as if to confirm the decision to exclude him, Armstrong immediately broke the gang's vow of silence. Appearing on TV the very next morning, Armstrong leaked Saturday's work and vowed "to contact groups like the National Federation of Independent Business, the Chamber of Commerce, the American Association of Retired Persons, the AFL-CIO, and put this proposition to them: If you are going to help me head off a massive tax increase . . . then now is the time to start cranking up the troops and getting cards and letters into congressmen and senators, because that is what is in prospect if something doesn't happen." Armstrong's broadside jeopardized the ongoing negotiations and cost him any influence inside the Gang of Nine. Though he still attended the meetings, Dole and Conable kept him away from the bargaining table. The gang broke into even smaller negotiating groups. Sometimes, Ball and Stockman would slip into another room, while the rest of the gang diverted Armstrong's attention. Other times, Ball and Stockman would meet outside of the normal gang. Thus the old Gang of Nine continued its work, albeit hampered by Armstrong's presence.

If Armstrong's presence was not enough to stymie the negotiations, the Democratic National Committee had mailed another fund-raising letter in late December. The letter finally reached the Republicans just as the Gang of Nine turned the corner toward an agreement. The letter, mailed to 3 million people, announced that Republicans "HAVE ALWAYS FOUGHT SOCIAL SECURITY" and concluded that "IT IS SIMPLY TOO DANGEROUS TO LEAVE THE FATE OF SOCIAL SECURITY IN THE HANDS OF THE REPUBLICAN SPECIAL INTERESTS WHO REALLY DON'T SUPPORT IT." The letter was not particularly successful, barely covering its production costs. Dole called it a "partisan potshot," while Conable warned Rostenkowski that "this type of letter makes it difficult for me to make an appeal to the sense of responsibility of my members." Yet in some ways, the letter helped restore balance in the Gang of Nine after Armstrong's broadside. It was an eye for an eye.

Taxing Work

By Friday the 14th, the group had completed a week of tough bargaining, most of it now at Blair House. They had discussed dozens of options for the short and long term and had agreed to a six-month permanent COLA delay ($40 billion in 1983–1989)—moving the annual benefit increase from July back to January—and a payroll tax acceleration in two roughly equal parts ($40 billion). At least on these items, the Gang of Nine had reached a 50–50 split. The group had also agreed on coverage of new federal employees and all nonprofit employees not already covered ($20 billion), an increase in self-employment tax rates ($18 billion), and an accounting maneuver involving payment of the military wage credits ($18 billion, of which $1.6 billion was for lost or uncashed checks). Democrats had finally agreed to coverage of federal employees, but only for new hires after December 31, 1984; Republicans had finally agreed to tax acceleration, but only in two equal pieces, one in 1984 and the other in 1988. The package also included about $1.4 billion in new benefits for women and recommended immediate removal of social security from the unified federal budget. The budget committees would finally lose any input on social security. The fact that they had been excluded from the National Commission and the Gang of Nine took its toll. It was a glaring defeat for Domenici.

Though the list of concessions was impressive, the package was still short, adding up to $140 billion in the near term and less than half the target in the long term. The gang needed more money, but neither side would agree to higher taxes or deeper benefit cuts. "The principle of equality was very important to the White House," one of the Democrats said, "but if we had gone to a strict 50–50 split, we would have needed $80 billion in benefit cuts. That was simply not acceptable to us. The key was to go *outside* either pure taxes or benefits, and find some new area of agreement."

The answer came from *taxation of benefits,* a combination of both options. By subjecting half of all social security benefits to the income tax, but only at upper-income levels, the gang could raise $27 billion in the short term and one-third of the target in the long term. Because the threshold amounts ($25,000 for a single beneficiary, $32,000 for a couple) in the taxation of benefits proposal were intentionally not indexed to rise steadily with inflation, upper-income beneficiaries would not be the only ones to come under its effects. Depending on the rate of inflation over coming decades, middle-income beneficiaries and even some lower-income beneficiaries would someday see their benefits taxed.

The idea had originated with Ball, long an advocate of the idea. He had won the Speaker's support back in November and had talked with most of the commission members about the proposal. Though the Senate had rejected the notion twice in 1981, it did raise a great deal of money. Ongoing taxation of benefits would generate huge savings in the next century. More important, it was all things to all people. Consider the label: taxation of benefits. Was it a tax increase or a benefit cut? In fact, it was both. "It could be called taxes or benefits, depending on which ax you wanted to grind," a White House participant said. "It was a tax increase to Democrats, but a benefit cut to Republicans." In reality, it was a deep benefit cut for upper-income retirees, achieved through the income tax.

Though taxation of benefits was an attractive option, there were two problems. One question was how to define the proposal. Though it was all things to all people, the group had to decide how to split it up. "The minute it would be announced, people would take out their calculators," a participant recalled. "Everyone would try to figure out who was getting the short end. We had to answer those questions first." Eventually, the gang decided to call taxation of benefits a 50–50 proposal: half a benefit cut, half a tax increase. The other question was how to protect both sides from blame. All of the participants knew the proposal would cause a firestorm of controversy when it finally went into effect in 1985. "Nobody wanted to take credit for that baby," a member said. "It's too hot. You cannot trace the authorship." Even though the concept came from Ball, it was disguised so that no one could be blamed later.

Taxation of benefits was not the only example of artful labeling as the gang moved forward. Tax increases were called "tax acceleration"; COLA cuts were called "permanent delays." These labels helped both sides swallow proposals they had once considered unacceptable. The labels also took advantage of public opinion. Perhaps the public would not understand what was happening to their program. It was a way to disguise the pain, a way to help the public accept cuts. If there was a lesson here for other dedistributive policies, it was to confuse, not educate.

Neither Reagan nor O'Neill was directly involved throughout these discussions. They were kept posted on the progress of the negotiations but did not sign off on the proposals. Both were waiting to see if the gang produced a final agreement. Only then would they make the final decisions. Moreover, neither had the substantive expertise to become involved in the detailed bargaining. Stockman and Ball were the only participants who knew enough about the specifics of the social security program to make the trades. By keeping their distance, both Reagan and O'Neill could easily disown the Gang of Nine if it failed. Unlike the case of the Gang of Seventeen, there would be no summit meeting between the President and Speaker to make the final bargains. Those would have to be in place *before* the two principals gave their consent.

Sticking Points

With taxation of benefits penciled in by midweek, the negotiations moved quickly forward. As one White House aide said, "That was the breakthrough, if there was one. Once we broke through with that, everything else was easy. That put us at around $160 to $170 billion, and that's all we needed in the short term." All that remained were three basic questions, all resolved Friday night and Saturday morning.

First, would the Democrats get some kind of tax relief for workers? The answer was yes. That was Kirkland's price for AFL-CIO support. Though he was not part of the gang, he made his position clear: without a credit on the payroll tax increases, he would not endorse the final commission package. He was quite willing to fight it out in Congress. Kirkland had initially demanded credits on any and all payroll tax increases, but he gave in when Republicans offered him a "one-time-only" credit on the 1984 boost. Conservatives continued to oppose the idea as hidden use of general treasury revenues, but Kirkland's support was essential. At least for 1984, workers would pay 6.7 percent into social security, while employers would jump to 7.0 percent.

Second, would the Republicans get some kind of social security stabilizer? After all, they had made it an issue in the formal commission and needed some concessions of their own to sell the package to the President. Again the answer was yes. Republicans had originally wanted a new COLA formula based on the lesser of wages or prices only triggered in when social reserves fell too low. That kind of COLA would give social security some protection against poor economic performance. Republicans wanted the stabilizer to take effect immediately, whereas Democrats wanted to wait. Ball and Moynihan were willing to accept the general notion of a stabilizer, but only some distance into the future, hopefully when it would never be needed.

By early Saturday, the gang had solved this impasse, too. Republicans would get their stabilizer starting in 1988. However, even though such a stabilizer might save large sums of money under pessimistic economic assumptions, it never had a price tag in the secret negotiations. Perhaps Democrats did not want to acknowledge just how much money it would raise if the worst-case outlook came true; perhaps the Republicans did not want the public to know either.

Third, would the gang be able to reach an agreement on the final one-third of the long-term solution? The answer was no. Even with taxation of benefits, the package would hit only about two-thirds of the long-term total, or 1.2 percent of the 1.8 percent of taxable payroll needed. The gang simply could not agree on the final piece. Republicans wanted an increase in the retirement age, whereas Democrats wanted another tax increase. The final choice would have to be left to Congress. It was too late to work through the conflict, but not enough to scuttle the entire package. "Besides," as one member concluded, "Danny Rostenkowski would need something to do anyway."

Closing In

By midday Saturday, the Gang of Nine had a package worth $168 billion and 1.2 percent of taxable payroll. Defining taxation of benefits as a half-and-half proposition and the military wage credits as a tax increase, the package was split into 32 percent benefits and 68 percent taxes in the short term, but 27 percent benefits and 39 percent taxes in the long term, with 33 percent still open for debate. Republicans had managed to hold down the short-term tax increases, but only through taxation of benefits and military wage credits, not through benefit cuts. Yet if Republicans could pass a retirement age increase in Congress, the long-term splits would improve significantly. Filling in the last one-third with retirement age, they would win a 60–40 split.

Compared with the Trowbridge plan that Reagan had accepted in December, the Gang of Nine package had more tax increases and less benefit cuts. But compared with the liberal proposals that Republicans had rejected in November, it had less tax increases and more benefit cuts. In addition, when compared with any of the preceding plans, the Gang of Nine package was the most complex. The first liberal package, for example, had only seven pieces. The final compromise package had seventeen, reflecting a conscious effort to build a more complicated legislative proposal. It would confuse the public and help cancel out interest group opposition.

The final question, of course, was whether the package would work in either the short or long term. The answer was that it would have to work; the gang had gone as far as it could. Even with the stabilizer on the COLA, the Gang of Nine knew it would be tight. Had the negotiators still been using the old economic forecasts, which assumed higher inflation, the proposal would have generated $185 billion in savings and revenues, right on the mark. Though there would be an immediate infusion of money in 1983, particularly from the $18 billion military wage credits, there would still be three lean years from 1985 to 1987 as the social security system waited for the next tax acceleration, due at the start of 1988. Like the Carter 1977 package, the new package was backloaded. Much of the money came later. Nevertheless, neither side would accept a fail-safe provision to protect the program against emergencies: Democrats would not accept automatic benefits cuts, and Republicans refused automatic tax increases or the use of general revenues.

The final package, as published by the National Commission, is summarized in Table 8. Interestingly, the summary had its own version of the "magic

TABLE 8. Major Provisions of the Bipartisan Social Security Package, January 1983

Proposal	Short Term (billions)	Long Term (percent of payroll)
Cover all nonprofit and new federal employees	$20	.30%
Prohibit withdrawal of state and local employees	3	—
Taxation of benefits for upper-income retirees	30	.60
Six-month COLA delay	40	.27
Tax acceleration	40	.02
Self-employment tax increase	18	.19
Lump-sum military wage credits	18	—
Additional long-run savings	—	.58
Benefit sweeteners (additional cost)	(1.4)	(.17)
TOTAL	$168	1.80%

Source: Report of the National Commission on Social Security Reform, January 20, 1983.

asterisk," this time labeled as "Additional long-run savings." The final one-third of the long-term deficit would be left to Congress but was still included in the report along with a footnote describing the two obvious solutions: (1) retirement age increases or (2) taxes.

Saturday Afternoon

After taking the package to O'Neill and Reagan for their signatures, the gang would have to return to the commission. After all, the National Commission had provided the cover for the secret bargaining. A strong commission vote would give the package a bipartisan flavor. With only hours left before its January 15 deadline, the full commission would be called together for the final blessing. It would be the first time the commission had gathered since December 10. "We wanted at least an 11–4 vote," a gang member said. "It had to look like the commission was in agreement." The major stumbling blocks to the majority were Pepper and the business representatives; Archer and Armstrong were already counted out.

Pepper would be the first to move. Having opposed even a three-month COLA delay, he would be asked to accept six months. Nevertheless, he would vote yes. Perhaps Pepper saw the compromise as the best he could get. Perhaps he was concerned about getting a bill out of the more conservative Ways and Means Committee. Perhaps he did not fully grasp the impact of the COLA delay on future benefits, believing it to be a one-time six-month delay with a return to the old July 1 date the next year.

The business representatives would be next. Meeting Armstrong and Archer on Friday the 14th, they expressed serious reservations about both the size of the increases and the employee tax credits. Why should employees get a tax credit when employers did not? Conservatives were also outraged by the amount of general treasury funds involved in the package, particularly the $18 billion in military wage credits and the tax credits for workers. Armstrong and Archer were hoping to hold all four business representatives against the compromise, leaving a majority of nine to six in favor.

The gang had answered some of the concerns with the one-time-only tax credit, but the business opposition remained solid until Saturday afternoon. "That's when the White House started work on them," a Gang of Nine member said. "You should have seen it. Fuller, Beck, and Trowbridge all got calls from the President. It was tremendous pressure. I'll never forget the look on Mary Fuller's face after she got her call. She was as white as a sheet and told us that she was going to support the package." Waggoner, however, was unmovable and would join Archer and Armstrong in dissent.

There were still several calls to make as darkness fell on Washington. As Greenspan said, "The last thing was the tricky problem of getting everybody within an hour's time to all agree to this document, all contingent on everyone else's agreement. What we had going is that the President would agree if the Speaker would agree, if the commission would agree." Around four o'clock, the call went to O'Neill. He was in Palm Springs, California, playing golf with Rostenkowski in the Bob Hope Desert Classic tournament. It was still early in the day, and they were on the course. The Gang of Nine marked time watching the Redskins beat the Vikings 21–7 and waited for the return calls. Meanwhile, Stockman and Baker walked across Pennsylvania Avenue to talk with Reagan.

Despite Rostenkowski's reluctance, O'Neill finally agreed to the package early in the evening. Reagan also signed off. In the span of not more than twenty minutes, the two principals agreed, the commission debated the package, and the final vote was held. The compromise passed twelve to three, with Archer, Armstrong, and Waggoner opposed. "It was pretty tense right up to the end," Conable said. "We would meet for two or three hours, then go consult with our principals or interest groups. It is impossible to say who blinked first." Despite the hard work, there was no celebration at the end. "We were concerned that cheers would break it apart," one commissioner remembered.

The minute the Gang of Nine proposal passed, it became the National Commission agreement. It would be labeled as such throughout the congressional debate. "I didn't want to vote for the package," members of Congress would be able to say, "but the National Commission made me do it." The commission label would provide a shield against public outcry and a way to explain a painful vote back home. The package would be sold as the product of a year-long bipartisan study, not two weeks of secret negotiations.

The President and Speaker began selling the compromise immediately. Reagan said he believed "the American people will welcome this demonstration of bipartisan cooperation in offering a solution that can keep a fundamental trust," while O'Neill promised to place the agreement "at the top of the agenda of the new Congress." In short order, the House majority and minority leaders also issued statements of support. Those statements would also protect members of Congress back home and provided a way to transfer the blame up the line to the party leaders. "I didn't want to do it," members would be able to explain, "but the party made me do it."

Mutual Fear

There were a number of explanations for the agreement, but most boiled down to one simple word: FEAR. Both sides were equally worried about what the other could and could not do.

The White House, for example, was worried about the budget, the 1984 elections, Claude Pepper, an increasingly rebellious right wing, and the Speaker. The package solved many of the problems. Upon greeting reporters immediately after the final commission vote, Baker said, "This is certainly not consistent with the idea of a presidency in disarray. It shows the President dealing with one of his major problems and doing so in a bipartisan way. He could have washed his hands of this and left it to Congress. Instead, he demonstrated leadership and political courage." The social security compromise also set a precedent on the budget: all federal programs, including defense, would get a COLA freeze. Stockman had finally won a defense cut. "When the compromise was adopted," the secretary of defense admitted, "it meant that other government programs would have the same rule applied to them."

The White House also worried about Congress. What if O'Neill could pass a bill on his own, a bill containing tax increases and general revenues? Would the Senate follow suit, ducking the issue and forcing a presidential veto? Though some White House aides believed they could have gotten a more conservative bill from Ways and Means, it would have carried a very high political price. "We knew the negotiations were heading toward a more liberal package," a presidential aide said, "but finally decided that the risks of waiting for Ways and Means, and scuttling the commission in the process, were too great. We could have gotten something better, yes, but it would have been very, very hard."

Finally, if Reagan had even the slightest intention of running for reelection, he had to get the issue resolved quickly. It was, according to one aide, "his cross to bear, and it was time to move on." According to Conable, "Baker caught me on the way out of the Saturday meeting and said, 'This will be great for the President, won't it?' And I said, 'Absolutely not. It's a terrible package. He's going to take a lot of political hits on this. But it's a lot better than what he would've had if he'd left it up to the House.' It's not a great package, but it's a lot better than it could have been."

The Speaker, in contrast, was worried about the President, his fragmented Democratic party, Pepper versus Rostenkowski, the Senate, and the future of social security. Whereas the White House worried about a possible Democratic bill, O'Neill worried about a possible stalemate. "Forget Pickle and Pepper, forget the differences on ideology, forget their personal dislike, it would still be hard to get the House to agree on any single set of solutions," one Democratic representative said. "Any number of solutions could have been put together, but none would pass."

For starters, social security was hurting the Democratic party, too. "The voters do not want a legislative stalemate," one pollster told the Speaker.

"Voters blame the current economic problems on past Democratic policies rather than current ones. The Democrats cannot return to the programs of the '60s." In short, the social security issue was played out. It was time to find another reason to vote Democratic.

Moreover, despite Reagan's repeated mistakes on the issue, there was a fear that the President just might succeed with a veto strategy on social security. Even if the House could pass a bill, it was not clear that the Democrats would come out ahead by confronting the White House. "The feeling in 1981 was 'Let the Republicans hang themselves on the issue,'" a leadership aide remarked, "but the Democrats knew that the public would turn against both parties if nothing was done."

The Speaker also understood the potential for conflict between Pepper and the Ways and Means Committee. Pepper, Rostenkowski, and Pickle would all want a say on any legislation. O'Neill simply did not want to choose between them. In all likelihood, Ways and Means would have produced a more conservative bill than the Gang of Nine. Rostenkowski had already talked to the White House about his ideas in early January, and they did *not* include any tax credits—not even one-time only. Moreover, Pickle's subcommittee had already shown what it would do with social security: retirement age increases and deeper benefit cuts. O'Neill knew that a House compromise would be very difficult indeed, producing a bitter contest between liberals and moderates within his own party.

The Speaker also cared about the program. He openly worried about public confidence. This was FDR's program, not some small domestic issue. "It was going beyond politics," one of O'Neill's aides said. "It was a damn good issue in 1982, helped bring in 26 new Democrats, but it was getting to the point where something had to be done. I think the Speaker honestly felt that the problem needed to be solved."

Thus the White House worried that the Speaker could pass a bill, while the Speaker worried that he could not. It was a case of mutual fear and uncertainty. Yet both sides also believed they had won a good compromise in the National Commission. Reagan was persuaded that the package was the best he could do. As governor of California, he had often shown an almost complete unwillingness to compromise at first, only to go for the best he could get later on. As President, he was showing the same bargaining strategy on social security, waiting until the last moment to move. Though the package contained clear violations of long-standing Reagan principles—tax credits, tax increases, general revenues—he understood that it was far better than a long battle in the House.

O'Neill was also persuaded that the package was a very good deal, and he was clearly right. In exchange for a six-month COLA delay, Democrats had won a number of extremely valuable precedents. The tax credit was one-time only and the general revenues were small; but both would set the stage for future action. With inflation running under 4 percent in 1983, the six-month COLA delay would not hurt much. The precedents were worth much more than the Democrats had paid in cuts. In short, the party would have to give up a major political issue but received a very good package in return. Moreover, the package would move through the House of Representatives first, allowing some tampering. Perhaps the Democrats could back off on federal employees a bit; perhaps they could fix the COLA ever so slightly.

CONCLUSION

Washington seemed to sigh in relief Saturday night. The social security crisis was almost over. On Sunday morning, for example, Daniel Schorr, a reporter with the Cable News Network, asked Greenspan whether he agreed that "this may be one of the great, positive things that's happened to the political and economic life in this country?" To his credit, Greenspan answered, "Let's look at it a week from today."

The agreement also carried resounding endorsement of the social security program. Benefits would be lower for future generations—particularly because of higher taxes and a new retirement age—but the basic system had survived again. Even Archer and Armstrong supported that one provision. In one of the few unanimous votes on the commission, the members recommended that Congress "not alter the fundamental structure of the Social Security program or undermine its fundamental principles." Radical reform was off the agenda.

The January euphoria created its share of myths about the National Commission. At times, the myths were promoted by members of the commission itself to protect the compromise. Suddenly, this once-lifeless commission was resurrected as a great bipartisan success. In reality, the commission had succeeded mainly as a front for secret bargains. After setting the targets in November—no small accomplishment indeed—it had turned back the clock on Congress, providing some shade from the sunshine. By giving the leaders a chance to lead, by putting politics back into politics, the commission had provided the political cover needed for compromise.

Still, the social security compromise needed every political advantage it could get as it entered Congress. By wrapping the agreement in the National Commission flag, supporters hoped it would survive the interest group onslaught. As the product of a bipartisan commission, the compromise would have a better chance. The social security battle was far from over that January 15.

16

A Legislative House of Cards

Everyone would be hurt by the compromise. It was a package of shared pain. Thirty-six million retirees would lose an average of $120 from the COLA delay; another 3 million would pay an average of $700 each year under taxation of benefits; thousands of future federal employees would be forced into social security; 9 million self-employed workers would pay an average $500 increase in taxes each year; and 110 million other workers would pay an extra $200 in 1988 and 1989. If income taxes were raised to cover lost federal revenues from the one-time-only tax credit, all taxpayers would end up paying. Even the President and Congress carried a share of the pain. As federal employees, they were finally forced into the social security program. Even the Social Security Administration was forced to join.

THE STRATEGY

The compromise having touched almost everyone, the question was how to sell the agreement to Congress. "This so-called compromise is a very fragile one," a lobbyist for the elderly warned. "If any one component is knocked out, it will fall like a house of cards." Indeed, the agreement faced intense opposition from several huge interest groups, including the postal workers, retired federal employees, the American Association of Retired Persons, the National Federation of Independent Business, and the self-employed. "We have no choice but to oppose it flatly and with all the resources we have," vowed the 14-million-member American Association.

And the general public was not particularly enthusiastic about the package. It still opposed the tax increases and benefit cuts and was confused by the complicated package. Further, new economic assumptions in early February suggested that the agreement might not be enough to solve the short-term problem. Without additional savings, the social security system might not make it through 1985.

Thus as the package started its journey through Congress, there was no guarantee of success. "The longer it gets poked at," one commission member concluded, "the more likely it is to become unraveled, and we'll have a generational war, with young people refusing to support the fundraising system." Moreover, as Conable noted, "any change in the basic balance threatens the whole package. Grumblement is to be expected, but failure is to be feared." Unfortunately, the National Commission package had left one-third of the long-term problem open for debate. Congress would have to do something.

Facing these obstacles to passage, supporters developed a three-pronged battle plan. First, the package had to move as fast as possible. The longer it waited, the greater the opportunity for interest group action. Here, supporters hoped to win passage before the Easter recess. Because members of Congress would be anxious to leave for home, there would be a flurry of activity just before the vacation. Perhaps social security would slip through—forced up against a recess deadline, Congress might act. Second, the package had to be kept clean. Anytime a bill is headed for automatic passage, it attracts other issues. "We are already hearing on both sides of the Capitol that the compromise will move forward without a hitch," Conable warned in late January, "and that, therefore, it becomes an appropriate vehicle for bearing additional freight." Third, the package had to be sold as an all-or-nothing proposition. There could be technical changes but no major additions or subtractions. "I wanted to amend the package," members of Congress would be able to say, "but it would have destroyed the compromise." Again, members would be able to mute some of the criticism back home.

Even with the President, the Speaker, the majority leaders, and the National Commission solidly in support, it would be a very tough fight in both chambers. Pepper remained a question mark in the House. What would he do if the House passed a retirement age increase alongside the COLA delay? Armstrong remained a question mark in the Senate. He had agreed not to filibuster against the agreement, but he was ready with a wide range of amendments. And what if the bill became a hostage in some other battle having absolutely nothing to do with social security?

THE HOWLING

True to his November promise, Rostenkowski scheduled Ways and Means Committee hearings for February 1. Neither the public nor the interest groups would have very much time to decide whether they supported or opposed the package, and they would have even less time to organize a counterattack. The interest groups were particularly unhappy about the tight legislative schedule. With only two weeks to draft their testimony, most groups waited to see how Congress would react. If the package was destined for failure, the groups would attack, taking credit for the defeat. If the package was destined for success, the groups would hold back, reserving their influence for other battles.

The Public

Congress, of course, waited to see how the public would react. "When the President and the Speaker agree," Armstrong said, "they usually get their way—but not always. We have not yet heard from Middle America. If they howl loud enough, there is some chance of amending the package."

Yet the public did not howl. Though Congress received mail on social security, it was drowned out by other issues, particularly the nuclear freeze and something called withholding on interest and dividends. Of the two issues, interest withholding was hotter at the beginning of the new year. Withholding had passed in 1982 as a way to make sure people reported their savings interest on their income taxes. Banks would be forced to withhold a portion of each customer's savings interest for the Internal Revenue Service, in the same way that employers withhold a portion of their employees' wages. Because the new procedures would cost time and money, the banking industry mounted a massive campaign to win repeal. Some banks even provided their customers with stamped preaddressed postcards to Congress. The mail simply over-whelmed all other issues, including social security, and led most members of Congress to look for ways to reduce the heat back home. The public was certainly howling, but not about social security.

Nevertheless, the public opinion polls did not show much support for the individual pieces of the agreement. The public supported coverage of federal employees and the self-employment tax increase, but over half still opposed the three major funding options: taxation of benefits, a six-month COLA delay, and tax acceleration. Without these critical pieces, of course, the package would fall far short of the needed targets.

On most questions, there was little difference among age groups. However, opposition to the COLA delay was strongest among the young, perhaps reflecting their very negative image of aging. Sixty-one percent of people under 30 opposed the COLA delay, compared with 49 percent of the near-retired and 57 percent of the retired. Apparently, the near-retired were somewhat more willing to accept a benefit cut in return for promised solvency. The younger groups were also more opposed to the tax increases and the taxation of benefits. Surprisingly, even though people over 65 were clearly affected by taxation of benefits, half supported the idea, while another 10 percent were not sure.

Despite the opposition on separate items, the public seemed to favor the overall package. When asked by the Harris poll whether they favored or opposed "Congress passing this new legislation on social security as recommended by the special commission," 48 percent of the respondents were in favor of passage, 37 percent were opposed, and 15 percent were not sure. Though the question wording pushed respondents to favor passage, if only because the legislation came from "the special commission," there was very little howling here, either. Wrapping the agreement in the National Commission flag seemed to be working. Moreover, there was some advantage in the level of confusion over the package. Most of the young, more educated groups were willing to give an opinion one way or the other on the package; only 8 percent of people under 30 were not sure how they felt about it. However, 26 percent of the retired said they were not sure whether they favored or opposed the agreement. Many did not know what taxation of benefits would mean or how the COLA delay would reduce their benefits.

Despite lukewarm support for passage, the agreement did not appear to reduce public fears about the future. When asked in 1981 whether they believed "the social security system will have the money available to provide the benefits you expect for your retirement," only 30 percent of the respondents in a CBS News/*New York Times* survey said yes. When asked again in mid-January 1983, only days after the celebrated National Commission agreement, just 27 percent of the respondents said yes. Confidence was even lower! Whether those fears would abate soon was unclear. Confidence had taken only a few years to fall but might take decades to rebuild. Certainly, Congress would have to finish the work on the long-term problem to have any hope of restoring confidence among young workers.

Finally, the public did not give Reagan much credit for the package. Approval of his handling of social security improved only slightly after the National Commission report. Just before the compromise, 75 percent of the public gave Reagan a negative rating on social security; by February, the rating had fallen to 73 percent; by March, to 72 percent; by April, to 68 percent. The total improvement was but 7 percent. That was when the pollsters finally stopped asking the question, turning to other issues to fill their questionnaires.

The FAIR View

As the interest groups and Congress read the opinion polls, they found little guidance for their own decisions. The public remained opposed to the key funding options, frightened about the future, angry toward the President, but increasingly confused about the issues. In deciding whether to oppose the package, the gray lobbies had to ask whether the public could tolerate another two years of social security politics, particularly given the growing number of elderly who were baffled by the basic arguments. The business lobbies had to ask whether they could afford a battle in Congress, even if they could win.

Interest group support and opposition were particularly important to conservatives. "The question is how strongly outside groups will weigh in," Armstrong said. "If they weigh in powerfully, then we've got a horse race and a chance to make significant improvement. If they don't, then I think it is a relatively small number of members of Congress who are going to fight that battle."

Federal employees decided first. They opposed one of the few items that Armstrong strongly favored. Regardless of high public support for coverage of federal workers, the Fund for Assuring an Independent Retirement (FAIR) was ready to fight the package as soon as it was announced on January 15. A loose coalition of 6 million current and retired federal employees, FAIR opted for a media campaign against the package, budgeting $500,000 for television and radio spots.

FAIR's reasons were clear. First, federal workers were worried about the survival of their own civil service retirement program. If all new employees were covered by social security, there would be fewer workers to support civil service retirement. "No one will be paying into it if younger workers are taken out," one lobbyist concluded. Second, the federal unions were in business to protect their employees, not to save the social security system. Some of the groups expressed little concern about what would happen if they succeeded in defeating the compromise package. Third, federal employees were under attack on a number of fronts beyond social security. The Reagan administration had proposed a pay freeze, a hiring freeze, reduced retirement benefits, a higher retirement age, and new rules on promotions and firings. Social security seemed to be just one more part of a broad assault on federal workers by a hostile White House.

Whether FAIR's complaints were accurate—and the evidence suggests that some were unfounded—its strategy was simple. Federal employees wanted a separate floor vote on the issue. As the lifeblood of congressional incumbency and reelection, the unions had considerable support among individual members of Congress. Federal workers deliver benefit checks, solve constituent problems, implement legislation, and generally make life easier for members of Congress. If the employees could force a separate vote, they just might win. One radio spot summarized the issue as follows:

VERY SHORTLY CONGRESS WILL CONSIDER A BILL TO PROP UP SOCIAL SECURITY.
(SOUND OF A TRAIN PULLING OUT)
AMONG OTHER FEATURES, THE BILL WOULD RAISE TAXES, REDUCE FUTURE BENEFITS, AND FORCE MILLIONS OF NEW WORKERS INTO THE SYSTEM AT A COST OF BILLIONS TO ALL TAXPAYERS.
(SOUND OF A TRAIN GATHERING SPEED)
THE ALARMING PART OF ALL THIS IS THAT CONGRESSIONAL LEADERS PLAN TO RAILROAD THIS BILL INTO LAW BY REQUIRING LEGISLATORS TO VOTE SIMPLY YES OR NO ON THE ENTIRE PACKAGE WITHOUT REGARD TO THE MERITS OF EACH PART. THIS IS CONTRARY TO THE VERY TRADITIONS OF OUR DEMOCRACY, AND A POOR WAY TO BUILD PUBLIC POLICY. IS THIS RIGHT?
(SOUND OF A TRAIN STOPPING SUDDENLY)
JOIN US IN CONTACTING OUR REPRESENTATIVES TODAY. AN OPEN RULE GIVES EACH REPRESENTATIVE AN OPPORTUNITY TO TAKE A STAND ON EACH CRITICAL ELEMENT OF THE BILL AND IT WILL SIDETRACK ANY ATTEMPT TO RAILROAD A PACKAGE PAST THE AMERICAN PEOPLE.

Because the House had stronger rules on debate, the strategy was tailor-made for the Senate. Indeed, FAIR concentrated most of its fire on the upper chamber.

A Marriage of Convenience

With the federal employees already out front against the package, attention turned to the business and aging groups. Would they join the attack?

The answer from most business lobbies was no. With Trowbridge and Beck already on board, the National Association of Manufacturers and the Business Roundtable would follow suit. Further, the Chamber of Commerce was still confused on payroll taxes. The White House asked the business groups to toe the line on social security, and most did. All except the National Federation of Independent Business. The federation, representing small business, saw the agreement as "like putting a nail in the coffin" of their constituents, already beset by a recession. The National Federation was on its own but hoped some elderly groups might join.

The answer from most aging lobbies was also no. With Ball so clearly linked to SOS and the National Council of Senior Citizens, it would have been difficult to repudiate his leadership. Besides, it was a very good package. The COLA delay was a small price to pay for so many precedents. "We wouldn't look to unravel the compromise for that alone," a National Council lobbyist said. The aging groups would still fight the COLA cuts in public, but they had already signed off in private. "We have to give our people a chance to be heard," one lobbyist said. "We have to be able to represent our constituents on this one, but we'll be on board." The aging groups also knew there were few other alternatives for saving social security. Because they could not come up with a consensus position of their own, they eventually offered a lukewarm endorsement of the compromise package. The groups also knew it would be hard to defeat the package, and most groups went along. All except the American Association of Retired Persons.

The American Association opposed the agreement for three basic reasons. First, the organization believed that the benefit cuts and tax increases were too severe, concluding that the package was a "lousy agreement," as one staffer said. Because its membership included more upper-income retirees than the National Council, the American Association was solidly opposed to taxation of benefits. Here was one provision that would clearly hurt its membership. Second, looking at public opinion among its 14 million members, the organization could find little evidence of support. Once again, its large size created problems. Opposition was easier. Third, the group also saw opposition as a chance to set itself apart from the other elderly groups. It was an opportunity to lead, not follow.

The American Association was on its own. One SOS leader was particularly critical of the association's decision: "They've made a mistake by going out so hard against this package. They've thrown in with the conservative groups and have hurt their reputation. They've always been criticized for being too conservative, and this proves it. And they're going to get hurt because they're not offering any alternatives. They're against everything but don't have any proposals that make sense." Indeed, the association's list of options included a bizarre assortment of ideas: excise taxes on alcohol and tobacco, repeal of oil and gas loopholes, a windfall profits tax on natural gas—all of the money to be earmarked for social security. On Capitol Hill, the ideas were rejected out of hand. Congress did not want a major tax reform bill, too.

It was out of this isolation that a remarkable interest group marriage was made. The giant American Association joined with the smaller National Federation of Independent Business to stop the social security agreement. Finding no mates within their own interest communities, the two groups pooled their resources on Capitol Hill.

For a short time, the marriage was strong. Members of Congress shuddered at the thought of such a powerful alliance generating mail back home. However, as the legislative process moved forward, the American Association–National Federation alliance was under increasing pressure to draft its own alternative, to "put up or shut up" in the words of one House Democrat. But it was almost impossible to find a position that would satisfy both groups. The National Federation wanted to remove "welfare" from social security, while the American Association wanted new taxes. Eventually, the alliance came up with its own proposal for a vast infusion of general treasury funds, exactly the option that Armstrong and the congressional conservatives found most distasteful.

Thus as long as the two groups focused on opposition, their marriage was strong; once the two groups turned to serious counterproposals, the alliance was broken. Though the groups continued to struggle against the package into March, the alliance was a victim of pressure to say something more than no. In short, the two groups were defeated both by their own rivals within the interest group community and by their inability to draft a passable package.

In the end, the National Commission's package of shared pain canceled out most of the interest group opposition. Business groups were unhappy with the payroll tax increases but knew they could have been higher; aging groups were unhappy with the COLA cuts but knew they could have been deeper. With a compromise in hand, members of Congress finally demanded that the interest groups stop their attacks. Liberal groups liked the package anyway, while business groups knew they could not win on the floor. Moreover, congressional leaders made it clear that this bill had to pass. A desperate fight against the package might end up costing much more future influence than it was worth.

Now the question was how to convert the compromise package into legislative reality. That job would start in the House, the origin of all new revenue legislation.

THE HOUSE

There were four basic steps in building a social security bill in the House: (1) full Ways and Means Committee hearings, (2) Social Security Subcommittee hearings, (3) subcommittee markup, and (4) full committee markup. Only then could a bill move to the House floor for passage.

Even before the hearings began, the House confronted another controversy.

On Tuesday, January 25, House Majority Leader Wright asked Reagan to give up the third year of his tax cut in return for passage of the social security bill. "It would be grossly unfair and enormously unjust to require these sacrifices of the old," Wright said, "and not exact any sacrifice at all from the wealthiest." Senate Minority Leader Byrd also demanded some linkage between the two issues, telling reporters, "I certainly don't want a six-month delay in social security while leaving in place the third year of the tax cut." Such linkage would, of course, earn an immediate presidential veto. Within hours of the statements, however, O'Neill and Moynihan had persuaded their Democratic colleagues to drop the idea. "To reopen the negotiations at this time couldn't be done," Moynihan warned. "It's a bipartisan agreement and has to stand on its own."

Gaining Speed

With the brief storm over, Rostenkowski announced his intentions to pass a bill in the House by the first week of March, move to a conference with the Senate by mid-March, and push for final enactment before the Easter recess began on March 25. It would be a record-setting pace, beginning at nine o'clock on Tuesday, February 1, with full Ways and Means Committee hearings. The hearings would last several days and were clearly not designed to discover new ideas on social security reform. Rather, the full and subcommittee hearings would be used to develop momentum for the package—what one staffer called "Big Mo"—while giving the interest groups a chance to vent their frustrations on the record. Friendly witnesses would be scheduled early, hostile witnesses late.

   Thus the full committee hearings started with testimony from the National Commission on Social Security Reform. With the television cameras on, Greenspan endorsed the package, then answered questions from the committee. The following exchange between Commission Chairman Greenspan and Representative Conable, a Ways and Means member, was typical of the friendly testimony:

CONABLE: Is there any part of this, Mr. Greenspan, that you think could be taken out and the compromise still preserve its essential outline?

GREENSPAN: I am certain that if you press me for every single line and word, I might suggest that it is possible, but on anything substantive, anything which resembles a critical element in this negotiation, I would say no. We struggled very hard.

CONABLE: In your long-standing capacity as an economist associated with the government in various ways, have you made any effort to estimate what might happen if this agreement fails?

GREENSPAN: In the event that somehow or by some means Congress fails to resolve this question . . . I am most fearful that the international financial markets would take this as a terribly negative signal, that our domestic markets would perceive it as a verification of their already deep-seated view that the Federal budget is out of control, that it will create a reign of inflationary forces, and that . . . would push long-term interest rates up from where they are, would abort a nascent recovery and I think create problems for this Nation which I have very great difficulty even contemplating.

Such dire predictions were designed to help members of Congress explain the difficult legislation back home. "I had to vote for the bill," members would be able to say, "because of what would have happened if I didn't."

Despite the importance of social security, attendance at both the full and subcommittee hearings was poor. Indeed, at the start of the full committee meetings, only 22 out of 35 Ways and Means members were present, a level of participation that steadily dropped as the parade of witnesses continued. By the second day, only 6 were present for the opening gavel. Members wandered in and out on occasion; but most understood that the important decisions had already been made by the National Commission or would be made in private negotiations between party leaders and the social security experts. Nevertheless, the hearings produced almost 1,300 pages of testimony, giving the interest groups their one chance to show support or opposition.

The Subcommittee Markup

With the hearings over, the markups began on Tuesday, February 22. A markup is a simple process for building legislation. Committees and subcommittees start with a proposal and "mark it up" with whatever changes they might want. Once the finished product is printed as a bill, it moves up the line.

On social security, the subcommittee markup involved translation of the National Commission package into legislative language. Rostenkowski had wanted Pickle to take a first crack at a bill, both to protect the full committee from conflict and to respect the normal process. Having waited two years to build a rescue bill, Pickle deserved his chance. Contrary to usual practice, however, neither the full committee nor the subcommittee had a formal bill to work on. No one had introduced the commission package as a separate piece of legislation. Nothing would be printed until the full committee made its final decisions. "There can't be a formal bill at this point," a minority staffer said at the time. "We need a working document, but we can't have any bills floating around. They'll just become targets. It's better to write a committee bill *after* we've made the agreements, instead of forcing a choice between two or three bills at the start." (In the Senate, however, Dole and Moynihan introduced formal legislation, titled "A Bill to implement the consensus recommendations of the National Commission on Social Security Reform." The bill was given the coveted number S. 1, making it the symbolic first priority on the Senate agenda.)

As in most other legislative markups, the Social Security Subcommittee would start with a document comparing the current law with proposed changes. The subcommittee could then vote on each section, proposal by proposal. Clearly, in order to write that markup document, a number of decisions had to be made. Someone had to decide just what the proposals would be, what the subcommittee would and would not consider. In this case, it was the Democratic majority and its staff. Because the Republicans were led by Archer, who had already announced his absolute opposition to any compromise, few expected the package to pass unanimously, and fewer still expected the Republicans to be consulted at the subcommittee level.

Most of the decisions were made long before the markup began. Though the subcommittee made a variety of technical changes, the bulk of the commission recommendations passed easily, including a new social security stabilizer based on the lesser of wage or price increases whenever the system got into trouble. The only major changes involved the one-time-only tax credit and removal of social security from the unified budget. In the National Commission package, workers would have paid higher social security taxes in 1984 and applied for the one-time credit on their 1985 income tax returns. In the subcommittee package, workers would never see the tax increase at all. Instead, the Treasury would simply pretend that the higher taxes had been paid, forward the money to the trust fund, and thereby avoid needless paperwork and a 1984 election-year tax boost. Workers would pay a 6.7 percent tax, but the Treasury would act as if they had paid 7.0. Employers, in contrast, would get no credit.

On the unified-budget issue, the subcommittee decided to ignore the National Commission recommendation. Under pressure from the House Budget Committee and its chairman, James Jones, the subcommittee left social security in the budget. It would still be subject to annual debate and the temptations of budget directors. Jones had persuaded the subcommittee that such a large program could not be left out of the unified budget, that there had to be some truth in budgeting. Hiding $140 billion in spending from the public would not protect social security from future trouble, either. This was not a victory for Domenici but a gesture to the hardworking House Budget Committee.

Throughout the markup, Archer offered one amendment after another, some to show opposition to the package and some to improve the bill. One of his amendments would have covered all federal workers with less than fifteen years of service (rejected 9–1); others would have removed taxation of benefits from the bill (rejected 8–3), given employers a one-time-only tax credit (rejected 7–4), reduced the self-employment increase (rejected 7–4), and reformed the social security benefit formula (rejected 7–4).

A Slight Delay

Despite the machine-gun pace, two disputes threatened the package. The first involved Pickle's effort to provide a social security fail-safe, some way to protect the program against the worst that could happen. Pickle's proposal combined three devices: (1) interfund borrowing, (2) an accounting game called "normalized" tax transfers, and (3) general revenue loans. According to the markup document, under that third option social security would be permitted to "borrow, for a limited period, from the general fund." Though the subcommittee agreed to interfund borrowing and normalization, there was a Republican outcry on general revenues. It was too much. Unless the Democrats changed that item, there would be no Republican support at the full committee or on the floor. Yet the proposal still found its way into the full committee markup document—never passing the subcommittee, never failing, just never coming up for a vote. It would be up to the full committee to strip it out.

The second dispute involved the remaining one-third of the long-term deficit, willed to Congress by the commission. Archer offered three different long-term plans, each involving deep benefit cuts. All were easily defeated. Pickle had long favored a jump in the retirement age, but the question was how to slip it past Pepper and the Rules Committee. Pepper had announced his opposition in the full committee hearings two weeks before, promising never to let it reach the floor for a vote. Yet Pepper's own option, a tax increase in the year 2015, had no committee support, producing a serious stalemate. Eventually, Rostenkowski and O'Neill worked out a compromise: Pickle and Pepper would be allowed to offer their respective solutions on the House floor. Each would get a fair shot at the bill. The only restriction was that each would have to offer a pure version of their amendment. Pickle could not blend a retirement age increase with something more attractive; Pepper could not mix a tax increase with benefit sweeteners. The two amendments would have to offer very clear choices.

The social security bill was now finished at the subcommittee level, containing almost $170 billion in the short term and a temporary patch on the final one-third in the long term. With the Republicans still angry about the fail-safe, the subcommittee sent the bill to the full committee on a 7–4 vote.

To Committee

Though the Social Security Subcommittee did most of the work on the rescue bill, two other Ways and Means subcommittees were also involved. The Public Assistance and Unemployment Compensation Subcommittee added a routine extension of emergency jobless aid, and the Health Subcommittee added a major reform of the Medicare program.

The Medicare reforms changed the way hospitals would be paid. In the past, hospitals had been paid on a *retrospective* basis, submitting bills only after the patients had been treated and released. All charges were automatically paid as long as they did not exceed a generous definition of reasonable cost. Under the reforms, hospitals would be paid on a *prospective* basis, receiving clear advance notice of how much they could expect for each kind of illness. That way, hospitals would have some incentive to hold down costs. This dramatic reform was added onto the social security package with almost no debate or controversy. It was a perfect example of insider legislation, surprising most of the interest groups; it would have been a difficult fight on its own but had a free ride on the social security bill.

   With the major pieces of the bill ready, the full committee began its final markup on Wednesday, March 2, still well ahead of Rostenkowski's schedule. There was little conflict as the committee began reading through each section of the bill. Though Democrats offered an amendment to strike coverage of federal employees from the bill, it was easily defeated on a voice vote. It was more a gesture of sympathy to federal workers than a serious effort to delete the item. Because it was a voice vote, every member of the committee could claim a vote for or against the amendment as needed. Indeed, one of the Democrats even joked that the committee needed an especially loud "no" vote from the Republicans. When one of the conservative Republicans joked back that there ought to be a recorded vote, with each member clearly identified on the issue, the laughter stopped. Such a recorded vote would force the Democrats to oppose the federal employees in the open. They could do it on a voice vote, but not on the record. The full committee also decided to reverse its subcommittee's decision on the unified budget. Social security would be pulled out of the budget, but only starting in 1988.

   The only major fight came after almost an hour of steady voice votes supporting the subcommittee. Republicans could not accept the general revenue fail-safe. Though acknowledging the need for some kind of fail-safe, they vowed to vote against the full package on that single provision. Conable and his Republicans gambled that Rostenkowski wanted a large committee majority badly enough to give on this one item, and they were right. Whereas the subcommittee bill contained explicit authority to borrow from the general fund, the full committee bill simply required the President to notify Congress whenever trust fund reserves fell too low. That was the fail-safe, nothing more than a simple report. "It was a contract to make a contract," one Republican said. "It was no fail-safe at all, just mumbo jumbo."

   Nevertheless, Rostenkowski wanted a large committee vote for the bill. That would help him win on the floor. The Ways and Means Committee vote would be a cue for other members, a show of strength. "It was the way the powerful chairmen used to work," one member said. "They would get as many votes on a bill in committee so they could go to the floor as strong as possible. No one would dare challenge the committee if all of the members had voted for the bill." Like the leaders of old, Rostenkowski hoped to steamroll the House.

   The final committee vote came just as the Democratic party launched its last fund-raising letter. Coming right before the full committee markup, the letter first congratulated the National Commission, then warned: "THE REAL TEST—THE BIG TEST—IS STILL AHEAD. DEMOCRATIC PARTY MUST NOW, MORE THAN EVER, CONTINUE MASSIVE EFFORT TO DEFEND AGAINST DRASTIC CUTBACKS. THE RECOMMENDATIONS SO FAR ARE NOT—REPEAT NOT—BINDING. TO HAVE REAL AND LASTING EFFECT, CONGRESS MUST STILL PASS SOCIAL SECURITY LEGISLATION." The letters had come full circle. After attacking Reagan's May proposals, opposing the National Commission, and criticizing any benefits cuts, the letters now supported the compromise legislation. Republicans had to ignore the attacks in the hopes of resolving the issue once and for all.

In the end, Rostenkowski's coalition building worked. On the final roll call for passage, 32 of his members voted aye, and only 3 voted nay. It was a surprising majority and would be difficult to break on the floor. "Everybody is so concerned about the future of social security that they're willing to do things to solve the problem that they ordinarily wouldn't do," a Democrat said in explaining the large majority. "If this bill were to fail, people would be terrified." A Republican agreed: "It has to pass. The alternative is chaos. For better or for worse, this package is going to stumble through."

All that remained now was to give the legislation a title and a number. Because neither Rostenkowski nor Pickle had served on the commission, the legislation was titled "A Bill to assure the solvency of the Social Security Trust Funds, to reform the Medicare reimbursement of hospitals, to extend the Federal supplemental compensation program, and for other purposes." Unlike S. 1, there was no mention of the National Commission. The social security bill was given the number H.R. 1900. Rostenkowski had wanted a "nice round number" that members could recall, and 1900 was the next one available. With its formal title and number in place, Ways and Means took the bill to the Rules Committee for a ticket to the floor.

To the Floor

There were three options for the rule allowing debate on H.R. 1900: (1) an open rule, allowing unlimited amendments to the bill, (2) a closed rule, allowing no amendments, and (3) a modified closed rule, allowing only specific amendments. Rostenkowski asked for a modified closed rule, permitting only two amendments, one from Pickle on a retirement age increase and the other from Pepper on a tax increase. An open rule would expose the bill to endless amendment as House members struggled to fight the package of pain. Despite FAIR's lobbying for an open debate, Pepper and the Rules Committee adopted the modified option. The House would be protected from itself.[1]

The rule provided a simple chain of debate. The House would consider Pickle's retirement age amendment first. After voting on the proposal, the House would turn to Pepper's tax increase amendment. The voting order would favor Pepper, chairman of the Rules Committee. If both amendments passed, only the second would stand. The rule also gave the House nine hours of debate: one for the rule, two for each amendment, and four for the final bill. Clearly, there were few opportunities for individual stalling tactics under the rule.

Few observers gave Pickle much chance as the debate began on Wednesday, March 9, at ten in the morning. The first problem was that Pickle's amendment contained an increase in the retirement age to 67. Though many House members might have supported a boost to 66, if only because it was smaller, a jump to 67 involved more political costs. Yet, no matter how he tried,

---

[1]The following narrative is based on my personal notes, confidential interviews, and the *Congressional Record*.

Pickle could not raise enough money with a jump to 66. Because he was restricted to a pure retirement age increase, he had to move up to 67.

The second problem was labor opposition. An increase in the retirement age would mean more time on the job for workers. Though many social security experts assumed there would be few assembly-line workers left by the year 2022, organized labor was not so sure. "That kind of change might be nothing to doctors or lawyers," one labor lobbyist said, "but it would be torture for most of our people. Most of them can't wait to get to retirement. You try working in a steel mill or on a factory line until 67. Our people earn their money through hard physical labor and can't stay with it two extra years." Moreover, even though longevity was steadily increasing, it was not clear that future retirees could count on two extra years of good health. Pickle's amendment might take two healthy years at the front of retirement and replace them with two bad years at the end. Finally, even though workers could still retire at 62 under Pickle's amendment, they would have to take a cut from 80 to 70 percent in early retirement benefits.

Thus most of the Democratic leadership opposed Pickle's amendment. Pepper defined it as a benefit cut and said he would not support any package containing a retirement age increase. The prospects for passage seemed dim. Yet Pickle knew something the Democratic leadership did not: a Whip count of House Republicans showed solid support for the amendment. Though many Republicans were undecided about or opposed to the full package, most would still vote to improve the bill wherever possible. "We won't vote for final passage," one Yellow Jacket conservative said at the time, "but we sure as hell will vote for the retirement age. We'll always try to change it for the better." Armed with strong Republican support, Pickle needed only 60 Democratic votes for victory.

When the amendment finally came up for a vote in midafternoon, Pickle had the needed support, winning 228–202. All but 14 of the 166 Republicans voted aye, while 76 Democrats joined in. The full Ways and Means Committee voted 24–11 in favor, with all 12 Republicans on board. Rostenkowski had voted early to signal his support to the rest of his Democrats, and 11 joined him. Without Rostenkowski's voting "cue," Pickle's amendment could not have passed. Of Pepper's 58 freshman Democrats, 17 voted for and 41 against. According to Pickle, however, there was a reservoir of Democrats who would have voted in favor had their support been needed.

There were several explanations for Pickle's victory. Some said it was a personal reward for Pickle, reflecting House support for his long struggle for serious social security reform. "Members felt a lot of affection for Jake," a Ways and Means staffer said. "He had been publicly humiliated by the Speaker in 1981 for trying to solve the crisis. People wanted to see him vindicated." Others said it was a personal defeat for Pepper, reflecting Republican anger over his rhetoric in the 1982 election campaigns. "A number of members had been hit by Pepper in the midterms," a leadership aide noted, "and saw this as a chance to get back for fresh wounds." Still others blamed the Democratic leadership for not taking the amendment seriously enough, failing to lobby against it until the very last moment. Still others blamed Pepper for even letting the amendment to the floor, a major tactical error by the Rules Committee.

Yet the final vote also reflected a fairly clear liberal–conservative split in the House and involved a brief return of Reagan's once-powerful 1981 budget and tax cut coalition. Ninety percent of liberal Democrats voted against Pickle; 94 percent of conservative Republicans voted for. With those kinds of party and ideological splits, there is simply not much room for friendship. Moreover, a tax increase would have been more difficult to sell back home.

Pickled Pepper

Pepper was visibly shaken by the Pickle vote; he had expected an easy defeat and was surprised by the result. Now he had but one chance to regain control: he had to win on his tax increase amendment. Under the rule, Pickle's amendment would be automatically tabled if Pepper's amendment passed.

The chamber grew quiet as Pepper rose to speak. Though most members could not vote for a pure tax increase amendment even in an odd year, his speech might doom final passage of the bill. "There are only a handful of floor debates that make a difference," a leadership aide said, "and this was one of them. Pepper wasn't talking about just his amendment but about the full package. He was telling the House to vote no." For thirty minutes, Pepper talked of his support for the elderly. With tears in his eyes, he asked, "What parent in America wants to be a burden upon his or her children no matter how faithful and loving they are? And yet here we twiddle over giving them a few more dollars a month, keeping them from being crushed from poverty down to misery, giving them the right to sustain that dignity." It was a moving speech and prompted a standing ovation from the packed House. Even conservative Republicans acknowledged Pepper's oratory.

When his amendment came up for a vote early that evening, Pepper fell far short of the needed majority, losing 132–396. Only one Republican voted in favor, while the Democrats split evenly 131–131. The full Ways and Means Committee voted 29–6 against. Of Pepper's 58 freshman Democrats, 35 voted for and 22 against.

Now the question was whether the full package would pass. On the left, Pepper would not vote for a bill containing a retirement age increase; on the right, Archer would not vote for a bill containing a payroll tax increase. What would the center do? Speaking just before Pepper's amendment lost, O'Neill urged his fellow Democrats to support the final package regardless: "The real purpose of this bill as we originally submitted it was to straighten out the crisis. On both sides we agreed with that. I hope you will vote for final passage." That brief statement allowed his Democrats to vote with the package, and the bill passed just before eight o'clock by a 282–148 margin. Sixty-nine conservative Republicans voted no, joining 56 liberal Democrats, and leaving the center in support. Repeating their earlier committee margin, Ways and Means members voted 32–3 in favor. And despite Pepper's earlier opposition, his freshmen also voted in favor, splitting 44–14. They had supported him on the amendments, but they had their futures to worry about. A no vote would not help in their first reelection campaigns. Perhaps they were just following Pepper's lead. Having agreed to the Gang of Nine proposal when it was presented to the commission, he cast his vote "aye," too.

The House finally had its bill, right on Rostenkowski's schedule.

THE SENATE

Though the Senate Finance Committee held social security hearings in mid-February, it waited patiently for the House to act before starting its own markup. The House would be the leader on this issue. Dole wanted to see how the House handled the retirement age issue, holding back until he could see the final House bill. "He didn't want to get caught again," an aide reported. "He wanted to make sure that the House moved first, and moved in the right direction." Moreover, Dole was worried about Senate "self-starters." He hoped that a clean House bill might discourage additional riders in his own chamber.

Unlike in the House, there would be no subcommittee markups in the Senate. First, Armstrong, the subcommittee chairman, was not committed to the compromise bill. He had voted against the National Commission package and just might try to pass a conservative reform bill. Dole wanted to avoid that kind of unnecessary political conflict. Second, the Finance Committee was small enough to hold a markup on its own. With 20 members, it was still manageable. Dole certainly did not want to make the same deals twice. Third, like other Senate committees, Finance rarely relied on its subcommittees for legislative markups.

To Committee

The full committee markup began on Thursday, March 10, one day after H.R. 1900 passed. The Senate bill, still numbered S. 1, did not differ from the House legislation on most items, but it did include a number of minor changes. The Finance Committee wanted a larger tax credit for self-employed workers, a deeper cut in windfall benefits for federal employees, use of tax-free bonds in determining whether retirees faced taxation of benefits, slight changes in normalized tax transfers, a variety of small technical changes, and social security in the unified budget. In all, there were over sixty differences between the two bills. Though most of the Senate changes were not controversial, there were three major disputes.

First, the Senate wanted a stronger fail-safe than the House. The Ways and Means version was far too weak for the more conservative Finance Committee. After a surprisingly brief debate, the committee adopted a fail-safe offered by Sen. Russell Long: whenever trust fund reserves fell too low, the President would notify Congress. If, in turn, Congress did not act within sixty days, the President would be forced to cut the benefit COLA to meet the crisis. Because the provision would take effect in 1985, at least there would be no benefit cut in the coming election year. Though several Democrats objected to the fail-safe, the committee finally agreed that some fail-safe was better than none. It would go into the bill.

Second, under pressure from Armstrong, the committee voted to eliminate the earnings ceiling on social security benefits. Under that ceiling, beneficiaries lost $1 of benefits for every $2 of earnings, but only after they had earned $6,600 (if they were at or above the normal retirement age) or $4,920 (if they were below) in any given year. The ceiling had long been a target of conservatives because it seemed to penalize higher-income retirees for continuing to work. Though it applied only to retirees under age 70, Armstrong insisted on the change as the price for his support on the full committee bill. It would go in the Finance package, too.

Third, the committee decided on its own version of the long-term solution. Instead of taking the House retirement age increase, the Finance Committee adopted a two-part option: half the savings would come from a 5 percent benefit cut starting in the year 2000, the other half from an increase in retirement age to 66, coming in one-month jumps from 2000 to 2012. The benefit cut had been offered back in November by liberals on the National Commission, and it was easier than a full jump to age 67. Moreover, the 5 percent benefit cut could always be repealed during the coming golden days. Politically, the Senate version was easier to sell back home. It would go into the bill.

With these major and minor changes in place, the Senate Finance Committee voted 18 to 1 to pass the bill. The lone dissenter was Symms of Idaho, not Armstrong. Though Armstrong had voted against the National Commission package in January, there were enough changes in the Finance Committee bill to win his support. Unlike Archer, Armstrong had decided to compromise and won several important changes in the process.

After the vote, Dole congratulated his committee and promised swift Senate action. Unfortunately, a self-starter got in the way.

A Hostage

The self-starter was Sen. John Melcher, Democrat from Montana, and the issue was withholding on interest and dividends. The banking lobbies, led by the American Bankers Association, had persuaded Melcher to offer an amendment to the social security bill to repeal withholding. Never mind that the issue had nothing to do with social security; the bill was a good vehicle for the amendment. And because the Senate had virtually no rules on floor debate, Melcher could do whatever he wanted.

As the author of the withholding legislation, Dole was vehemently opposed to repeal of the item and would not let the amendment come to a vote. "We have Republicans and Democrats climbing over one another trying to get a piece of the action because everyone's frightened with the mail they've gotten," Dole said. After the Senate refused to table Melcher's amendment, and thereby remove it from debate, Dole blocked a final vote, creating his own stalemate. Knowing that the amendment would easily pass, Dole stalled his own social security bill, waiting for help.

The breakthrough eventually came from another unlikely marriage: Reagan and the AFL-CIO. The President wanted to move on to other issues and was angry at the banking lobbies for attacking him on withholding. Noting that "it would be far better if the bankers spend less time lobbying and more time lowering interest rates," Reagan concluded that he had "had it up to my keister with the banking industry." The AFL-CIO, in contrast, did not care about withholding and was much more concerned about the unemployment section of the rescue bill. Emergency jobless aid was due to expire on March 30 if Congress failed to act and had been added to the social security bill as the fastest track for passage. Now Melcher had become an obstacle. Though most Senate Democrats favored repeal of withholding, the AFL-CIO joined with the Republicans to end the stalemate.

Eventually, the Senate leadership used a very simple device for ending Melcher's two-day assault. The 1974 Budget Act required all spending and revenue legislation to move through the normal budget process before reaching the floor. Unless the Senate granted a waiver from the act, Melcher's amendment would be out of order. "Are those who predicted that the package will fly apart because of partisan consideration or personal political advantage correct?" Majority Leader Baker asked before the vote for a waiver. In this case, the Senate said no on Melcher's request, 54–43. Dole immediately asked the chair to rule Melcher's amendment out of order. In a rare appearance as President of the Senate, Vice President George Bush gladly complied, and the withholding stalemate was broken.

Final Amendments

With the social security bill freed from bondage on Tuesday, March 22, the Senate moved toward quick passage. Most of the two dozen floor amendments failed, but one more stumbling block remained: federal employees. The FAIR coalition had long since concentrated its fire on the Senate, corralling members outside the chamber and in the hallways. Tactics that could not work in the rule-bound House now seemed perfect for the Senate. Unlike in the House, there were no rules to keep this issue from a final vote. The floor debate was scheduled for Wednesday, March 23.

The debate was simple. Unless Congress changed the civil service retirement rules by 1984, new hires would be enrolled in two pension plans—social security and civil service—and would pay a total of 14 percent on their wages. That would hardly make federal employment attractive. Yet if Congress waited for the Post Office and Civil Service Committee to act in the House and the Governmental Affairs Committee to act in the Senate, social security coverage of new hires might never come. Those two committees were dominated by members who were sympathetic to federal employees. The question was how to make those committees act. One side (Republicans) favored covering employees immediately, thereby forcing the committees to move now or make new hires pay later. The other side (Democrats) favored waiting for a new civil service retirement plan, thereby linking federal coverage to committee action.

The contest turned on two amendments: one to cover new hires in 1985, the other to cover these employees only when and if a new civil service plan was enacted. The first amendment, which gave Congress over a year and a half to pass that new system, was defeated 45–50, with a mix of Democrats and conservative Republicans against. The conservative Republicans did not want any delay in coverage, preferring the 1984 date, while the Democrats fell in line with the FAIR coalition.

The Senate then passed the second amendment on a voice vote. The employee unions had had their chance and won. The voice vote protected both parties from political fallout, allowing Republicans and Democrats alike to claim whatever position helped them most. The Senate then moved on to several remaining amendments, refusing to add a section on health insurance for unemployed workers to the bill. The final vote on passage came at nine o'clock Wednesday night. The Senate bill, now renumbered H.R. 1900 because it had originated in the House, passed 88–9, with right-wing Republicans aligned against.

The Senate finally had its bill, only hours before Rostenkowski's deadline. Though liberals had won an important victory on federal coverage, the Senate bill was much more conservative than the House package, particularly on the fail-safe. And though both bills followed the general outlines of the National Commission package, there was still room for considerable conflict.

CONCLUSION

With two bills now passed, all that was left was a conference between the House and Senate. Both chambers seemed equally intent on preserving their versions of the legislation. Indeed, in one of the very last motions in the debate, Dole asked the Senate to "insist upon its amendments" in conference and won unanimous agreement. There was only one day left before the Easter recess; the conference would have to start Thursday morning at 8:30. And the House would be rested.

17

Finishing Touches

Despite the separate victories, there was one "small" problem: neither bill could pass in the other chamber. Both bodies had made their positions clear. This was a test of institutional strength, with both promising never to yield. Now the question was who meant business. With less than twenty-four hours before the Easter recess, Congress still had no final bill. The House and Senate were at yet another impasse and would have to go to conference. It was time for one more compromise.

Like all other conference committees, this one would be outside the normal legislative process, with some protection against interest groups and the public. Though the conference would have to work within the boundaries of the two bills, there would be an opportunity for quiet negotiation. Though the conference committee was open to the public, it would be easy to shield negotiations from public view. Rostenkowski and Dole would slip into a back office. Who could say what they were talking about?

As with the 1981 minimum benefit conference committee, there would be only two votes on the social security bills: one for the House, one for the Senate. Because the members would come from the committees that wrote the bills (Ways and Means and Finance), Pepper would not attend. The conference committee would meet in the Ways and Means hearing room, with Rostenkowski as chairman. Every disagreement between the two bills would have to be ironed out. The compromise bill would then have to return to the House and Senate for final passage.

WHEN WORLDS COLLIDE

The social security conference began at nine o'clock Thursday morning, March 24, less than twelve hours after the Senate had passed its bill. Because the

Senate had finished only the night before, there were no copies of its bill. "You could piece it together from the debate," a Ways and Means staffer said, "but they had no formal version to lay side by side next to ours. That gave us an initial advantage. Some of the Senate conferees didn't know what was in their bill."

Despite five dozen differences between the two bills, Rostenkowski wanted to have a compromise on the floor by the end of the day. The Easter recess still loomed as a magic date after which social security somehow could not be rescued. Rostenkowski also wanted to win most of the disagreements. Otherwise, he would lose face in the House. If Rostenkowski wanted to be Speaker someday, this was a chance to test his mettle.

Rostenkowski had a three-part strategy for defeating the Senate. First, he would move the conference as fast as possible. He knew that the Senate was still exhausted from the long social security debate. He wanted to take charge quickly. The Senate conferees would not be allowed to sleep late on Thursday morning. Second, Rostenkowski exploited Senate fears of Claude Pepper. After all, Pepper was still Rules chairman. Though Pepper was not on the conference committee, Rostenkowski often talked of Pepper's opposition to specific items in the Senate bill. "Gee, we'd like to go along with you on this one," he would tell his Senate counterparts, "but Claude won't budge." Third, just in case the Senate came down too strong on some provision, Rostenkowski and his House partners set priorities among the sixty differences. They would create a working list of items they could use in trades.

Moreover, both sides were anxious to finish. The Easter recess was now only hours away. Several Ways and Means Committee members, for example, were scheduled to leave for Japan on Thursday night; members of both bodies were ready to go home. As Conable noted, the intense activity surrounding the rush to recess created some incentive for compromise: "Exhaustion achieves what good intentions and logic cannot."

Setting Priorities

On the surface, most conferences involve a very simple choice: one side has to give in on each disagreement. On a complex bill, however, the choices are much more complex. One side might recede on a major issue in return for a range of trivial items. According to the House conferees on H.R. 1900, there were at least five options on each disagreement with the Senate.[1]

First, there were some items that the House considered absolutely essential. The House would not yield on the retirement age increase. It had cost too much on the floor. Second, there were some items that the House was willing to trade. The House conferees were willing to give a little on Armstrong's phased-in elimination of the earnings test in return for something else. Third, the conferees knew that the Senate would want some kind of fail-safe. That had cost too much on their floor. Thus, the House conferees began thinking of the price tag. In the end, Rostenkowski concluded that any fail-safe would be very expen-

---

[1] The following discussion is based on personal notes and confidential interviews.

sive—the House would have to win on almost every other disagreement. Fourth, the House conferees looked for small ways to help the Senate look good. "Why bloody their noses on everything?" one conferee asked in a closed caucus right before the conference. "We'll be seeing them again on a tax increase this summer." The House would win on the big issues but would try to even the score on the small items. Fifth, the House conferees vowed never to yield on any item where the Senate had not acted. If the House bill had a provision that the Senate bill did not, the House would keep it. Something would always beat nothing. But because the House had a stronger position than the Senate in drafting the bill, there would be many times where nothing in the House bill would beat something in the Senate version. Sixth, there were some items that the Senate did not want to win. The House conferees did not believe the Senate truly wanted to let federal employee coverage wait until a new civil service plan was ready.

Since the conferees had to return to their home chambers to sell the final bill, both sides had to win something. With so many options on each disagreement, the conference allowed both sides to claim victory. The Senate might lose on every issue except one and yet argue that the one trade was worth the price; the House might win on dozens of minor issues, building a huge margin of victories, and still lose the most important items. Both sides knew they would meet again on other issues and tried not to humiliate each other. As Rostenkowski told his fellow House conferees in a closed caucus, "We want to lose whenever we can, because we're going to beat the hell out of them on the big ones."

In working through the list of disagreements, both sides used a number of factors to set priorities. If an item had passed by a slim margin in committee or on the floor, it was seen as an easy victory for the other side. If, however, it had moved with near-unanimous committee support or a large majority on the floor, it had to be part of a major trade. Because the House bill had passed 32–3 in the Ways and Means Committee, it already had a strong position as the conference began. Though the Senate bill had also passed by a strong committee majority, it had suffered on the floor, a hostage of interest withholding. The long Senate debate had weakened its position in the conference, undermining its image of strength.

Thus reading down the side-by-side provisions of the two bills early in the day, the House conferees decided to stand firm on most items. They were willing to give a little on Armstrong's earnings proposal, agreeing to a new formula that would reduce social security benefits $1 for each $3 earned, albeit only for those at or above the normal retirement age and only starting in 1990, but would not cave in on complete elimination. They were also willing to compromise on a tax credit for the self-employed. They were even willing to take a Moynihan amendment to reduce fraud and abuse by having all social security cards printed on banknote paper. "Let Moynihan win one," a House conferee said at the time, "but not much of one." On most disagreements, however, Rostenkowski and his House colleagues decided not to budge.

Most of these priorities were set in a private House caucus. The House conferees knew they had the edge in the bargaining and decided to test the Senate. They had lost many conferences with the Senate in the first two years of the Reagan administration, and they clearly relished their new power. As they read their list of differences, the conferees traded jokes, designing a conference strategy that would make the Senate fight for even the most trivial amendment. Throughout the process, the House conferees counted the savings and costs of each Senate amendment. If a Senate provision would cost money, it was automatically rejected, regardless of merit. Though the House members certainly enjoyed their work, they took the social security rescue very seriously.

It was clear that Rostenkowski cared less about the substance of the bill and more about a House victory in the institutional struggle. Rostenkowski was determined to win the conference, as a signal of his effective leadership. Whereas other House conferees talked about the technical substance of this change or the long-term policy merits of that amendment, Rostenkowski asked two basic questions about each disagreement: (1) How much did it cost? (2) Why should the House cave in? Since the House had already ironed out its political and policy disagreements in passing the original bill, this was a game between the institutions. Both sides had strong institutional loyalty.

To the Victors

Conferences are usually very casual affairs. The committee reads through the so-called side-by-sider comparing the two bills and votes on each item. Where there are serious disagreements, a conference often will pass over the issue, moving to the back rooms for further talks.

The very first issue to come up in the social security conference was coverage of federal employees, one of the most controversial provisions of both bills. There was no conspiracy to bring the issue up first; it was simply the initial section of the bill. The House wanted coverage to start in 1984 regardless of other action, whereas the Senate wanted to delay until a new civil service retirement plan was ready. Rostenkowski had to make a quick decision about the issue: either postpone a vote on coverage or hit it right away. "The problem with waiting," one of his staffers recalled, "was that the issue would cost even more to win later. If we beat the Senate at the start, they wouldn't be able to hold out for something big, and it would set the tone for the rest of the conference."

The key question was whether the Senate was bluffing on coverage. After all, the original Finance Committee position was almost identical to that of the House. Perhaps the Senate would gladly give up on federal coverage without a fight; perhaps they even wanted to recede; perhaps they had only voted for the amendment because of lobbying pressure, hoping the conference would strip the provision out of the bill.

Public positions to the contrary, the House gambled that the Senate actually wanted to lose on the issue and brought the issue to an immediate vote. The Senate conferees voted 4–3 to recede, Republicans against Democrats, giving the House a major victory, or at least the appearance of one. "We ended up with the version we initially wanted," a Republican Senate aide said. "If the House wanted to claim a big one, so be it." In short, the Senate never wanted to pass the House amendment but was forced to do so by the interest groups. Given a chance to back away from the issue in the conference, the Senate gladly complied.

As the conference moved forward, the House won on other issues: small business would not get a one-time-only tax credit in 1984; social security would be taken out of the unified budget (but only starting in fiscal year 1993); the retirement age would go up to 67. Of the sixty differences, the House prevailed on forty-nine. By midafternoon, it was clear the House was in control. Of the twenty-two times the House had a provision in the bill where the Senate did not, the House won every time. Something beat nothing in each contest. But of the eighteen times the Senate had a provision in the bill where the House did not, the Senate won only half of the time. Nothing beat something nine times, a rare reversal of poker odds. Moreover, of the twenty-two times the House and Senate offered competing versions of the same item, the House won eighteen. It was a very good day for Ways and Means.

A Last Stalemate

By late afternoon, there was one remaining issue: the fail-safe. Neither side was bluffing. Both agreed that something was needed, but the House would not accept automatic COLA cuts. Yet this was the one issue where the Senate had to stand firm, refusing to cave in. Without some kind of fail-safe, Armstrong would defect, as would the conservative Democrats. The White House was already hearing of serious problems over in the Senate and hoped the fail-safe could bring conservatives back into the fold.

As night fell, the conference was still in deep trouble. The conferees had resolved fifty-nine issues, but the one that remained could derail the entire bill. Several Senate Democrats had walked out of the conference after the federal coverage vote and were already working to block the final bill. Dole desperately needed a redeeming victory. Meeting in the back rooms of the Ways and Means Committee, far outside the public spotlight, Rostenkowski and Dole struggled with the issue. Rostenkowski knew that Pepper would never let the conference report reach the floor with the Senate fail-safe; Dole knew that the bill might not pass the Senate without it.

As Rostenkowski and Dole continued to talk, the time pressure grew. It was already six o'clock. Even if the printers worked quickly, a final conference report would not be ready until ten, giving the House and Senate little time to reach a final compromise. Many members of Congress had left the Hill for the day. Worse yet, some were already on the way back to their home districts for Easter. Rostenkowski and Dole both knew that the opponents would stay in town longer than the supporters. Feeling that the bill was sure to pass, some of their allies had left early. Conservatives, believing they might be able to win enough votes to stop the bill and keep it in legislative limbo during the recess, stayed around. Thus as the conference continued, the Senate leadership tried to keep its supporters in town.

By seven o'clock, Rostenkowski and Dole had finally reached a major trade. The Senate would drop the fail-safe if the House would change the stabilizer. Recall that the House had passed a stabilizer that would change the COLA formula if social security got back into trouble. If trust fund reserves fell below 20 percent, the COLA would be changed to the lesser of wage increases or price increases. The problem was that the House version came into play only in 1988, offering little protection in the first years of the compromise. When the smoke finally cleared, the two chambers had agreed on a 1985 effective date and a 15 percent trigger level.

Republicans certainly knew that the stabilizer carried dramatic savings. When SSA actuaries finally calculated the impact of the change several weeks later, it came out as a potential $55 billion benefit cut. Little wonder that Republicans were willing to take the political risks. Though the stabilizer would never be used under optimistic or intermediate assumptions, it would be triggered if the pessimistic forecast came true. Because the social security computers were so slow, Democrats did not know the true impact of the final agreement when it was offered. Moreover, even though many social security experts knew just how large the cut could be, they did not want Pepper to find out. Otherwise, the conference report would never have reached the floor.

With this sixtieth agreement in hand, the conference met one last time in public. The House and Senate each cast a vote in favor of the compromise. On the House side, only two Republicans said no, both Yellow Jackets. On the Senate side, two Democrats said no, both Boll Weevils.

House Odds

The House emerged victorious from the social security conference for several reasons.

Perhaps the Senate wanted to lose. "All we wanted was a bill that we liked," a Senate staffer said. "We all wanted to cover federal workers as soon as possible, but couldn't do it given our rules. We all wanted an increased retirement age, but quibbled about when and how much." Indeed, compared with Dole's original long-term package, the final House bill was quite acceptable. Dole wanted a retirement age increase, and he got one. Moreover, as one House member remarked, "The Senate appointed the foxes to guard their chicken coop. Most of their people were conservatives who already supported us on the issues."

Perhaps the House was better prepared for the conference. Remember that the House bill had passed two weeks before the Senate version. "The Senate was hurt because they were tired and distracted," a House conferee said. "They had a number of close votes on their bill and were divided and angry. Dole was still hot about withholding and let it get in the way." Further, throughout much of the conference, Dole was the only senator present. Most of the Senate conferees were not interested in the issues and had returned to their offices. Though Moynihan was in and out, the rest of the group did not stay beyond the first fifteen minutes. Once federal coverage was over, the Senate conferees were indifferent.

Perhaps Rostenkowski was more determined to win than Dole. In a contest of wills, Rostenkowski made it clear that he did not intend to lose on the major items. He had built the legislation in his committee, he had pushed it through the Rules Committee and onto the floor, and he was not going to let a bunch of senators take it away from him in conference. The House had always led on social security and considered itself the rightful owner of the issue. "He was just coming into his own as chairman," a Democratic member said, "and decided that, by God, he was going to show the Senate and Washington who was in charge. Whether Dole was too tired or what, Rosty walked all over him."

Whatever the reasons, the conference produced a House victory and also saved the Senate from its own lack of rules. The conference had stripped out most of the special interest amendments added on by the Senate. Small business, federal employees, and the self-employed all lost key battles in the conference.

A FINAL RIDE

The true heroes of the day were the employees in the Government Printing Office. Receiving a cut-and-paste copy of the conference agreement at eight o'clock, they had to produce a clean copy by ten. House and Senate rules demanded at least four copies before the final votes. Most members would have to rely on the leadership for cues on the final vote.

With the copies in hand, the House convened just after 10 P.M. Rostenkowski rose to praise the conference; Pickle rose to praise Rostenkowski and Conable; Conable rose to praise the House. It was, in the words of one House member, "a love fest."

With the congratulations over, the three members described the conference report in greater detail, listing the numerous House victories. That was the easiest way to sell the agreement. Because the House had already voted to pass the social security bill once before, all the members wanted to know was whether they had prevailed in conference. And they had. "We all relinquished some long-cherished objectives in this process," Conable concluded. "It was painful, but the sacrifice was well worth the effort and the result. This conference report may not be a work of art, but it is artful work."

After less than twenty minutes of debate, the House passed the report 243–102, with 88 members absent and a majority of Republicans against. Despite his opposition to the higher retirement age and his earlier vote against the bill, Pepper voted aye, as did 3 out of 4 Democrats.

Conable's first words upon leaving the floor were, "It was just like the good old days." Ways and Means was once again the great legislative engine on social security, rolling up a huge committee majority on its bill and winning easily on the floor and in conference. Conable and his Republicans were once again part of the game, a key part of Rostenkowski's strategy for passing the bill. Little wonder Conable was reminded of the good old days.

The Senate also convened at 10 P.M., but there were few congratulations. The Senate knew that the House had won most of the disagreements. Armstrong rose to announce his opposition to the conference report. "They had taken the fail-safe out," Armstrong said. "I cannot swallow that. That gets to the stomach-turning point. . . . Because with the fail-safe out, we cannot be sure we are not going to be back here in 1985 or 1986 patching up this system." Long rose to announce his opposition, too. The bill is a "travesty," Long said. He "could not support any legislation that financed social security by merely increasing the national debt." Whereas the House had passed the conference report with little dissent, the Senate began another long debate. Once again, Dole was stalling his own bill while the leadership brought supporters back to the Capitol. White House limos were put on call for any senator who needed a ride from home.

The interest groups smelled an upset. With so many supporters gone, it just might be possible to defeat the conference report and reopen the bill. Senators were collared in the hallways; switchboards were on fire. Sensing a potential upset, the groups made one last attempt. Whereas the House had been calm in passing the conference report, the Senate was in turmoil. Maybe the bill would fail. Federal employee unions returned to the Capitol and battled alongside the American Association of Retired Persons and the National Federation of Independent Business. All they asked was a no vote on the conference; let Congress go home and listen to the people. That would give the groups time to use their grassroots strength to kill the rescue. It now appeared that an unlikely coalition of liberal Democrats and conservative Republicans could defeat the bill.

As the threat grew stronger, supporters rose to the defense. Moynihan issued a stern admonition to his fellow Senate Democrats: this was a Democratic bill that had just passed the House of Representatives 2 to 1. "A Democratic leadership has been willing to cooperate in this singular bipartisan effort to save the single most important domestic program our party has ever brought this Nation," Moynihan said. Turning to Sen. Jennings Randolph, a Democrat from West Virginia who had voted for the original social security bill forty-eight years earlier, Moynihan asked how he would vote. "I will vote aye!" Randolph replied. "I do so with the inner knowledge that I do right. It is a vote for the people, our citizens of this great and good land!"

With Moynihan working to preserve some semblance of support among his Democrats, Baker and Dole embarked on a parallel course among moderate Republicans. It was already clear that the Republican right wing would vote nay. Helms, John East, Orrin Hatch, and the rest of the conservative bloc would not be swayed by White House pressure. Whether Reagan supported the bill or not, they would not violate their principles. It was Armstrong who was the problem. Having supported the Finance Committee before, having compromised on the Senate floor, Armstrong now opposed the conference report.

Addressing the Senate at 1 A.M., March 25, Armstrong ripped into the conference agreement, warning of imminent failure. Asking only for a "reasonable assurance, not an absolute ironclad guarantee," Armstrong concluded that the bill would not work. His argument seemed to have some impact on his fellow senators, including the 19 Republicans who would be up for reelection in 1984. "When Armstrong sat down after his speech," one senator remembered, "the conference report was in limbo. It looked like it was going to lose."

Majority Leader Baker then made his appeal. Recalling that he had never seen "the Congress of the United States pass a bill that we agreed was perfect," Baker acknowledged Armstrong's concerns. Yet concluding also that "there are times when the country demands that we do something," Baker asked his colleagues to "get on with the business of fixing the social security system." Keeping his remarks to fifteen minutes, Baker said, "There will be the inevitable cleanup hitter. There will be the corrections that have to be attended to next month or the month after that or in the next session because we learn from our experience." This was not a perfect bill, Baker said, "but we are not a perfect body. This is not the last word to be spoken." In short, the Senate had to move on. This was the best they could get in the Ninety-eighth Congress. This was the time to "move it," even if parts of the bill were not perfect.

With the debate quickly winding down, the conference report came to a vote fifteen minutes later. It was not clear whether the bill was actually in trouble or not. Supporters were certainly concerned, and the White House lobbying apparatus was in full motion. Yet the conference report passed 58–14, with 28 senators absent and not voting. Armstrong later concluded that Baker's speech was the key to the margin of victory, but perhaps his early optimism had been wishful thinking. The social security rescue bill had triumphed. It would be enrolled on parchment paper and sent by special messenger to the White House the next morning for a presidential decision. The Senate immediately took its Easter recess, adjourning at 2 A.M. Congress had finished the rescue only two hours behind Rostenkowski's schedule.

A WORK OF ART?

Short of a complete economic collapse, the compromise would protect social security through the 1980s and into the next century. That sixtieth House-Senate compromise had provided the margin of safety.[2] If the economy worsened, social security would switch to the new COLA. That one piece of the rescue could save as much as $55 billion under worst-case conditions.

It was almost impossible to tell whether the long-term package would work. It certainly improved the outlook, but the future was still cloudy. A new baby boom, a cure for cancer, a third world war, or any one of a dozen other events could easily turn the social security golden days into lead. If the package

[2]Interestingly, according to Robert Myers, the stabilizer would not have been enough to prevent the 1983 crisis. (Personal correspondence.)

now seemed to be a work of art in the short term, preserving the system for another two decades, it was an unfinished canvas in the long term.

If the program got back into trouble after 1992, there would be one new advantage in making repairs: social security would be outside the budget process, removed from the unified federal accounts. The program could not be used to give the illusion of a smaller deficit. The change would also hide a huge chunk of federal spending from the public and Congress. The question was whether any program ought to be protected from annual debate. Shouldn't Congress and the President be forced to choose between new missiles and social security COLAs? between nuclear carriers and Medicare? By moving social security from the unified budget, government might be tempted to buy everything, no matter how high the deficit.

The compromise demanded sacrifices from everyone: workers, businesses, federal employees, the self-employed, Presidents, members of Congress, and the elderly. Almost everyone lost something, whether through lower benefits or higher taxes. And if the economy worsened, retirees would lose even more of their COLA under the new formula.

Still, much of the savings in the bill came from younger generations: the baby boomers and those born after them. Whether as employees or employers, they would pay higher taxes in the short term, would retire with smaller relative benefits in the long term, and would have to work longer under the new retirement age. And if any single group suffered more than others, it was people under age 23. They would feel the full impact of the higher retirement age after 2025 and would receive the lowest returns on their taxes. Because they had virtually no representation in Washington and such low voting rates back home, it was easier to inflict more pain on them in the long term.

Further, without some boost in fertility above the 1982 rates (1.8 births per woman), these young workers might just be left with no social security at all. Under a pay-as-you-go system, they would need plenty of workers to fund their benefits, and that required an increase of fertility. Moreover, whatever happened to their social security, they would still have to work longer, giving up two years of healthy retirement in their 60s for something less in their later years. At least on social security, the advice to the young seemed simple: either have more children of their own or invest in private pensions. A new baby boom was the easiest way to ensure continued social security in the next century. Alternative investments would provide a margin of safety.

Despite this uncertain future, the baby boomers had reason to feel confident about receiving social security benefits in the next century—not because of the rescue bill but because of raw political power. By 2030, one-fifth of the population would be over 65, up from 11 percent in 1980. If past voting rates among older Americans remained stable, the baby boomers could have considerable clout. Just as the elderly forced Congress to protect their COLAs in the 1980s, the baby boomers could force Congress to protect their COLAs in the 2030s. Social security would continue to rest on the power to tax, and the baby boomers could force the politicians to act. If the baby boomers could get into the habit of voting, they would control much of what government would do far into the next century.

CONCLUSION

There was never any doubt that Reagan would sign H.R. 1900, the Social Security Amendments of 1983. The only questions were when and how. The White House decided to wait until Congress came back from the Easter break, planning an elaborate signing ceremony for April 20. With over 300 special guests invited, the signing would be held on the South Lawn of the White House, complete with television coverage and a special Republican National Committee film crew. "You'll see plenty of the ceremony in the 1984 elections," one White House aide said later. "There aren't too many times that Reagan and Pepper shake hands, and we've got this one on film."

The only problem with the ceremony was the weather. Washington had a sudden cold snap, pushing temperatures down past freezing. With hundreds of empty seats, the White House scrambled for extras, using tourists to fill the roles. With the lawn now filled, Reagan spoke first, congratulating the commission and the Democrats. "None of us here today would pretend that this bill is perfect," Reagan said. "Each of us had to compromise one way or another. But the essence of bipartisanship is to give a little in order to get a lot." Indeed, the White House had to compromise even to get O'Neill and the Democrats to attend the signing ceremony. In an unusual departure from normal practice, O'Neill was allowed to address the gathering before the signing, calling the event "a happy day for America." Baker also spoke, concluding, "There are issues that are more important than any of us, or perhaps all of us, taken together. The preservation of the social security system is one of those issues."

With the speeches over, Reagan signed the bill, using twelve pens, one for each letter of his name. Conable, Dole, Moynihan, O'Neill, Pepper, and Rostenkowski would each get a souvenir. Because the legislation was the twenty-first act passed and signed into law in the Ninety-eighth Congress, it was numbered Public Law 98-21. The social security rescue was over.

PART FIVE

Conclusion

18

Making Tough Choices in the American System

After three years of starts and stops, Congress and the President had finally reached a consensus on social security reform. They had defined a problem, drafted a package of solutions, and defeated the opposition. It looked as if the American system worked. Despite all the obstacles, the crisis was over. The checks would go out on time, July 3. Government had produced an agreement, if only at the last moment.

Yet there were some who found the negotiating process distasteful. After all, most of the package was hammered out behind closed doors. The process was secret, with gangs of leaders sneaking through back alleys to avoid the press. There were some who argued that anything outside the public spotlight had to be tainted and corrupt, that responsible government could come only in the sunshine. Here, the question was less whether the system worked and more whether it worked *well*. The answer, of course, depends on what the system was designed to do.

If the system was built for stalemate in the absence of consensus, it had worked quite well. The system had remained in limbo on social security for three years, unable to move forward in the congressional subcommittees or in the budget process. The system could not work without a consensus, and none existed. There was no agreement on either the size of the coming crisis or the appropriate solutions. Congress and the President could reach a compromise only by leaving the normal process for a secret negotiating gang.

If, however, the system was built for quick action in policy emergencies, it had not worked well. The social security crisis had first appeared in 1980; the final rescue passed in 1983. Social security was on pay-as-you-go time and needed fast repairs, not a three-year delay. Moreover, if the system was built for public education on complex policy questions, it had not worked well, either. There was little time for education or rational analysis. This was a move-it-or-lose-it system of government, with few windows for political action. At least on dedistributive issues, the key to success lay in packaging, not in public education.

Nevertheless, despite its failings, the American system had shown one advantage: it was flexible. Unable to break the legislative stalemate through normal channels, Congress and the President had created a new form of government. A secret gang built a compromise, wrapped it in a bipartisan flag, and rammed it through Congress. There was no other way to move. It was government by fait accompli. Congress would have to take all of the package or none.

Looking at social security, the answer to future policy emergencies was not major constitutional reform toward a more efficient government. Nor was it a national commission at every turn. It was innovative leadership and a willingness to adapt. Here, the National Commission on Social Security Reform did not succeed where all others had failed—the Gang of Nine did. The National Commission did not set the deadline that created pressure for compromise—a House-Senate conference committee did. The National Commission did not make the final decisions—Reagan and O'Neill did. There was no magic in the commission; nothing that could save it from stalemate in November 1982; nothing that could keep it going when the President and Speaker refused to talk. Merely appointing a blue-ribbon commission, even with a bipartisan label and congressional members, could not create consensus where none existed.

The lessons for future commissions are clear. First, if Congress and the President do not want to solve a problem, no amount of "commissioning" will work. Commissions cannot supply the leadership that others lack. Second, if Congress and the President do decide to move, commissions can provide cover. They can provide the needed hiding place. Commissions will rarely be the source of final agreements. The best they can offer is a set of closed doors for the principals.

BUILDING A CONSENSUS

There were at least five steps in reaching a consensus on social security reform, each with lessons for other dedistributive issues. As Congress and the President turned to Medicare reform and budget deficits, they could look back to social security as an example of how to make painful choices.

First Step: Decide to Move

Before Congress and the President could reach a compromise, key participants had to decide to talk. Not everyone believed in solving the crisis. Some conservatives felt it would be better to let the system collapse. Only then could truly radical reform emerge. Some liberals felt it would be better to keep the issue alive for the 1984 presidential campaigns. There were ample incentives to stall for time.

In order to reach an agreement, Democrats had to give up their one golden political issue and Republicans had to face the realities of a tax increase as part of any solution. Having failed with his 1981 proposals, Reagan eventually decided to try again because of a failing budget, images of disarray, and the coming presidential elections. Having opposed Pickle's 1981 effort to build a rescue bill, O'Neill eventually decided to talk because of his own fragmented party, growing conflict between his chairmen, and loyalty to social security. Whereas Reagan wanted to resolve the issue before the 1982 congressional elections, O'Neill preferred to wait. It was only after the campaigns that O'Neill decided to talk.

The most powerful incentive to move came from Conable's crisis. In setting a deadline for July 3, the House-Senate minimum benefit conference demanded action. By painting the consequences of stalemate in the worst possible terms—bankruptcy of the trust fund, delayed checks, election defeats—the conference committee hoped to create pressure for political compromise. If Congress always acts, but only at the very last moment, it was critical to let Congress know just when that last moment would arrive. By picking the summer of 1983 instead of 1982, the committee gave Congress time to ride out the midterm campaigns, dispose of this painful issue well ahead of the next elections, move on to more popular distributive topics if any still existed, and gear up for the long presidential season.

Second Step: Pick the Players and Find a Place to Work

Once Congress and the President found the will to negotiate, they needed to narrow the number of participants to a select few. Despite the steady dispersion of congressional power over the 1970s, social security demanded leadership from the top down. Individual members of the House and Senate could not speak for the Speaker or President; staffs could not be trusted with the issue; subcommittees did not have the authority to draft bipartisan compromises. This issue had to be tackled by a small group of leaders. Decisions had to be centralized in both branches of government. In the executive branch, the departments lost control to Stockman and Darman. In the House, Pickle lost control to Rostenkowski and O'Neill.

After winnowing the list of key players, Congress and the President had to find a place to hide. Eventually, most of the crucial decisions came *outside* the normal process. The National Commission defined the size of the coming crisis, while the Gang of Nine drafted the package of solutions. Leadership was almost impossible any other way. By hiding the tough choices from the public and interest groups, Congress and the President could finally talk. Since bargaining rarely starts with the last, best offer, the intricate process of give-and-take had to be protected from endless political sniping. Democrats and Republicans had to be able to make offers and counteroffers without worrying about the morning headlines.

In many ways, the secret process helped diffuse any blame for the final package. It was difficult to tell who was responsible for what. Who was to blame for taxation of benefits? for the COLA cuts? for the increased retirement age? Most of the package could be blamed on a secret gang or a long-dead National Commission.

Though congressional sunshine has many advantages—more account-ability, less hidden influence, fewer abuses of power, more access for the unrepresented—it also brings problems, particularly on dedistributive issues. Leadership is clearly more difficult in an open congressional system. There are more players fighting for attention, more delays in the legislative process, and more pressure points for interest groups. As Congress faces more and more dedistributive choices, negotiating gangs may well become the standard device for resolving party differences outside the public spotlight. This may be the era of gangs in government. With the public and interest groups firmly opposed to most of the major options on the dedistributive agenda, Congress and the President are well advised to build prenegotiated packages outside the consti-tutional system, returning to the normal process only at the last moment.

None of this is to say that Congress could never have reached an agreement without secret gangs and national commissions. It would have been very difficult, but it would have happened. Social security checks would have gone out on time. Though the debate would have been hot, Congress was not about to let the program fail, not with 36 million constituents involved. Yet without the Gang of Nine, there would have been very great problems reaching a full solution before the 1984 election. It would have been easy to patch the system for a couple of years, creating another series of scares and driving public confidence even lower.

Third Step: Define the Problem

Even with incentives to negotiate, a group of players, and a place to work, Congress and the President had to agree on a common set of economic and demographic assumptions. This was crucial for defining the size of the problem and the targets for a package. This was not, however, a purely technical question. The two sides had been using different assumptions to shape the political debate. Democrats had used more optimistic assumptions to claim there was no problem. Republicans had used more pessimistic assumptions to inflate the size of the crisis and increase the pressure for deep benefit cuts. In the end, the choice of assumptions was a political question.

Here, it was not enough to agree on just one set of assumptions at the start of the negotiations. With the National Commission having defined the size of the crisis with one set in November, the Gang of Nine had to draft a package with another set in January. Since the assumptions were so inaccurate over even short periods of time, Congress and the President were forced to negotiate new figures at each step of the process. It was a new political game and a way to hide important choices from the public eye. The choice of one set of assumptions over another determined the kinds of solutions needed to plug the coming deficits.

At least for defining the social security problem, the National Commission gave the numbers an aura of legitimacy. By endorsing a single set of assumptions, the commission provided some protection for Congress and the President. On their votes for final passage, members could point to the targets as a defense. Even though the numbers involved a political compromise of their own, the National Commission provided a valuable stamp of approval.

Fourth Step: Build a Package

With a set of short- and long-term targets, Congress and the President had to develop a package of solutions. Here, the principle of shared sacrifice was key. Given interest group pressures, no package could have succeeded by concentrating on just one segment of society. And no one segment could have provided enough money on its own to cover the deficits. By taking a little from everyone, Congress and the President could cancel out some of the opposition. Though the Gang of Nine never reached a perfect 50–50 split between revenue increases and benefit cuts, it remained a noble goal.

In many respects, building the package was the easiest step in the process, particularly with most of the decisions out of the public sunshine. It involved picking from and adding to the long list of options. Where there were breakthroughs, they involved finding a solution that could be defined as both a tax increase *and* a benefit cut at the same time. The participants knew what the solutions were but needed an opportunity to experiment with different combinations. Having ruled out radical reform, the Gang of Nine needed only to mix and match until it reached the targets. The fact that the gang could not reach an agreement on the final one-third of the long-term deficit reflected political problems on Capitol Hill, not technical problems in finding a solution that would work. As with many other policy issues, the solutions were quite clear. It was a matter of weaving them into an acceptable compromise.

Fifth Step: Sell the Compromise

Once the Gang of Nine had finished its work, the compromise had to be sold in a number of political "markets," starting with the National Commission. Part of the effort involved the all-or-nothing approach. By portraying the rescue package as the only option, the gang forced the commission and Congress to accept it or reject it, with nothing in between.

Part of the effort reflected the move-it-or-lose-it tactic. At least on this dedistributive issue, there were very few windows of opportunity. One came at the start of the Reagan term. The first six months of office offered a brief chance to set the congressional agenda. The second window came at the start of the third year, with the new Congress. Reagan and congressional leaders had another brief chance to win passage.

Unlike many other kinds of issues, dedistributive policy must be tackled at the furthest point from the next election. Members of Congress are willing to gamble that the electorate will forget over time. The problem with the dedistributive calendar is clear: if the President refuses to confront the issues or if the issues do not even arise until the second or fourth year, government may be unable to react quickly.

A final part of the marketing effort involved breaking what one scholar calls the "traceability chain."[1] Members had to have some cover back home. Though members work to establish traceability chains on some issues—public works projects, tax cuts, economic progress, and so forth—they did not want to be linked to the social security package. It was too painful.

One way to break the chain was to blame the National Commission. Congress could point to the commission as the cause of any pain, shifting the blame to a body that no longer existed. The Senate, for example, transferred responsibility in the rescue bill's title: "To implement the consensus recommendations of the National Commission on Social Security Reform." A second way to break the chain involved artful labeling. By using such terms as "tax acceleration," "taxation of benefits," and "permanent COLA delays," Congress could deflect some of the criticism surrounding tax increases and benefit cuts. The public might feel some pain but not know why. A final way to break the chain was to blame the legislative process itself. Members of Congress who worried about their federal employees back home could point to the closed rule in the House or the voice vote in the Senate. And some of the pain could be traced to the conference committee and the mysteries of that legislative process.

Ultimately, members would need a long list of explanations for their votes on social security: "The commission made me do it." "The Speaker/President asked for my vote." "There was no choice." "The bill could not be amended." The list helped break the link between individual members and the bill.

Unfortunately for Congress, these political devices placed an emphasis on finding the perfect solution. By establishing absolute targets for the crisis and selling the solutions as the only answers, Congress and the President inflated public expectations about the future. Once again, they were setting a trap by promising that there would never be any need for further action.

With good luck, there would be little need for further repairs in the 1980s. However, there would always be need for legislative adjustment, reflecting problems in how society changes over time and the continuing conservative opposition. This program was too large to ignore, whether part of the unified budget or not. Social security would never escape the budget pressure, and many believed that it should not. In mid-1984, the Brookings Institution, a moderate think tank in Washington, recommended that the social security COLA be changed as part of a broad attack on the budget deficit. As Alice Rivlin argued, "Everybody should take their lumps in this national fiscal crisis."[2] Perhaps she was right. PL 98-21 would not be the last social security bill.

Still, the issue would always be politically hot. Indeed, Reagan inaugurated yet another round of social security rhetoric in 1984. "What we need to do," Reagan said, "is a revamping of the program." The interview brought an immediate Democratic response. "President Reagan has had a lifelong itch to

---

[1]This concept is advanced by Douglas Arnold, a Yale University political scientist.
[2]Quoted in the *National Journal*, June 23, 1984, p. 1213.

tamper with social security," O'Neill said. "This week, he started scratching again." It looked as though the fight was already on again to be carried through the 1984 presidential campaign and beyond.

A WORLD WITHOUT SUNSHINE

Though dedistributive issues call for strong leadership at the top, there are no guarantees in Congress. The Gang of Nine, for example, was plagued by fear that none of the agreements would survive on the House or Senate floor. This is not to argue that party leaders should have absolute power to dictate support. Nevertheless, when the normal process cannot handle an issue such as social security, there must be questions about whether the system itself needs repair.

Though major constitutional reform is not necessary given the system's flexibility, some streamlining may be in order. Subcommittee government in the House and the rise of individualism in the Senate present serious problems for dedistributive leadership. Some formal centralization of such issues in the party policy committees may be one option, particularly when the President fails to lead.

Although sunshine is still an important part of the congressional process, the opportunity for closed-door negotiation needs to be returned to Congress. There must be room for politics on Capitol Hill. Building a legislative compromise is not a neat, rational process, and it cannot be sterilized to the point where hard choices are no longer made.

There are obvious problems with a closed negotiating process, however. Both the represented and the unrepresented are unable to express their views to Congress. On social security, commission members had strong ties to interest groups, but few spoke for minorities and women. Despite the high incidence of elderly poverty among those groups, there was no chance to address their problems through detailed hearings. That was one cost of a secret gang—and one of the reasons why sunshine was first brought to Congress in the 1970s. Sunshine was a way to open the political process to the unrepresented and was still a valued end. It simply got in the way of action on social security. And it continued to present problems for dedistributive issues.

Moreover, neither the commission nor the gang did much to increase public knowledge on social security. Public understanding remained abysmally low throughout the long drive to reform. Whether the public could have learned a great deal was always in doubt. Social security was a highly technical program, with considerable room for confusion. Nevertheless, government was obligated to try. An educated public is essential for the democratic process.

CONCLUSION

Whether Congress and the President would be able to build artful compromises on the growing list of other dedistributive issues was still in doubt after the social security rescue. Whether the bill signaled new leadership or merely a last-second miracle was open to question. The political process did not change with the rescue. Nor did election pressures.

Yet there were signs that government had found some courage to face the future. There was talk of dealing with the budget deficits by increasing taxes and of tackling Medicare reform with a package of shared sacrifice. Even in an election year, members of Congress were talking about setting national priorities. Though Congress and the President would not be able to pass works of art every time, there were encouraging signs that they had found the keys to handling dedistributive issues: equal sacrifice, face-to-face negotiation, and protection from the public spotlight.

PART SIX

Epilogue

19

Success!

There can be little doubt that the 1983 rescue succeeded. It's all in the numbers.

Social security's balance sheets began to grow almost immediately. Fueled by the accelerated tax increases on the 75 million baby boomers born between 1946 and 1964, almost all of whom were in the workforce by the mid-1980s, the rescue package pulled social security back from the brink, at first slowly, then accelerating with each new bump in the payroll tax.[1] By the end of 1991, the old-age and survivors trust fund had $268 billion in reserves and was set to top a trillion dollars sometime in 2001.

The number of beneficiaries and taxpayers also grew, though not precisely because of the 1983 rescue. By 1992, there were roughly 40 million social security (OASI) and disability insurance (DI) beneficiaries, up from 36 million in 1983. More important for financing, there were 132 million taxpayers, up about 17 million. The ratio of workers to beneficiaries remained relatively stable at 3.3 to 1.

MEASURES OF SUCCESS

The short-term financial story is nothing but success. Without the rescue, according to Robert Myers, the staff director of the National Commission and former chief actuary of the Social Security Administration, the checks would

[1]Unless otherwise noted, the financial figures used in this chapter are from the Board of Trustees of the Federal Old-Age and Survivors Insurance and the Federal Disability Insurance Trust Funds, *The Annual Report of the Board of Trustees of the Federal Old-Age and Survivors Insurance and the Federal Disability Insurance Trust Funds* (Washington, D.C.: U.S. Government Printing Office, April 3, 1992); also unless otherwise noted, all figures are drawn from Alternative II.

have been delayed. "By July 31, the fund balance would have been $12 billion, which would have been insufficient to meet the $12.8 billion of benefit payments to be made in the next three days. So the 'Social Security boat would have hit the iceberg,' and checks would have been delayed until a few days later when additional payroll taxes came in."[2]

Because of the 1983 rescue, the trust fund ratio—that is, the amount of reserve "in the bank," so to speak—that had fallen so precipitously began to rise. By the end of the 1980s, the social security trust fund had accumulated roughly nine months of reserve. The 1980s had been very, very good to social security. According to Myers, "The fund balance at the end of 1989 was $163 billion, or 2.6 times as large as the estimate made in 1983. Since then the fund has increased significantly and was about $330 billion at the beginning of 1993, or 13 months' benefit payments, which is a vastly more favorable situation than prevailed a decade ago."[3]

Along the way, the social security actuaries were finally freed from the II-A forecast that had been forged at the height of the 1983 crisis. It was unceremoniously dropped from the annual trustees report in 1991 after a special technical panel of actuaries and economists concluded that its "purpose is not obvious and its preparation detracts from the resources needed to prepare the other three projections."[4]

In fact, the purpose of II-A had once been quite clear. It was a device for moving the Reagan administration's outrageously optimistic budget assumptions out of the way during the 1983 social security crisis. The Reagan budget forecast was so optimistic, writes Sidney Blumenthal, that it "was soon sardonically referred to, even within the Administration, as Rosy Scenario."[5] While such optimism might have been necessary for selling Reagan's budget and tax cuts to Congress, it did not belong as the basis for the intermediate, or best-guess, social security forecast. That is why the social security actuaries split the intermediate forecast in two—II-A to be reserved for Reagan, II-B to be the real best guess. With the social security crisis over and the author of "Rosy Scenario," David Stockman, gone, II-A had outlived its usefulness.[6]

Beyond the mid-1990s, however, the future looks far less certain. Social security was, and still is, vulnerable to poor economic performance and changing demographic realities. Even though inflation held steady and low during the mid-to-late 1980s, the 1991 recession cut into social security revenues as workers were laid off. This does not mean that the social security fund balance

---

[2]Robert Myers, "Effect of 1983 Amendments on Social Security," *The Actuary* (May 1992), p. 9.
[3]Robert Myers, "Social Security's Financing Problems—Realities and Myths," *Journal of the American Society of CLU & ChFC* (March 1993), pp. 38–45.
[4]The report of the Social Security Technical Panel can be found in *Social Security Bulletin*, Vol. 53, No. 11 (November 1990), pp. 2–34; its appendixes can be found in Vol. 53, No. 12 (December 1990), pp. 2–25; the quote is on p. 14.
[5]Sidney Blumenthal, "The Sorcerer's Apprentices," *The New Yorker* (July 19, 1993), p. 30.
[6]Even as the social security trustees dropped II-A, they rejected the technical panel's advice to change the old labels from Roman numerals to "low cost," "best estimate," and "high cost," which is how the President and Congress have perceived the sets all along.

stopped growing. Rather, it simply did not grow as fast as predicted just the year before. The net result was a slight decline in the projected trust fund ratio. The recession also served as a reminder that social security depends on a healthy economy. If the deficit weakens the economy, ceteris paribus, social security suffers.

More important for the immediate future, the old-age and survivors companion trust funds, disability insurance and Medicare, were both facing problems of their own. The disability fund would be exhausted by the mid-1990s, Medicare shortly thereafter. It was not that either disaster could pull the old-age and survivors fund down with it. Rather, the emerging crises in these once-healthy funds also served as a reminder of the fragility of America's social safety net. Having borrowed money from both funds in 1982 (recall Conable's crisis) and since repaid it, social security could be asked to return the favor. More important, regardless of what happened to these companions, social security was on a return course toward crisis in the next century.

Despite the shadow of crisis yet to come, the 1983 rescue remains nothing short of miraculous. Indeed, absent the 1983 package, the long-term forecasts would be much worse. Taxation of benefits and the rise in the "normal retirement age" have kept the brink of social security collapse beyond the horizon, even as the economy continues to underperform relative to past forecasts. And even as futurists rightly worry about the next century, it seems reasonable to assume, as economists Henry Aaron and Gary Burtless of the Brookings Institution do, that Congress and the President will make sure the long-term deficits "are unlikely to materialize."

The public hardly expects the program to never change. Looking back to 1983, Aaron and Burtless argue that "it is hard to credit the notion that ordinary citizens, to say nothing of those whose expectations were rational, thought current law would remain unchanged. It is equally hard to take seriously the view that the public now thinks Congress will do nothing to change Social Security over the next 75 years." Looking forward into the 2000s, the two authors therefore suggest that "a more plausible view is that in the future, as in the past, Congress will periodically modify the Social Security system to maintain solvency. In that event, either payroll taxes will have to go up or benefits will have to be cut."[7]

That future repair is much easier assumed than done, of course. With 75 million baby boomers uniquely interested in the outcome, it will be no small debate in Congress. Thus, the question for the next chapter is which side will win out, and whether the adjustments needed to handle the baby boomer retirement are so large as to provoke a political crisis of unprecedented proportions.

One way to predict the outcome of that battle is to ask whether and how the politics of social security changed in the wake of the 1983 miracle. First, did the 1983 social security rescue calm the public and restore confidence? Second,

[7]Henry J. Aaron and Gary Burtless, "Fiscal Policy and the Dynamic Inconsistency of Social Security Forecasts," *American Economic Review*, Vol. 79, No. 2 (May 1989), p. 95.

did Congress and the President show a more measured, even rational, hand in dealing with aging policy once the six-year social security crisis was over? And third, has the politics of social security cooled off in the wake of the financial success of the 1980s? The answers suggest that the future modification of social security could be very hot, indeed.

PUBLIC OPINIONS

Back-to-back security crises in the late 1970s clearly eroded public confidence. The question is whether the 1983 rescue and its financial success made any difference.

The answer is "yes, but." Using surveys collected over a quarter century, Sally Sherman traces the decline of public trust to passage of the social security COLA in 1972 and the financial debacle that followed. With annual expenditures exceeding income by 1975, driven in large part by a technical flaw in the benefit COLA, headlines began carrying the news of impending shortfalls and technical flaws in the benefit formula. "These ominous developments did not go unnoticed by the public," Sherman writes. "Confidence in the future of the Social Security system declined considerably in the late 1970s. In 1975, 63 percent of the public had expressed confidence in the future of the program, and 37 percent had little or no confidence. By 1978, these proportions were virtually reversed, and the percentage who were 'not at all confident' had doubled."[8] Jimmy Carter's assurances following the 1977 rescue that the program was now safe for 50 years apparently had little effect.

Public confidence in social security hit rock bottom in January 1982, just as the Greenspan Commission began work. Asked by the ABC News/*Washington Post* survey whether "Social Security will exist or not when it's time for you or your spouse to retire," 47 percent said "no." Interestingly, those figures did not rebound immediately with passage of the 1983 rescue. Asked the same question in January 1985, 45 percent still said "no." A rather different question asked by the CBS News/*New York Times* poll yielded similar results. Asked "Do you think the Social Security system will have the money available to provide the benefits you expect for your retirement," 58 percent said "no" in 1983, compared with 52 percent in 1990. A drop of 6 percentage points is hardly significant given the normal 4 to 5 percent margin of error in most opinion polls. At least according to these surveys, the 1983 rescue had a limited impact on confidence.

What, then, to make of Sherman's conclusion that "confidence in the future of the system began edging up" following the 1983 rescue and had nearly reversed itself by the end of the decade? The answer may be that the public is simultaneously positive and negative about social security. People may be much more confident about social security *as a system* than as a source of future

[8]Sally R. Sherman, "Public Attitudes toward Social Security," *Social Security Bulletin*, Vol. 52, No. 12 (December 1989), p. 4.

TABLE 9. Confidence in the Social Security System

Year	Very & Somewhat Confident	Not Too or Not at All	Don't Know
1975	63%	37%	0
1976	57	42	1
1977	40	50	0
1978	39	60	1
1979	—	—	—
1980	—	—	—
1981	42	57	1
1982	32	67	1
1983	34	64	2
1984	32	68	0
1985	35	61	4
1986	39	58	4
1987	—	—	—
1988	49	45	6
1989	—	—	—
1990	52	44	4
1991	50	45	5

Source: American Council of Life Insurance. Question not asked in 1979, 1980, 1987, and 1989.

support *for themselves.* There is no doubt, for example, that public confidence in social security as a system rebounded sharply after the 1983 rescue. Asked by the American Council of Life Insurance "How confident are you, yourself, in the future of the Social Security system," the people surveyed showed a steady increase after 1984. Table 9 shows the trend.

Two patterns emerge in the data. First, even a legislative miracle takes time to sink in. Indeed, public concerns hit a peak one year after the social security rescue passed. One reason for the lag is sheer skepticism. Having been through a similar denouement only years before, the public had ample reason to hold off judgment. All had been declared solved in 1977, too.

Another, more troublesome reason is that at least one organization in Washington, the National Committee to Preserve Social Security and Medicare, seemed to like the public unsure. Founded in 1982 by the son of President Franklin Roosevelt, Jimmy, the National Committee generated 1.5 million petitions to Congress in 1983 asking members to "take no action which would be destructive to the Social Security and Medicare benefits which have been solemnly promised to our people."

Even after the rescue, the committee continued sending the literature. Mailed in official-looking 14- by 17-inch envelopes marked "URGENT! IMPORTANT SOCIAL SECURITY AND MEDICARE INFORMATION ENCLOSED" and printed with directives to the postmaster—"TIME DATED OFFICIAL NATIONAL COMMITTEE DOCUMENTS ENCLOSED/EXPEDITE FOR IMMEDIATE DELIVERY"—the literature from the National Committee got the attention of its target, 20 million households. Once this public got inside the envelope, the scare was on. Labeling the 1983 bill a "stop-gap" measure, one Roosevelt letter noted that "never in the 45 years since my father, Franklin Delano Roosevelt, started the Social Security system has there been such a severe threat to Social Security and Medicare benefits." For a small contribution of $10, the committee promised to keep up the fight against the "rich and powerful forces" bent on destroying social security.

The literature was designed by a conservative direct-mail firm in California, which was paid 5 cents per letter and an administrative fee equal to 15 percent of all mailing and production costs under a 19-year contract with the National Committee. Despite the costs, the committee soon boasted its own political action committee ($6 million in 1988) and growing political weight (100,000 volunteers for local campaigns). With $29 million in the bank by 1986, it was nothing short of a hit.[9] And with 50 staffers in Washington by 1988, including one former acting commissioner of the Social Security Administration and 12 registered lobbyists working Congress and the executive branch, the committee had the muscle to work the hidden legislative process. As to the content of the letters, the committee's director of public affairs merely explained, "People have accused us of scaring seniors with our mailings. But are people upset at us or because of what they read? And if they're upset at what they read, is it our fault that these problems exist? We're not making these things up."[10]

The National Committee was not the only group to continue talking about threats to social security, however. Consider the following quotes compiled by *Congressional Quarterly* in 1984: (1) "The battle is not yet over. . . . I am personally appealing to you to enlist your immediate help in preventing Medicare and Medicaid from being gutted"; (2) "We will be battling to preserve Social Security and Medicare—two programs facing serious threats to their continued existence"; and (3) "Greetings from your friends in the Nation's Capitol who are working on nothing else but making sure your Social Security benefits are not taken away. . . ."[11] The first is from a fund-raising letter by the late Thomas P. O'Neill, Jr., who was then the Speaker of the House; the second is from a new group called the Association of Informed Senior Citizens; and the third is from an organization called the Social Security Lobby for Senior Citizens. With so much incoming fire, it is surprising that confidence rose at all.

The second pattern in Table 9 involves the substantial reservoir of doubt regarding the future of social security. Much as we might want to attribute the concerns to scare tactics among fund-raisers, there is an equally plausible explanation based on the age of the respondents. As noted earlier in this book,

---

[9]These figures are drawn from Crocker Coulson, "Geezer Sleaze," *The New Republic* (April 20, 1987), pp. 21–23.

[10]Michelle Murphy, "Elderly Group Continues to Thrive," *Congressional Quarterly* (March 26, 1988), p. 779.

[11]Pamela Fessler, "Tactics of New Elderly Lobby Ruffle Congressional Feathers," *Congressional Quarterly* (June 2, 1984), p. 1310.

TABLE 10. Confidence in Future
Benefits

Year/Age	Will Money Be Available for Benefits?	
	Yes	No
1983		
18–29	14%	79%
30–44	16	75
45–64	41	46
65+	48	13*
Total	27	58†
1990		
18–29	18	71
30–44	22	71
45–64	53	34
65+	70	11
Total	35	52

Source: CBS News/*New York Times* poll. Question: "Do you think the Social Security system will have the money available to provide the benefits you expect for your retirement?"
*Of the 65+ respondents, 31 percent were already receiving benefits, which appears to be much lower than expected, possibly suggesting a flaw in the sample.
†Six percent of the total sample were already receiving benefits.

young people are considerably less likely to have confidence in the future of social security, in part because they are so far from future retirement. The closer people age toward retirement, *(a)* the greater the belief that they might actually make it and *(b)* the greater interest they have in learning about the stability of social security. Thus, older Americans might be either more receptive to positive messages about the impact of the 1983 rescue and the fact that they continue to receive their checks or more susceptible to negative rhetoric about continuing, unnamed threats, or most likely both. How they might reconcile the cross-pressure is any pollster's guess, but at least for now, according to the data in Table 10, they seem to believe their checks.

Whether younger Americans will become more trusting toward social security as they age is still in doubt. As long as the rhetoric about future crises remains hot—and there is no evidence that it will soon abate—they may remain doubtful about their own benefits. Although the Social Security Administration has become somewhat more aggressive in advertising its financial health in recent years and making individual records much more easily available, its primary marketing motto might still read "nothing succeeds like success." No one yet knows how well that will hold as social security enters its next period of crisis in the 2010s and beyond.

MOVING ON?

With the social security crisis over, Congress and the President were free to set a new agenda for older Americans. Having deferred action on a host of pressing elder-care issues, congressional committees, lobbying groups, and White House planners could finally work through the backlog, hopefully applying the lessons of the 1983 rescue toward more rational outcomes. The question is what Congress and the President did with the breathing room. The answer, for the most part, is catastrophic health care, one of the most curious legislative issues in recent memory. Its final resolution is not a shining example of deliberative policymaking.

The Diagnosis

The story begins with the State of the Union address in February 1986, when Ronald Reagan gave his blessing to those who wanted to "free the elderly from the fear of catastrophic illness" and "to reform this outmoded social dinosaur." The basics of the bill that emerged from the next two years of study, debate, and sweetening are too complicated to summarize here. Suffice it to note that the result had three major features: (1) it set a cap of approximately $2,000 (in 1990) on how much individual beneficiaries would be required to pay for most existing Medicare services, (2) it put prescription drugs under Medicare coverage for the first time, provided that individual beneficiaries met a yearly deductible of $550 (again in 1990), and (3) it paid for itself through a rather complicated premium—all participants would pay an added amount of $4 starting in 1989 on top of the then-monthly premium of $27.90, while upper-income beneficiaries would pay a "supplemental premium" that acted very much like an income tax surcharge.

The prescription drug provision was a sweetener added by the House to the much more modest proposal made by Reagan's Secretary of Health and Human Services, Otis "Doc" Bowen, in late 1986. After six years of holding back under budget pressure, according to John Rother, public policy director of the AARP, "many members of Congress felt this was their only chance to put something back." The pay-as-you-go premium was dictated by the White House and budget reality. The federal government simply did not have the dollars to cover the bill from general revenues. If the elderly wanted catastrophic care, they would have to pay for the premiums out of their own pockets. Although those beneficiaries with deeper pockets (more income) would pay more, the concept of pay-as-you-go financing was essential to passage.

Lost along the way to final passage was long-term nursing care, often cited as the greatest threat to elderly finances. At the time Congress took up the catastrophic issue, roughly 1.4 million elderly Americans were in nursing homes of one kind or another, at an average of $22,000 a year. The problem with providing nursing home coverage was obvious. Covering the elderly then in nursing homes would be expensive enough, but the mere option of catastrophic insurance might actually encourage the elderly then *not* in homes, and their families, to use the new benefit. Estimates at the time suggested that for every one older American in a home, there were another four who could easily qualify. At $27.7 billion, Claude Pepper's threatened amendment to provide a long-term home-health-care benefit would have doubled the cost of the overall package. That is why it was never considered. Pepper withdrew his proposal under pressure from the House leadership.

The Treatment

Even without long-term care, however, the bill was an impressive achievement. Perhaps Congress and the President had learned how to make legislative miracles after all. Not that the bill was perfect, however. First, it was remarkably complex. Few beyond the close-knit core of committee specialists knew precisely what was in the bill or how the new premium would work. According to Rep. Pete Stark, "I don't think there are 300 members of the House who could tell you extemporaneously what Medicare benefits are," let alone explain the catastrophic plan. "I don't think nine of 10 seniors understand their Medicare benefits until they get sick."

Yet, as members soon found, this was one bill where surface knowledge would not do. Whereas most members of Congress can make do with a staff summary of a *Congressional Quarterly* report on a Congressional Budget Office analysis of a committee bill, catastrophic health care required much more depth, particularly when members went home to meet with increasingly agitated elderly constituents. Recall the old congressional adage that "if it can't fit on a bumper sticker, it's too complex."

Second, the program was overfinanced in its first years. Premiums started rolling in several years before the program was up full force. This "front-loading" was clearly driven by the need to meet the budget targets established under the 1985 deficit-cutting process authored by Senators Phil Gramm, Warren Rudman, and Ernest Hollings. According to *The New Republic*'s Jacob Weisberg, "This bit of clever bookkeeping was supposed to generate a short-term surplus of $5 billion to help fudge Gramm-Rudman budget projections; it won the support of President George Bush's White House but ensured that the program had no chance to develop a wide constituency before it came under fire from those who didn't want to pay for it."[12] Again, the details are less important than the potential distrust and uncertainty fostered among the elderly.

[12]Jacob Weisberg, "Cat Scam," *The New Republic* (October 30, 1989), p. 12.

Despite these harbingers of future controversy, the bill passed handily—86–11 in the Senate, 328–72 in the House—thereby becoming the single largest expansion of Medicare since its initial passage in 1965. It had absorbed enormous legislative time and energy, taking 18 months from start to finish. Congress and the President had worked hard to tame this highly complicated issue and had built a platform for future expansion to long-term nursing care, as well as possible national health care for all Americans. Moreover, it was mostly good policy. Even with the sweeteners, it would fundamentally improve life for millions of older Americans. The bill was signed into law at a full-dress White House ceremony, where Reagan said it "will remove a terrible threat from the lives of elderly and disabled Americans." It was a signal achievement of the One-hundredth Congress.

The Relapse

As a senior staff member of Sen. John Glenn's Governmental Affairs Committee during the One-hundredth Congress, 1987–88, I recall vividly the sense of accomplishment felt by many of us knowing that the bill had passed. Here in the final year of an eight-year administration, with a presidential campaign in full swing, Congress had passed a sweeping reform measure. Coupled with earlier passage of Moynihan's Family Support Act, the most sweeping welfare reform in 20 years, there seemed to be cause for celebration.

That is why what happened next is so utterly bizarre: *catastrophic health insurance was repealed the very next year*. Indeed, proposals for repeal were introduced even before the first premium dollar was collected. There were half a dozen bills waiting in the hopper only two months after the Reagan signing.

For some senior citizens, the new program represented a needless duplication of what was then an apparently cheaper private "medigap" insurance or employer-provided postemployment supplemental coverage. One senator compared the new system to the "Boy Scout who sees a little old lady standing on the corner who happens to be going the other way, but he decides he is taking her on across the street whether she wants to go or not."[13] Although duplication became a heated issue on the floor as repeal moved forward, the facts according to the Congressional Budget Office were that only 7 million of the roughly 26 million potential beneficiaries would be buying something they didn't need. They were already getting their medigap from their former employers either partly or completely free. The rest of the 26 million either did not have any private insurance at all (7 million) or would not need it once catastrophic came on line (12 million).

If duplication wasn't the real problem, perhaps the pay-as-you-go financing was. At least on the surface, it looked like a break with the past. Those beneficiaries who paid more than $150 a year in federal taxes were required to pay the supplemental premium—up to $800 per person, $1,600 per couple.

---

[13]These and other quotes that follow can be found in "Catastrophic-Coverage Law Is Repealed," *Congressional Quarterly Almanac, 1989* (Washington, D.C.: Congressional Quarterly), pp. 149–156.

Opponents of the premium argued that it violated the basic principle of social insurance systems such as social security—that all individuals should pay for their own. "In effect, we've told the American people, 'Don't save for your own retirement needs,'" said Bill Archer, one of the leaders of the repeal effort, "'because if you do, your savings and pensions will be penalized when you reach 65.'"

Here, too, the facts did not fit the rhetoric. Only 5.6 percent of participants would pay the full $800 premium, while 60 percent would pay no supplemental at all. And as to comparisons with other social insurance systems, social security has rewarded lower-income workers with higher rates of return from the very beginning, albeit through a complex benefit formula that few beneficiaries likely understand.[14] Basically, the program tells the American people that even if they can't save for retirement, there will still be a floor of support for all who put in a minimum amount of time in a job covered under social security. Because Congress passed the annual COLA in 1972, the program also tells the American people that their benefits will keep up with inflation. That is why the poverty rate among the elderly has fallen so dramatically over the past 20 years.

Yet, if social security and catastrophic health care shared a similar goal, they used very different financing mechanisms. First, social security involved all Americans in a social compact—workers paid in, and retirees took out; those workers then retired, new workers paid in, and the former workers took out. Catastrophic's pay-as-you-go financing involved only beneficiaries—all elderly paid an equal base, but higher-income elderly paid most of the supplementals. The effect was to single out one group of elderly. "It's a social experiment," Sen. Alan Simpson noted in supporting the program. "It's called pay for what you get, especially if you've got the wherewithal to do it." Second, social security's benefit formula made the so-called welfare component of each monthly check virtually invisible to beneficiaries. It was part of the plan for removing the stigma of providing a floor of support for needy elderly. In contrast, the effect of the supplemental premium was instantly apparent both to those who paid it and to those who received the benefit.

A Different Kind of Treatment

Ultimately, however, what killed catastrophic health care was panic. Whipped into a frenzy by the National Committee to Preserve Social Security and Medicare, as well as a plethora of other new groups such as the Seniors Coalition Against the Catastrophic Act, the elderly began writing Congress. Having cut its teeth on the so-called notch babies (representing elderly who had

[14]For persons attaining age 65 in 1992, the monthly social security benefit (the Primary Insurance Amount) was set by the following formula: (1) 90 percent of the first $387 of the Average Indexed Monthly Earnings (AIME), which converts a worker's lifetime of earnings into an equivalent value at the time of retirement, plus (2) 32 percent of AIME over $387 but under $2,333, plus (3) 15 percent of AIME over $2,333 up to a maximum total benefit of just over $13,000 per year.

supposedly lost benefits when Congress fixed the technical errors in the 1972 COLA), and having honed its techniques during the 1983 crisis, the Roosevelt committee was the first of the elderly groups to attack catastrophic insurance: "1989 INCOME TAXES FOR MILLIONS OF SENIORS WILL INCREASE BY UP TO $1,600 ($800 FOR SINGLES)—IT'S A TAX ON SENIORS ONLY AND IT MUST BE STOPPED!"

Again mailed to millions of households in official-looking envelopes, the literature had the effect of producing instant terror among the elderly, followed by terror on Capitol Hill. *The New York Times* and *Newsweek* carried photos of House Ways and Means Chairman Dan Rostenkowski trapped in his car as angry senior citizens demanded answers; the networks carried the footage. Members who happened to catch the story could not help but be worried about their next visit to a senior center.

Letters poured into Capitol Hill; new groups formed seemingly by the minute as a unique fund-raising opportunity appeared. A group called the Seniors Coalition Against the Tax mailed mock 1989 tax returns with $800 or $1,600 in the tax-due box. The Conservative Caucus got into the fray, too, mailing a fund-raising letter to Rostenkowski by accident. It just wasn't his year. "Your contribution is a good investment," the letter said. "It could help save millions of Americans (including you) from paying an extra $800 a year (and more) in taxes—year after year after year." Even the AARP was forced to back down from its earlier support for catastrophic insurance when it faced a revolt from its members.

Whether the outcry was driven, as Jacob Weisberg wrote, by "a core of greedy and not at all needy geezers who pretended to speak for a much larger pool of poor who stood to benefit" was hardly relevant.[15] The elderly were easily scared. AARP's Rother said, "The most prevalent misconception about the bill is that everyone was going to pay the $800. I can't tell you how many calls I've gotten from people who said, 'I live on my Social Security and a small pension, and I can't afford $800.'" "We're not confused," Simpson responded, "we're terrorized."

As if to add fuel to the fire, the Treasury Department released new estimates in January 1989 showing that the front-loading was even larger than first estimated. The supplemental premium was now projected to raise a staggering $4.3 billion more than expected, yielding a surplus of just over $6 billion. "How better do you want to demonstrate to people they're getting screwed," Rother would later ask, "than to collect their money and not provide their benefits?" Another estimate in February, this time by the Congressional Budget Office, showed the surplus up to $8 billion.

With more than 20 repeal bills introduced by midsummer, the question was not so much whether Congress would repeal but what, if anything, of catastrophic insurance would remain. The White House was almost completely silent, letting supporters and opponents alike imagine whatever they wanted about the President's position. The President simply refused to take a visible

---

[15]Weisberg, "Cat Scam," p. 11.

stand one way or the other, cutting congressional Republicans loose to vote as they pleased.

Being the local branch of Congress, the House acted first. Despite the best efforts of Rostenkowski and other supporters to hold catastrophic health care together, the chamber rejected all proposals for modification of the existing program and voted instead 360–66 to dump the entire program. The Senate struggled mightily as well, actually passing a bill 99–0 keeping small parts of catastrophic insurance alive by abandoning the supplemental premium and prescription drug coverage altogether. In a dramatic 15-hour meeting on November 17, the Senate finally capitulated to the public outcry. Bush signed the repeal bill, this time without a ceremony, on December 13. Simpson warned that "when the older Americans discover what they've lost, when they find out we've been swung around by our tails, my guess is we'll see a firestorm that outshines this one by megawatts." To date, that fire has not been ignited.

Prognosis

Obviously, the catastrophic flip-flop was the antithesis of the 1983 social security rescue. Where members had once stood together against unrelenting lobbying pressure to protect the social security package, they now caved in. What is important in comparing the two cases is the enormous potential for panic in Congress when members face highly organized, volatile interests. As Martha Derthick writes of social security, "Congress is not by nature inclined to shape policy on a comprehensive scale. It does not value rationality and consistency as presidential policymakers do. It does not do grand designs. Rather, it is an improviser, for only in that way can it reconcile the interests of its many members."[16]

Thus, no matter how careful the policy analysis leading to catastrophic insurance, no matter what the marketing strategy, there are organizations now in existence that appear to consciously seek opportunities to terrorize older Americans for short-term fund-raising aims. That those organizations were spawned during the 1983 rescue and endured in spite of what was clearly a success says something about the need to increase the collective courage of Congress and the presidency in responding to incoming fire and in designing understandable policy in the first place.

Anyone who assumes that future social security crises can be tackled with ease need only review the catastrophic insurance case and then read Derthick's concluding comment about Congress: "Action is *never* complete. Constantly changing in composition, torn always between its roles as policymaker for the nation and representative of particular constituencies and constituents, responsive by nature to a society that itself constantly changes, Congress engages endlessly in lawmaking." Strong-willed groups have little patience for economists, political scientists, or policy analysts who merely assume political

---

[16]Martha Derthick, *Agency under Stress: The Social Security Administration in American Government* (Washington, D.C.: Brookings Institution, 1990), pp. 191–192.

tension away.[17] Thus it will be with social security as it reenters crisis in the next century.

THE CONTINUING POLITICS OF SOCIAL SECURITY

Notwithstanding the catastrophic catastrophe, the social security playing field was relatively quiet from 1983 to 1990. No one talked much about new benefits; no one seemed interested in revisiting old conflicts. The rescue was working much better than planned; let sleeping dogs lie. There were still the occasional conservative critiques of the kind written for *Business Week* by Paul Craig Roberts, who argued that "the Greenspan Commission 'reforms' simply stick future generations with the bill for monstrous deficits. Thus a manageable crisis today will be unmanageable in a few decades."[18] And even though some, like *The New Republic*'s Robert Kuttner, declared the system "stable financially" but "unstable ideologically and politically," all was reasonably quiet as social security left the 1980s.[19]

That is when the politics of success struck back. In many ways, the current politics of social security is about what to do with the system's surpluses. Here is how political economist Herman "Dutch" Leonard put the problem in an edited volume titled *Social Security's Looming Surpluses: Prospects and Implications*, published in 1990:

> In the 1980s, social security fell victim to a new form of financial crisis. The pattern for many years had been that social security slipped from solvency toward cash crisis, only to be rescued each time. Now, its rescue promises, and is delivering a surplus of cash, swelling the trust funds' reserves. But this, too, is said to herald a crisis. What temptations will the buildup cause? What additional spending might be unleashed? What bankrupting benefit increases might come to seem affordable? How can the system be saved from the burden of having too much cash?[20]

Surplus Politics

How could surplus beget crisis? Two answers emerge, one likely wrong, the other much more persuasive.

The first was that the surpluses would prove too great a temptation for Congress and the President, who would spend them *(a)* to rescue Medicare from its impending crisis, *(b)* to boost existing social security benefits, *(c)* to finance a new national health care plan, or *(d)* to fund everything from the next

---

[17]See, for example, Paul Light, *Forging Legislation* (New York: W. W. Norton, 1992).
[18]Paul Craig Roberts, "Social Security Has Become a Giant Pyramid Scheme," *Business Week* (October 10, 1988), p. 28.
[19]Robert Kuttner, "Flawed Fixes," *The New Republic* (January 6 and 13, 1986), p. 15.
[20]Herman B. Leonard, *Social Security's Looming Surpluses: Prospects and Implications* (Washington, D.C.: American Enterprise Institute Press, 1990), p. 57.

savings and loan bailout, the space station, and the supercolliding supercon-
ductor to job training. In short, Congress and the President could not be trusted.

These fears were precisely refuted by the enormous terror inflicted on
Congress during the catastrophic insurance debacle. The public would never let
Congress tamper with the trust funds, not if the Roosevelt committee was still
in business. And there was not much evidence that anyone on Capitol Hill saw
the trust funds as an option for hidden funding of "soft" programs like savings
and loan bailouts. In 1989 alone, for example, members of Congress introduced
more than two dozen bills, resolutions, and motions of one kind or another to
protect the "sanctity" of the social security trust funds. The list of sponsors even
included Gramm and Rudman, although they must have known how the
growing surpluses were undermining their efforts at true deficit reduction.

The second, more persuasive answer was that the social security surpluses
were masking the true size of the federal budget deficit and in doing so were
being misused. "The current large excesses of income over outgo are being used
to hide the huge general-budget deficits," Myers writes. "Also, the availability
of such excesses year after year could make Congress and the Executive Branch
less cost-conscious as to new general expenditures, because the funds are so
readily available to be borrowed (and used)."[21] In 1992 alone, the surplus made
the federal deficit look $52 billion smaller. Further, because the social security
trust funds can only be invested in U.S. Treasury instruments, a growing
surplus reduces the need for outside dollars to fund the deficit. The federal
government has less to borrow from outside, but not less to repay in the future.
Sooner or later, the social security notes come due.

Granting the truth-in-budgeting case against growing the social security
surpluses bigger, there are only three possible solutions.

The first option is to order Congress and the President to never, ever again
add the surpluses into the deficit bottom line. Such an order would be
unenforceable, of course, and would run counter to reasonable accounting
practice, just as past statutes and resolutions requiring a balanced federal
budget have never worked. The social security surpluses are, after all else is
said, an asset of the federal government to be counted in a fair financial
statement of current conditions. Thus, even when social security is removed
from the Gramm-Rudman-Hollings budget process, which uses the surpluses
in setting annual targets, Congress and the President will likely continue the
practice in one way or another. Which President wants to stand before the
public (or Ross Perot, for that matter) and report a $50 to $100 billion jump in
the deficit?

The second option for unmasking the deficit is to invest the social security
surpluses in something other than U.S. Treasury instruments. Try state and
local economic infrastructure, housing notes, or high-tech industry, all of which
have been proposed. With the surpluses out of hand and out of mind, or so the
argument goes, the federal government would need to borrow more private or
foreign capital to finance a rising federal debt. The resulting increase in interest

---

[21]Myers, "Social Security's Financing Problems," p. 43.

rates might be enough to awaken Congress and the President to budget realities. Again, however, such a proposal is fraught with risk, not the least of which is choosing an alternative investment that can match the security of a U.S. note. One can almost see the Roosevelt committee going to work.

The third option is never to collect the surpluses at all. Myers made just such a case in 1991 in an article titled "Pay-As-You-Go Financing for Social Security Is the Only Way to Go." Reprising an argument he first made in 1985, back when the surplus was not yet a "problem," Myers based his case in part on the need to rebuild public confidence: "No longer would there be the confusion and the fear of 'thievery' and 'embezzlement' in connection with the use of trust-fund monies to balance the budget."[22] Such a step would be simple: cut payroll taxes. Less money comes in; less money accumulates.

The Moynihan Solution

Much as the third option makes sense, Congress and the President are addicted to the surplus. Moynihan tried twice to get the system to quit cold turkey, first in 1990 and again in 1991, and both times the system refused.

Moynihan's first try started on December 29, 1989, only days after Bush signed the repeal of catastrophic insurance, when he signaled his intent to propose a social security payroll tax cut. Backed by a strange assortment of conservatives (newspaper columnist George Will and the Heritage Foundation, a conservative think tank), a handful of liberals, a couple of odd lobbying groups (the American Association of Boomers), Senate Majority Leader George Mitchell (at first, that is), Senate Minority Leader Dole, and a respected former chief actuary (Myers), Moynihan rose to the floor the following January 23 to introduce his Social Security Tax Cut Act. No matter his belief that the bill would "strengthen the Social Security system, restore honesty and integrity to our Federal finances and provide a fair tax cut to 132 million Social Security taxpayers," S. 2016 never stood a chance. But what a debate it spawned.

Using some of his skills as a former professor at Harvard, Moynihan used the next two years to educate his colleagues on the true politics of social security. In decision-making style, he epitomized the senator as teacher. As I have described Moynihan's work on welfare reform, "the senator accepts the fact that rational decisions are almost impossible and pursues instead the imperfect search for truth. The primary interest is not perfect decisions, but better ideas, and the understanding that comes with reflection and study."[23]

Moynihan must have known his proposal was controversial—his December warning shot came just before a two-week sojourn in Africa. While Moynihan was away and either unable or unwilling to return phone calls, Washington had a chance to stew on his disarmingly simple proposal. Built explicitly on Myers's ideas, the bill would have cut the payroll tax on employees and

---

[22]Robert Myers, "Pay-As-You-Go Financing for Social Security Is the Only Way to Go," *Journal of the American Society of CLU & ChFC* (January 1991), p. 57.
[23]Light, *Forging Legislation*, p. 238.

employers each from 6.2 percent in 1990 to 5.1 percent by 1991. Although Moynihan had once opposed the pay-as-you-go idea, wanting to keep the 1983 reforms intact, he had clearly changed his mind. In introducing the bill, he explained why:

> It was just 7 years ago, in 1983, that the Congress approved a series of Social Security withholding tax increases designed to produce for the first time annual surpluses in the Social Security fund. The idea was to set the money aside to pay benefits in 25 or 30 years when there would be a larger number of retirees.
>
> I voted for that legislation, but in all honesty we should admit it is not working. The annual Social Security surplus is not really being set aside or invested productively. Instead the surplus taxes, taken from today's working men and women, are being used to hide the size of the Federal Government deficit and to help finance that deficit. Those surplus funds are used to purchase U.S. Treasury bonds and thus to help pay for current operating expenses of the Government—from the Pentagon, to the weather service to farm subsidies. And 25 or 30 years from now, when the Social Security system cashes in those Treasury bonds, our Government will have to tax the people again to pay off the bonds. And thus the people will pay twice for their Social Security benefits—once now and again in 25 or 30 years.
>
> It is simply wrong and it must be stopped.[24]

The more popular Moynihan's idea became, the more opponents looked for an ulterior motive. Some claimed the proposal was designed to force Bush to break his "READ MY LIPS/NO NEW TAXES" pledge—"It's an effort to get me to raise taxes on the American people by the charade of cutting them or cut benefits," Bush responded, "and I'm not going to do it to the older people of the country."

Others thought it might actually help Republicans on social security—"Let me tell you something," Vice President Dan Quayle told the Associated Press. "Cut these taxes the way Moynihan is talking about, you have to cut benefits at some time, and the President and the Republican Party now have an opportunity to show the American people, once and for all, that the Republicans are as committed to the integrity of this Social Security trust fund as anybody."

Still others hoped the proposal might reopen the old debate on whether social security was needed at all—"What Moynihan *tried* to do was the old bait-and-switch," said House Republican Whip Newt Gingrich, never known for obfuscation, "a pretend tax cut for a real tax increase later. What he *really* did was for the first time focus media scrutiny on Social Security and point out to people that their money is not going into a bank vault somewhere for their retirement later, but rather to mop up the deficit."[25]

Hard as his opponents looked for an ulterior motive, Moynihan had no

---

[24]*Congressional Record* (January 23, 1990), p. S. 154.

[25]Quoted in William McGurn, "Fumbling on Social Security," *National Review* (February 19, 1990), p. 20.

motive other than shining light on what he saw as a very serious issue. The proof was in the unrelenting opposition of his own party. Writing in June 1990, he expressed his surprise at the staying power of his proposal. "On the final Friday morning of 1989, at a sparsely attended press conference, I announced that I would introduce legislation to return the Social Security Trust Funds to a pay-as-you-go basis. Since then the proposal has been pronounced dead by assorted authorities. Yet, it does not die. It has acquired a kind of street life, and it is mentioned to me wherever I go. In almost forty years of political campaigns and public office of various sorts I have never seen a proposal (and a fairly abstract proposal at that) win as much support as rapidly as this has—except within the Democratic Party."[26]

Ultimately, Moynihan's proposal never came to a vote. After two days of debate, October 9–10, 1990, the proposal was ruled out of order on a procedural vote. Although it received 54 votes "aye," Congress required a supermajority of 60 to even consider, let alone pass, a bill that violated the Gramm-Rudman-Hollings budget targets.

Would the proposal have made any difference in deficit politics? Not likely, at least according to Brookings scholar Joseph White and his University of California at Berkeley colleague Aaron Wildavsky. Budget cutters have long believed that "the best way to eliminate the deficit is to make it seem bigger. . . . Trying to make budgeting easier by making it harder is a lot like trying to improve a winless college football team by scheduling it to play against the [Super Bowl–winning San Francisco] Forty-Niners."[27]

So noted, the proposal clearly created some momentum toward a much more comprehensive budget package in 1990. And it certainly enlightened the public. Moynihan's proposal provoked a *Time* lead story banner-headlined "Dirty Little Secret: A Plan for Cutting Social Security Taxes Exposes the True Size of the Deficit," a *U.S. News* report titled "Paycheck Politics: A Plan to Cut Social Security Taxes Makes Washington Flip Out," and a six-page *Brookings Review* multiauthor story titled "Four Reasons Not to Cut Social Security Taxes."[28] Moynihan got good press in all the right places, including *National Underwriter*, but was hit hard in friendly haunts. The most common phrase from his friends was "Moynihan's Right, but. . . ."[29]

Moynihan was undeterred, however, either by the 1990 vote or by the continuing controversy. He moved the bill again in 1991, only to lose by a greater margin on another procedural vote, 38–60, on April 24, 1991. But even in losing, he moved the issue to the front page again, forcing further hard conversation about the deficit. By moving the debate outside the Washington Beltway and into the popular press, he helped educate the public on a host of topics ordinarily left to academics and policy analysts.

[26]Daniel Patrick Moynihan, "Surplus Value," *The New Republic* (June 4, 1990), p. 13.
[27]Joseph White and Aaron Wildavsky, "Pretzel Logic," *The Brookings Review* (Spring 1990), pp. 7–8.
[28]*Time*, Vol. 135, No. 8 (February 19, 1990), pp. 48–49; *U.S. News & World Report*, Vol. 108, No. 4 (January 29, 1990), pp. 16–18; *The Brookings Review* (Spring 1990), pp. 3–8.
[29]This was the title of Henry J. Aaron and Charles L. Schultze's *New York Times* op-ed piece on January 18, 1990.

Ultimately, Moynihan's bill also served to remind the country of the continuing politics of social security. The program is too big to escape, too important to ignore. It will always be the subject of controversy of one kind or another.

CONCLUSION

As if to prove the point, President Bill Clinton became embroiled in social security politics only days after his inauguration. His mistake was not in talking about social security per se. In fact, he had been forthright throughout the campaign in talking about raising Medicare fees and taxing social security benefits. Although he had promised in Macon, Georgia, that "we're not going to fool with Social Security," he considered taxation of benefits a necessary sacrifice from older Americans. With taxation only applied to beneficiaries with incomes above $34,000 (for singles) or $44,000 (for married couples), it could be sold as part of asking the wealthy to pay their fair share.

Rather, it was a trial balloon on freezing the annual COLA that created the latest reminder that social security remains a third rail of the subway, at least as far as across-the-board cuts go. Here is how *New York Times* reporter David Rosenbaum played the front-page lead on Sunday morning, January 31, 1993: "President Clinton's economic advisers and Democratic Congressional leaders have concluded that retirees receiving Social Security benefits should pay a significant part of the price of deficit reduction, officials in the White House and Congress said this week. But the advisers and the top lawmakers disagree over how they should pay: whether through limiting cost-of-living increases in benefits or by increasing taxes on benefits."[30]

On one side of the debate was the new budget director, Leon Panetta, who favored the COLA freeze for its instant impact and shared sacrifice. On the other were several key senators, including George Mitchell and the Senate Budget Committee chairman, James Sasser of Tennessee. But one key member apparently not consulted before the balloon went up was the new chairman of the Senate Finance Committee, Daniel Patrick Moynihan. He got his chance to pop the balloon later that same Sunday morning on "ABC News." "The administration will do fine with me as chairman," Moynihan said, "if the President just won't step on any land mines, as his Cabinet kept doing all week, like proposing to take away cost-of-living allowances from retired persons—I mean, that's a real blow." Pushed further by host David Brinkley, Moynihan said, "That's a death wish and—let's get it out of the way and forget it right now."

The idea bounced around the administration until February 8, when Clinton met with leaders of the AARP to reassure them that he viewed social security as a special contract with the nation's elderly. But it lived long enough to generate a mass of new mailings from the National Committee to Preserve

---

[30]David Rosenbaum, "Clinton Weighing Freeze or New Tax on Social Security," *The New York Times* (January 31, 1993), p. A-1.

Social Security and Medicare, now headed by former acting Social Security Commissioner Martha McSteen; a knife-twisting blast from Gingrich, who promised "I'm going to do everything I can to keep the Democrats from tampering" with social security; and the following statement to AARP from a Democratic senator and chair of the Subcommittee on Aging of the Committee on Labor and Human Resources, Barbara Mikulski: "I'm a dues-paying, discount-seeking member of the AARP. You didn't create the deficit, and I don't know why they look at you all the time to correct the deficit."[31] Taxation of benefits was tough enough to protect as Republicans went to work against it.

Along the way, Clinton learned an important lesson about social security. Roughly 42 million beneficiaries will be listening, and so will their lobbying groups in Washington. Social security is extremely tough to talk about but impossible to ignore. He also learned that 1983 was long gone, that social security will always be political. Congress and the President have never been able to "depoliticize" the program, not by putting social security on autopilot, as Brookings Institution political scientist Kent Weaver calls the strategy, with automatic cost-of-living increases, and not with the 1983 rescue.[32] The rescuers, including Moynihan, had done their best to repair a hemorrhaging program. Once restored to health, social security took its place again as the anchor of America's social safety net, and as an occasional target for controversy. There is nothing easy about working on social security reform—it may be easy to assume that Congress and the President will fix the program, but it will always be tough to do.

[31]These quotes are drawn from Robin Toner, "Clinton's Social Security Test: Selling Sacrifice to the Elderly," *The New York Times* (February 7, 1993), pp. A-1, A-26.
[32]Kent Weaver, *Automatic Government: The Politics of Indexation* (Washington, D.C.: Brookings Institution, 1988).

20

The Next Social Security Crisis

Consider the following fact about the future of social security: the first of 75 million baby boomers will be eligible to join the American Association of Retired Persons in 1996. Having just turned 50, they will be asked not just to partake of the health insurance, read the magazine, use the travel service, join the mutual funds, buy drugs from the mail-order pharmacy, and use the motor club but also to contribute their numbers to a membership that will already be somewhere around 34 million.

If that does not make the point about the coming social security crisis, nothing will. Since 1 out of every 2 Americans over age 50 will belong to the AARP, the membership roster should top 50 million by 2010. It would be an AARP roughly double its current size of 1,600 employees; 251,000 volunteers in every House district across the country; $300 million in revenue from the various services listed above; and a $22.4 million research and lobbying budget.[1] The baby boomers could more than double all the figures.

Already labeled by Charles Peters, editor in chief of *The Washington Monthly*, as "the most dangerous lobby in America," the AARP would only get stronger. As Peters argues, "The image is that of the nicest kind of old fellows and old ladies, and, in fact, they are perpetuating a myth that the elderly are all needy. That's their fundamental lobbying technique, and our society has to face the fact that it's not true."[2]

While Peters overdraws the case—there are plenty of poor elderly who would be hurt by a COLA freeze, for example—there is no doubt that the

---

[1]These figures are drawn from Ron Suskind, "Whose Side Are They On, Anyway?" *SmartMoney* (February 1993), p. 98.
[2]Quoted in John Tierney, "Old Money, New Power," *The New York Times Magazine* (October 23, 1988); pp. 69, 98.

AARP often has the last word on social security policy. Clinton called the AARP, not the National Committee to Preserve Social Security and Medicare, when he wanted to pop the COLA freeze in 1993. Even though only 14 percent of its members join to support its lobbying activities (40 percent join for the travel service, discount cards, etc.), and even though large numbers of poor elderly simply cannot afford the dues and most certainly have no need of the mutual funds and special travel services, the AARP has never been bashful about speaking for all elderly.

Will the baby boomers join? The betting money should be on the AARP. The association already has a planning committee at work on how to make the appeal. "How is the association to play to a group whose motto was not to trust anyone over 30? When they hit 50, what will they do?" asks the AARP director of membership development. "Nobody knows how this generation is going to be addressing aging. It's uncertain whether they'll go kicking and screaming all the way or instead embrace their new status and discover it with a zeal no one else has."[3]

Whether the AARP can entice many baby boomers with its magazine, *Modern Maturity*, is doubtful, however. That is the last thing the baby boomers want to read as they fight middle age. What will draw the baby boomers at first will be the deals and discounts. What will hold them, however, is 2016.

2016

Most baby boomers have not thought much about 2016. Why should they? It is just a year somewhere in a distant future.

For now, the baby boomers are still mostly in their first careers and first marriages (divorce rates remain high) and are raising their first children. Nevertheless, unless the baby boomers start paying some attention to the future, 2016 may herald the start of a twenty-year political and social crisis. Baby boomers are making key choices today that may make their retirements difficult at best tomorrow. If the baby boomers continue on their present course of not saving, not investing, and not supporting deficit cuts, then 2016 may bring the intergenerational war many worry about in the present—not between the baby boomers and their parents, but between the baby boomers and their own children.[4]

Two events make 2016 very important to the baby boomers. First, 2016 is the year the first baby boomers will turn 70. They may be able to ignore 50, even 60, but 70 will be inescapable. Short of a major policy change, the first baby boomers will be well into retirement by then. Second, 2016 is the first presidential election year after social security outgo will first exceed tax

[3]See Karen Riley, "Boomers Find Early-Bird Special in New Retirees Interest Group," *Washington Times* (February 5, 1992), p. C1.
[4]For an overview of the baby boom, see Paul Light, *Baby Boomers: A Social and Political Reappraisal* (New York: W. W. Norton, 1988).

income—although the fund balance will continue to rise for about 10 years owing to interest receipts, the turn toward deficit will have begun. The program will not be anywhere near the kind of immediate crisis that hit in 1983, assuming the surpluses are still there, of course. Even if nothing is done, checks will continue to go out on time well into the 2030s.

Yet, given the uproar over catastrophic insurance, can anyone doubt the uproar as social security outgo crosses over into the red? Unless there is some radical change in the current forecasts—and recent experience suggests that further changes will likely be negative—2016 will give the baby boomers, and the AARP, their first chance to express concern about social security. "Generation X," the baby bust born right behind the baby boom, will have a chance to weigh in, too. They will be in the prime of their working lives but will be threatened with the crisis, too. Their taxes will likely rise and future benefits decline.

If current projections hold true, the baby boomers will be asking a great deal from both their own children and the baby bust. As the ratio of workers to beneficiaries shifts, the tax rates required to maintain a reasonable standard of social security benefits will rise. According to the 1992 *Report of the Trustees of the Federal Old-Age and Survivors Insurance and Disability Insurance Trust Funds*, assets will continue to rise rapidly until "15 years after the turn of the century," when the baby boomers hit retirement en masse. Thereafter, in the traditionally dry language of the trustees' reports, "tax rates scheduled in present law are expected to be insufficient to cover program expenditures and it will be necessary to use interest earnings and to redeem assets held by the combined OASI and DI trust funds to make up the shortfall."

Translated, by 2016, social security will be using its interest earnings and drawing down its reserves, cashing in its Treasury notes, and running an annual income/outgo deficit. The problem is obvious. In 1992, there were 100 workers for 30 beneficiaries. By the peak of the baby boom retirements in the 2030s, there will be but two workers for every beneficiary, 50 beneficiaries for every 100 workers. As Myers argues, "the 1983 estimates showed the fund balance building up rapidly in the 1990s and the next five decades, reaching a peak of $20.7 trillion in 2045. The current estimates show a rapid build-up in the next three decades (though not nearly as rapidly), but reaching a peak of *only* $5.6 trillion in 2023."[5] The "cause" of the decline? Continued deterioration of the long-range economic forecasts. Should the social security actuaries lower their fertility estimate, as the technical panel recommended, the figures will be even lower.

Depending on the estimates, the social security trust funds will be exhausted sometime in the 2030s, a prognosis that prompted former Social Security Commissioner Dorcas Hardy to title her recent book *Social Insecurity: The Crisis in America's Social Security System and How to Plan Now for Your Own Financial Survival.* Her take on the 1983 rescue is simple: "since 1983 it has been

[5]Robert Myers, "Social Security's Financing Problems—Realities and Myths," *Journal of the American Society of CLU & ChFC* (March 1993), p. 8.

extremely difficult to get people to pay attention to the issues that confront Social Security. The surpluses provide the illusion that all is well—at least until 2010."[6]

More troubling is the notion that the current social security forecasts may be overly optimistic. Some, like American Enterprise Institute researchers Ben Wattenberg and Karl Zinsmeister, believe the fertility assumptions are too high. Writing of what they call a birth dearth, they argue for national policies to stimulate higher fertility. Not only do larger populations produce larger economies, they produce better national defense and a larger base of people, industry, infrastructure, and taxes to pay the bills, including social security.[7] The fear that America is somehow depopulating itself has even led to a new lobbying group called the Committee on Population and Economy, formed to unite Americans who believe in the "injunction to be fruitful and multiply."

Others believe the current life-span projections are too short—that people will be living longer. Instead of assuming that the life span is finite, why not assume that society will continue to make gains far into the future? "As for future life expectancy," Rand Corporation researcher Peter Morrison commented in reviewing the 1986 social security assumptions, "a number of recent studies raise disturbing doubts about the assumed future levels. They may understate future life expectancy in old age, lengthening considerably the period over which retirees would be eligible to receive social security benefits. Misjudging this possibility could prove to be an extremely expensive error."[8] It is true that the actuarial estimates have been changing to account for some improvement in life expectancy, but for Morrison and others, the estimates are still much too optimistic.

Ultimately, even small changes in the long-range assumptions have enormous impacts on the projected future of social security. If children are not born, they never grow up; if they never grow up, they never get jobs; if they never get jobs, they never pay taxes; if the elderly live longer, they draw more from social security. Although there has been an "echo" boom as the baby boomers have children—births hit 4.1 million in 1992, compared with 3.1 million in the mid-1970s—the demographic facts appear immutable: the number of future taxpayers available to support the baby boomers is falling fast.

The world could look even more troubling if death rates fall even further than in the worst case. According to an analysis of the worst, worst case (low fertility/low mortality/low immigration) by population experts Jacob Siegel and Cynthia Taeuber, "there could be serious dislocations in the economy as it tries to adjust to changing needs for jobs, goods, and services. Societal aging calls for increasingly larger financial contributions to the federal treasury by

[6]Dorcas Hardy and C. Colburn Hardy, *Social Insecurity: The Crisis in America's Social Security System and How to Plan Now for Your Own Financial Survival* (New York: Villard Books, 1991), p. 15.
[7]Ben Wattenberg and Karl Zinsmeister, "The Birth Dearth: The Geopolitical Consequences," *Public Opinion*, Vol. 8, No. 1 (December/January 1986), pp. 6–13.
[8]Peter A. Morrison, "Changing Family Structure: Who Cares for America's Dependents?" Document No. N-2518-NICHD (December 1986), The Rand Corporation, Santa Monica, California, pp. 14–15.

workers on behalf of older non-workers. Tax rates could become oppressively high and serve as a disincentive to work. The productive capacity of the economy could be diminished as the proportion of persons of working age shrinks and vast expenditures have to be made for the 'maintenance' of elderly persons."[9]

Should the baby boomers plan for this worst, worst case? Absolutely not. The kind of society envisioned by the highly pessimistic projections does not leave much room for social security anyway, and the kinds of draconian measures that would have to be taken now to anticipate such a world might actually make the pessimistic scenario more likely. Ultimately, the baby boomers must plan for a future in which social security benefits are highly dependent on the willingness of society to bear the burden, but in which there is enough economic growth and past investment to make the burden bearable.

TWO FUTURES

Short of having another baby boom, which is hardly likely given recent fertility rates, there are only two ways the baby boomers can face the crisis. Each is based on a very different image of the future.

The first is to dampen the scope of the crisis by sharply cutting the federal deficit, rebuilding the economy, increasing productivity, improving the educational system, and taking immediate steps to raise the "normal retirement age." The combined effect would be to increase the economy's capacity to handle a needed tax increase in the future. Such action would not solve the long-term problem, unless the retirement age went up dramatically, but it would set the stage for easier remedy in the future. By at least trying to fix the problem, the baby boomers would also earn at least some respect from those they would be about to tax. As Robert Ball argues, "We owe much of what we are to the past. We all stand on the shoulders of generations that came before. They built the schools and established the ideas of an educated society. They wrote the books, developed the scientific ways of thinking, passed on ethical and spiritual values, discovered our country, developed it, won its freedom, held it together, cleared its forests, built its railroads and factories, and invented new technology."[10] The work of one generation to build for the next is part of what social historians Eric Kingson, Barbara Hirshorn, and John Cornman call the ties that bind.[11]

In this future, there is more than enough economic growth to support the baby boomers in retirement, more than enough in savings to provide needed care, and more than enough compassion to assure that the baby boomers retire

[9]Jacob Siegel and Cynthia Taeuber, "Demographic Perspectives on the Long-Lived Society," in A. Pfifer and L. Bronte, eds., *Our Aging Society* (New York: W. W. Norton, 1986), pp. 113–114.
[10]Quoted in Eric Kingson, Barbara Hirshorn, and John Cornman, *The Ties that Bind: The Interdependence of Generations* (Washington, D.C.: Seven Locks Press, 1986), p. 25.
[11]See Kingson et al., *The Ties that Bind.*

in comfort. Social security is easily repaired sometime in the early 2000s in a spirit of thanks for what the baby boomers did to build the future. The 2016 election is not much different from any other presidential election.

The second option is for baby boomers to join the AARP and the National Committee to Preserve Social Security and Medicare, and prepare to fight it out with the baby bust and anyone else who happens to be in the workforce around 2020. In this future, the nation's infrastructure continues to decay, the educational system remains in disrepair, and savings are never put aside. The baby bust struggles to get by, and the baby boom's own children enter the future unprepared for intense global competition. What matters most in such a scenario is the children's willingness to pay when social security hits the crisis.

This willingness to pay depends on far more than just the amount of the tax—though current projections suggest the figures could be very high, indeed. Just as the baby boomers support today's social security payroll tax because they see it as fairer than other federal taxes and as a source of needed support for their parents and grandparents, their children will have to support it on the basis of love and respect for their parents and grandparents, too. If the 2016 election becomes a referendum on the baby boom's stewardship during their years in power, how will their children vote? If the baby boomers fail to even try to alleviate the future burden they know is coming, will their children and young siblings have any reason for compassion?

It is not that the baby boomers cannot win a fight over social security in 2016 if they have to. Not if 60 percent of the likely voters in the election happen to be in retirement or very close to it. Fifty million AARP members would be a force to be reckoned with.

But the victory would come at great cost. Enforcing the kind of social security tax increase described in the more pessimistic future above is hardly the way to earn the compassion the baby boomers will need in 2030 and 2040, when they reach the outer years of retirement, when they need not just money but also individual care. The way to assure the social compact remains intact in the future is to honor the social compact that exists today—that is, to make sure the next three decades boast a record of stewardship and investment that will make future burdens bearable. Just as the baby boom's parents made decisions in the 1940s and 1950s to invest in their children, the baby boomers must decide to invest in their children's future, too.

APPENDIX A

A Brief Chronology

1981

January 5	Rep. J. J. Pickle begins work on a social security rescue bill
January 20	Ronald Reagan inaugurated
March	Budget Director David Stockman turns to social security as a solution to his "magic asterisk"
April	Stockman finishes work on White House rescue legislation, including early retirement cuts
April 7	Pickle bill passes Social Security Subcommittee
May 12	Health and Human Services Secretary Richard Schweiker announces social security proposals
May 20	Proposals rejected 96–0 by Senate
May 21	Reagan withdraws proposals
June 26	Social security minimum benefit eliminated in Reagan budget package
July 16	House Majority Leader Jim Wright introduces "Sense of the House" resolution on minimum benefit
July 31	Minimum benefit eliminated in House-Senate budget conference report
July 31	Minimum benefit restored in House
September	Stockman returns to social security for one last round of cuts
September 24	Reagan abandons social security cuts, proposes a National Commission on Social Security Reform
October 15	Minimum benefit restored in Senate

| November 16 | House-Senate minimum benefit conference committee starts work |
| December 16 | House and Senate approve minimum benefit conference report containing a December 31, 1982, deadline on interfund borrowing |

1982

January	White House presents new budget to Congress
February 23	Senate Budget Committee Chairman Peter Domenici presents alternative budget containing a social security cost-of-living freeze
February 27	National Commission meets for the first time
March	Gang of Seventeen budget negotiations begin
April 28	Gang of Seventeen summit between Reagan and House Speaker Thomas P. ("Tip") O'Neill; talks collapse
May 5	Domenici includes a social security solvency figure in his new budget
May 6	Domenici's effort fails
July–November	Congressional campaigns: no social security legislative action
November 1	Midterm congressional elections
November 11–13	National Commission sets targets for compromise; fails to agree on a package of solutions
December 10	National Commission has final attempt at compromise; collapses
Christmas week	White House representatives start secret talks with former Social Security Commissioner Robert Ball and Sen. Daniel Moynihan

1983

January 4	Gang of Nine is formed
January 5–15	Gang presents final compromise to the full National Commission membership; passes 12–3
February 1–3	Full Ways and Means Committee hearings on the National Commission package
February 9	Social Security Subcommittee markup begins
March 2	Full Ways and Means Committee markup begins
March 9	House passes social security rescue bill, H.R. 1900
March 10	Senate Finance Committee markup begins
March 23	Senate passes H.R. 1900 as amended
March 24	House-Senate social security conference committee starts work

March 24	House approves social security conference committee report
March 25	Senate approves social security conference committee report
April 20	Reagan signs PL 98-21

APPENDIX B

The Key Players

Archer, William	Republican representative from Texas; member, National Commission on Social Security Reform; member, Ways and Means Committee
Armstrong, William	Republican senator from Colorado; member, National Commission; chairman, Social Security Subcommittee of the Senate Finance Committee
Baker, Howard	Republican senator from Tennessee; Senate majority leader
Baker, James III	White House chief of staff; member, Gang of Nine negotiating group
Ball, Robert	Former social security commissioner; member, National Commission; member, Gang of Nine
Beck, Robert	Member, National Commission; chairman, Business Roundtable Social Security Task Force
Bolling, Richard	Democratic representative from Missouri; chairman, House Rules Committee until 1983
Byrd, Robert	Democratic senator from West Virginia; Senate minority leader
Conable, Barber	Republican representative from New York; member, National Commission; ranking Republican, House Ways and Means Committee; member, Gang of Nine
Darman, Richard	White House deputy chief of staff; member, Gang of Nine
Dole, Robert	Republican senator from Kansas; member, National Commission; chairman, Senate Finance Committee; member, Gang of Nine
Domenici, Peter	Republican senator from New Mexico; chairman, Senate Budget Committee
Fuller, Mary Falvey	Member, National Commission

Greenspan, Alan — Chairman, National Commission; member, Gang of Nine; chairman, Council of Economic Advisers, Ford administration

Keys, Martha — Member, National Commission; former Democratic representative from Kansas

Kirkland, Lane — Member, National Commission; president, AFL-CIO

Michel, Robert — Republican representative from Illinois; House minority leader

Moynihan, Daniel — Democratic senator from New York; member, National Commission; member, Gang of Nine

Myers, Robert — Executive director, National Commission, former social security chief actuary

O'Neill, Thomas P. ("Tip") — Democratic representative from Massachusetts; Speaker of the House

Pepper, Claude — Democratic representative from Florida; member, National Commission; chairman, House Aging Committee until 1983; chairman, House Rules Committee after 1983

Pickle, J. J. ("Jake") — Democratic representative from Texas; chairman, Social Security Subcommittee of House Ways and Means Committee

Reagan, Ronald — President of the United States

Rostenkowski, Dan — Democratic representative from Illinois; chairman, House Ways and Means Committee

Stockman, David — Director, Office of Management and Budget; member, Gang of Nine

Trowbridge, Alexander — Member, National Commission; president, National Association of Manufacturers

Waggoner, Joe — Member, National Commission; former Democratic representative from Louisiana

Wright, Jim — Democratic representative from Texas; House majority leader

Index

Aaron, Henry J., 38, 229, 244

AARP, *see* American Association of Retired Persons

ABC News poll, 150

ABC News/*Washington Post* polls:
on Reagan's performance, 118
on social security, 230

Accounting games, 101–102

Actuary, The, 228

Adequacy principle, 37

Administrative costs of social security, 39

Advocates of the Handicapped, member of SOS, 78

AFL–CIO:
ending stalemate, 202
involved in social security, 71
Medicare and, 73, 74
opposition to coverage of federal workers, 65
retirement age and, 105
in Save Our Security coalition, 78, 79

Age, retirement, *see* Retirement age

Age group, knowledge about social security by, 60

Agency under Stress: The Social Security Administration in American Government, 41, 239

Aging Committee (House), 116, 124

Aging in the Eighties, 56

AIME (Average Indexed Monthly Earnings), 237

American Association of Boomers, 242

American Association of Retired Persons (AARP), 71, 103, 238

American Association of Retired Persons (AARP) (*Cont.*):
beginnings of, 73–74
changes in social security benefits and, 72
denounces long-term benefit cuts, 162
future of, 247–249, 252
membership of, 76
opposition to agreement, 190–191
opposition to compromise, 185
recognition of, 76–77
in Save Our Security coalition, 78, 79

American Bankers Association, 201

American Business Conference, 74
member of Carlton group, 80

American Council for Capital Formation, member of Carlton group, 80

American Council of Life Insurance, 230

American Economic Review, 229

American Enterprise Institute, 250

American Federation of Labor-Congress of Industrial Organizations, *see* AFL–CIO

American Foundation for the Blind, 71

American Postal Union, 80

American productivity, 89

American system of government:
branches of, 4
choices in, 217–218

Anderson, Marty, 117

Annual Report of the Board of Trustees of the Federal Old-Age and Survivors Insurance and the Federal Disability Insurance Trust Funds, The, 227

Anxiety about bankruptcy, 59, 61

259